# DISCOVER EAST ASIA

Reader's
Digest

PUBLISHED BY THE READER'S DIGEST ASSOCIATION LIMITED

LONDON   NEW YORK   SYDNEY   MONTREAL

**DISCOVER EAST ASIA**

Translated and edited by Toucan Books Limited, London
for Reader's Digest, London

Translated and adapted from the French
by Robin Hosie

**For Reader's Digest**
Series Editor: Christine Noble
Editorial Assistant: Caroline Boucher
Production Controller: Martin Hendrick

**Reader's Digest General Books**
Editorial Director: Cortina Butler
Art Director: Nick Clark

*Discover the World:* EAST ASIA
was created and produced by
Hubert Deveaux & Co, Marie Garagnoux, Else for
Selection Reader's Digest S.A., Paris, and first published
in 2000 as *Regards sur le Monde: LA CHINE, LE JAPON ET LA CORÉE*

©2000 Selection Reader's Digest, S.A.
212 boulevard Saint-Germain, 75007, Paris

# CONTENTS

# INTRODUCING
# EAST ASIA

East Asia takes up less than one-tenth of the land
surface of the globe, and much of the region is
occupied by mountain, desert and steppe. Yet nearly a
quarter of the human race lives here. The peoples of East
Asia have a long record of cultural achievement, going
back almost 3000 years in the case of China. It is here that
such inventions as the magnetic compass, porcelain,
paper-making and printing have their origins. The
countries of the region are a mixture of similarity and
contrast. Japan, South Korea and Taiwan are technologically
advanced – major players in the global economy.
Mongolia and North Korea are the complete antithesis –
remote, one geographically the other politically, and
economically underdeveloped. Over them all looms China,
a regional superpower on the way to being a world one.

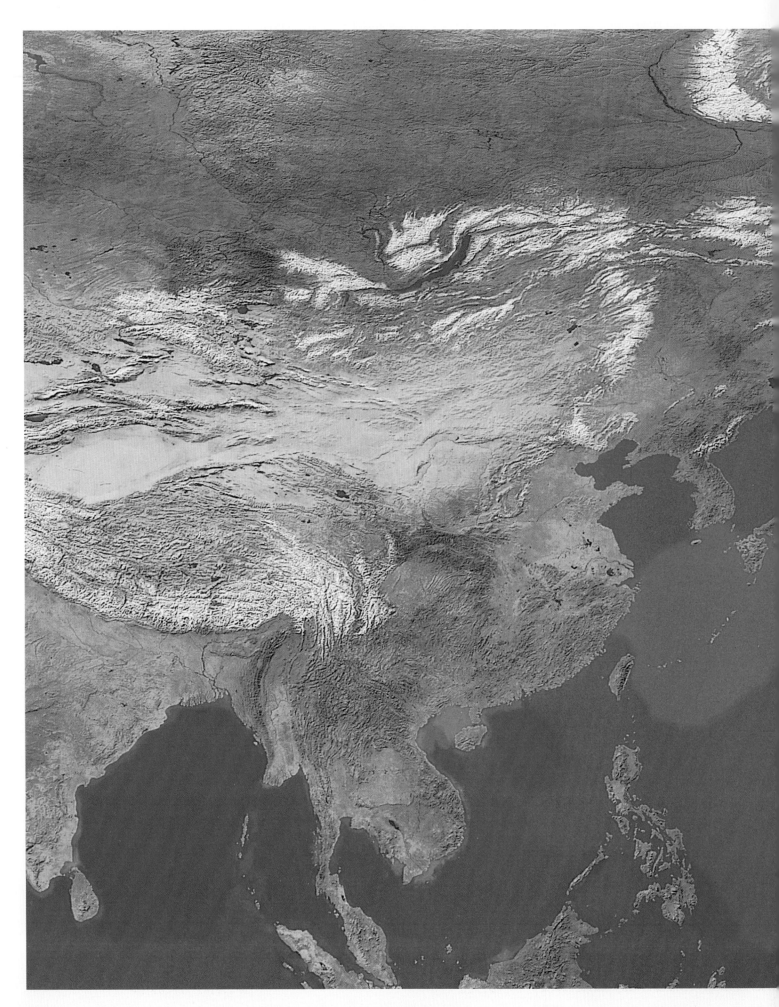

# Discovering old worlds

Until the recent past, the Western world looked on East Asia as the 'Far East', a remote, isolated and above all mysterious part of the globe. Those who inhabited this vast region, however, thought isolation was the fate not of themselves but of the peoples who lived beyond their frontiers. To the Chinese, whose civilisation stretches back for more than 3000 years, their land was *Zhongguo*, the 'Middle Kingdom' between heaven and earth – the centre not just of the world, but of the entire cosmos.

Two-thirds of East Asia is covered by mountains, confining major settlement to river valleys and deltas, and to relatively small patches of level, fertile land around the coasts. Some of the most crowded areas on the face of the Earth are to be found in East Asia, but so are some of its most sparsely populated areas. Despite its mountainous terrain, Japan has an average of nearly 877 people per sq mile (340 per km²), compared with just over 4 per sq mile (1.6 per km²) in Mongolia. This is only one of many contrasts in a region that stretches from the desiccated wastes of Mongolia to the monsoon-drenched coastlands of China.

East Asia's climate is dominated by the monsoon winds – a dry, bitterly cold monsoon in winter; a warm monsoon in summer, carrying a burden of moisture that falls as torrents of rain. The weather machine that powers the monsoons depends on something as simple as the difference between the heat-retaining qualities of land and sea. In winter, the interior of the Asian landmass, far from the moderating influence of the sea, is piercingly cold, and the air pressure is high. Icy, dust-laden winds chill the land as they sweep out towards the ocean. In summer, the pattern is reversed. The interior landmass

*Physical features* Snow-covered mountains, high desert and fertile lowlands etch the landmass of East Asia.

heats up faster than the ocean, and the warmed air rises, creating low pressure. This draws in winds that have sucked up moisture on their journey across the Pacific. As the clouds rise to cross the mountains they cool, unleashing their moisture as rain.

Nature can be hostile on a grand scale in Asia. Impetuous rivers, swollen by melted snows from the Himalayas and other mountain ranges, can burst their banks and devastate the surrounding land. Typhoons can punish the coast. Drought can bring famine and misery to the interior. As if to compensate for the violence of nature, at the same time as being inspired by its beauty, the artists and poets of these lands seem to search for calmness and harmony in their work.

These same virtues are also sought in four of the region's great faiths: Confucianism, Taoism, Buddhism and, in Japan, Shinto. Chinese communism, with all the fervour of a religion, turned against traditional faiths and set out to create a new society by smashing the old one. Temples were wrecked, holy relics profaned, monks beaten and humiliated. But after the death of Mao Ze-dong in 1976, his successors shifted their focus from wiping out relics of the past to building prosperity for the future, and took a more tolerant attitude towards traditional religions.

In the last quarter of the 20th century the 'Asian tigers', led by Japan and with Taiwan not far behind, dazzled the world with their brilliant economic performance. As the century came to a close, however, their challenge to the commercial giants of Europe and America seemed to falter. In the cold dawn of the new millennium, the future is looking less enticing for the Asian tigers. But the people of East Asia are used to overcoming setbacks: where they live, there is usually no alternative. And China, potentially the biggest tiger of them all, has begun to awaken, releasing the energies of its millions by accepting the principle of making private profit, under the slogan: 'To get rich is glorious!'

**Sugar-loaf landscape** Beneath the hauntingly lovely limestone hills of Guilin, China, immortalised by poets and landscape painters, the last inch of level land has been cultivated by generations of peasants.

**Two worlds in the sky** *Snow-topped peaks tower to 23 000 ft (7010 m) in Tibet's Nyenchen Thanglha range (below, left). The range divides Tibet into two different worlds. A settled way of life has developed in the valleys to the south, whereas the high plateaus to the north are still crisscrossed by nomads and their herds. To the nomads, the Bactrian camel is a prized beast of burden.*

**Obstacles on the Silk Road** *For centuries, China had a monopoly in the manufacture of silk. Demand in the countries of the West was insatiable, and the Silk Road became China's main link with the rest of the world. The merchants and their patient, plodding camels faced an arduous journey. They had to skirt two vast deserts: the Gobi, with its ferocious winds, and the Taklamakan, with its sandy wastes, only to face the Pamir Mountains, dominated by 24 757 ft (7546 m) Mount Muztagata (above).*

**The pony that won an empire** *When the Mongol warriors of Genghis Khan poured across the Great Wall and began their conquest of northern China in the 13th century, it was on sturdy ponies like the one below that they rode into history. These mounts, as tough as their riders, survive winter blizzards and summer droughts. Occasional rainfall can turn arid ground into temporary pastureland, as it has done in this valley in the Altai Mountains, straddling the border between China and Mongolia.*

**Born-again forests** For centuries, man and nature lived in harmony in Korea, though the mountains leave little space for crops. Then, in the 20th century, huge areas of forest were cleared. The result was an ecological disaster. These forests of pine, spruce, chestnut and birch on the outskirts of South Korea's capital, Seoul, are the product of a reafforestation programme, begun in 1960. Today, it is illegal to cut down a single tree without government permission.

**Sentinels of an island race** Japan, a chain of volcanic islands, is a civilisation of the sea. Along the shore of Cape Shiono, on the Pacific coast of the country's main island, Honshu, wave-battered rocks stand like sentinels.

**River of dreams ... and nightmares** In moments of tranquillity, the 3716 mile (5980 km) long Yangtze River inspires the dreams of poets and painters. In moments of fury, when the river floods, it brings terror and despair. Here, a boat battles its way through the spectacular Three Gorges section of the Yangtze.

**Warm bath in a cold climate**  *Japanese macaques are the most northerly monkeys in the world, living in mountain fastnesses that are on roughly the same latitude as New York. On hillsides that are rocky, forested and often covered in snow, the monkeys exist on a diet of fruit, nuts, grass and insects. When the weather turns cold they have learned to take advantage of the region's thermal pools.*

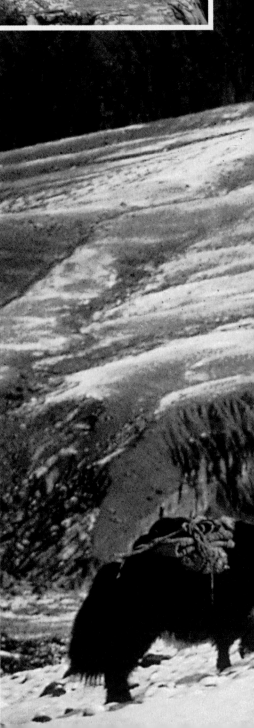

**Where great rivers rise**  *The eternal snows of the Himalayas and their outriding mountain chains are the source of many great rivers. The Ganges, the Mekong, the Brahmaputra and the Yangtze all begin as streams on the roof of the world. The Brahmaputra, which has the greatest discharge of any Indian river, rises in the Namcha Barwa chain (below), where the highest summit reaches 25 446 ft (7756 m).*

**Companions in survival**  *Life is hard enough for nomads on the high plateaus of Tibet, but it would be impossible without their partnership with the yak. They use the animal's densely matted coat to weave clothing and carpets. Its milk gives them the butter that enriches their tea, and can also provide oil for their lamps. Its dried flesh is a good source of protein to see  them through long journeys.*

# A brief history

Archaeologists are generally agreed that humankind originated in Africa. Our earliest-known ancestor was a hominid (human-like ape) known as Lucy, who stood about 3 ft 6 in (1.06 m) tall and lived in East Africa some 4 million years ago. But there is at least a possibility that this view may have to be revised – that there may have been more than one point of origin, with Asia having a claim to being one of the cradles of the human race.

Recent excavations in Japan have revealed evidence of a hominid settlement dating back 500 000 years. Peking Man, a forerunner of modern man, lived in China at about the same time, so it is possible that half a million years ago migration across East Asia was well established. Peking Man's skull was discovered in 1929 at Zhoukoudian, near Beijing, and he was identified as an example of *Homo erectus*, 'upright man', a group who used fire for cooking as well as for warmth. The skull disappeared in the 1930s, during China's war against Japan, but other remains of *Homo erectus* have been discovered in China. Some died violently, and there is evidence of cannibalism.

## China's 'Yellow Emperor'

By about 6000 BC, a thriving culture known as Yangshao had developed in the west of China. The peasants grew enough cereals to support both themselves and a scholarly or priestly class. They kept pigs and dogs, and made red-coloured pottery, decorated with geometric patterns. The Longshan culture of the east, which arose about 5000 BC, produced highly burnished black pottery. The Chinese date their history from the reign of the legendary 'Yellow Emperor' Huang Di (27th century BC). He has been credited with introducing many of the blessings of civilisation: medicine, the calendar, standardised units of measurement – even, through his wife, the breeding of silkworms.

## Barbarians to the East

The Chinese thought their land was the centre of the world: all other countries were inhabited by barbarians. But in Japan settlers, mainly from China and Korea, had driven out the primitive Ainu and were creating a culture of their own. They grew rice and made crude pottery without a wheel. The period 8000-300 BC was Japan's Jomon era, when independent tribes ruled by priests, and sometimes priestesses, worshipped the sun and the moon. One tribe, under a chieftain called Jimmu, conquered most of Japan. Jimmu became the nation's

***Storage jar***
*Amphora with cord-like decoration from China's Yangshao culture, c.6000 BC.*

***Funeral vase*** *A decorated two-handled vase, used in burials, dating from c.3000 BC.*

***Symbol of power*** *Jade was believed to have magical powers in ancient China. Discs like this, from c.4000 BC, were symbols of authority, and were buried with the dead to take on their last journey.*

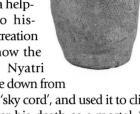

*Pottery without a wheel*
*The potter's wheel was unknown*
*in Japan when this clay vessel was*
*made, some 5000 years ago.*

### Goddess of the sun

In the Jomon era (8000-300 BC) the Japanese were nature worshippers, deifying the sun and the moon. In their mythology the sun goddess Amaterasu sent her grandson, Jimmu, to unify and rule Japan. In Japanese historical legend, Jimmu is the founder of the Japanese imperial line, with all the emperors who followed being of divine origin, in a direct line from the goddess. This belief was central to political thinking until it was officially rejected after Japan's defeat in the Second World War.

first emperor – in 660 BC according to tradition, though modern historians place his reign more than 900 years later. Myths were created around him to strengthen the imperial dynasty: he was said to be descended from Amaterasu, the sun goddess, making all the emperors after him semidivine.

Mythology often lends a helping hand to history. Tibet's creation myth tells how the first king, Nyatri Tsenpo, came down from heaven on a 'sky cord', and used it to climb back up, after his death as a mortal. The next five Tibetan kings returned by the same route. Korea preserves a legend that the god Hwanung created humankind after he descended to Earth on the peninsula's snow-capped mountains.

### The first man in the Land of the Morning Calm

When the god Hwanung, son of the creator god of the Universe, left heaven and arrived in Korea, 'Land of the Morning Calm', he met a female bear and a tiger, who asked him to turn them into humans. Hwanung set them a challenge: he would carry out their request if they could live for 100 days without setting eyes on the sun and with nothing to eat but a handful of garlic cloves. Only the bear passed the test: when she became human she gave birth to Tangun, the first man and Korea's first king. Tradition sets the date of his birth at around 2333 BC.

*Stuck with stripes* In Korean legend, the tiger failed a test to become human.

*In search of the ancestors* Excavations beside the banks of the Yangtze have uncovered the fossils of ancient ape-like creatures and prehuman remains whose dates have not yet been clearly established. Could human beings have evolved independently in Asia at about the same time as in Africa? This question has a special relevance for the Chinese and the Japanese, who set great emphasis on reverence for their ancestors.

## An age of thinkers

China began to emerge from the mists of prehistory about 1500 BC, under rulers called the Shang, from the Yellow River region. The Shang Dynasty was driven out in 1027 BC by the Chou, but rising prosperity during 800 years of Chou rule led finally to decadence and the breakup of the empire into warring kingdoms. Against this background of danger and uncertainty, different philosophers put forward answers to the question: how should society be organised? Three that have lasted to our own day are the doctrines of Confucianism, Taoism and Legalism.

## Unity under the Qin

The Chou Dynasty was overthrown by the Qin, whose ruler, Cheng, conquered and unified northern China and, in 221 BC, took the title of Qin Shi Huangdi, the 'First Qin Emperor'. In less than 50 years he reversed the decline of the past 500. Among his achievements, Shi Huangdi joined up exisiting sections of the Great Wall to keep out marauding Huns and built a road network. He had a mania for order, standardising weights and measures and imposing a rigid structure on society. Shi Huangdi saw tradition as his enemy, and embraced the doctrine of Legalism, which required absolute obedience. He burned books, abolished schools

*Statue from the tomb  Clay statues called haniwa were placed in the tombs of prominent people in Japan during the 3rd and 4th centuries BC. This figurine is 3 ft 8 in (1.12 m) high.*

### The message of Confucius: the family as a model for society

Confucius (c.551-479 BC) was born into poverty in the province of Shandong, at a time when the Chou empire was disintegrating. He became an official in the court of a local prince, and by the age of 22 was developing his theory of the just society. It owed much to the concept of the family: social harmony was the result of virtuous action. The subject owed obedience to the ruler in the same way as the son owed it to the father, the wife to the husband, or the young to the old. The emperor had a 'Mandate from heaven' to govern, but this mandate could be lost, even justifying rebellion, if he ruled unjustly. Natural disasters were signs from heaven that the mandate had been withdrawn. Confucius became a travelling teacher to spread this doctrine, and his sayings were written down after his death by his disciple Mengzi, the 'Second Inspired One'.

and persecuted Confucians – it is said that he had 460 of them buried alive, after cutting off their right hands.

## Expansion under the Han

The land groaned under the burden of high taxes imposed by Shi Huangdi, and the Qin Dynasty survived for only four years after his death. Rebellion broke out, the army mutinied, and in 206 BC a new dynasty seized power – the Han. Under Han Wudi (140-87 BC) the Confucian system was restored. At court, the emperor's numerous wives and concubines were watched over by eunuchs, who wielded enormous influence. The domains of Wudi would have stretched to Xinjiang in the west, present-day North Korea to the north-west and Vietnam to the south. Civil servants

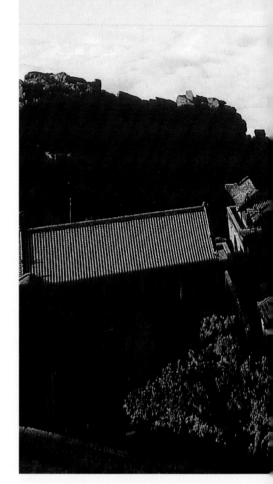

*Sacred mountain  Lapped by a sea of mist, Tai Shan in Shandong Province is the holiest of China's five sacred mountains, and the focus of many legends. One of them is that the palace of the regent of the world, who represents the heavenly emperor, is located on its slopes. Another is that it arose from the head of the god who created the world. The 5000 ft (1524 m) mountain is particularly sacred to Taoists.*

were chosen by examination, as Confucius had advised. High-quality ceramics were invented; so, too, was paper, fostering the keeping of records and the spread of learning. The economy prospered, with the Han Chinese trading as far away as the spice island of Java and exchanging silk for horses along the Silk Road.

### Rewards and punishments

The short-lived Qin Dynasty imposed order with an iron fist. Their doctrine of Legalism meant rewards for those who obeyed their rules and severe punishment for those who broke them. Weights and measures were standardised, and the work of the peasants was supervised by officials.

## Confucianism reaches Japan and Korea

When Prince Shotoku gave Japan its first constitution in AD 604 he took China as his model. The codes of conduct and the system of ranks and duties that Shotoku laid down were directly inspired by the teachings of Confucius. Centuries later, the Meiji Emperor gave a new 'spin' to the Confucian doctrine of the Mandate of Heaven: the emperor was divine, so his right to rule could not be questioned. In Korea, the Yi Dynasty (1392-1910) also adopted Confucian principles for the orderly running of society.

*Honouring the past* In our own day, South Korean devotees of Confucius pay homage to the Yi Dynasty, which adopted his teachings.

## Back to nature

The reputed founder of Taoism was Laozi, the 'old master', who was born c.570 BC. The word *dao*, meaning 'path', is a reference to the effortless way in which nature works. Mankind should avoid choice and striving, and live as naturally as water flows downhill. The ordered society so prized by Confucius was rejected by Taoists because it was artificial. Taoism inspired a love of nature among poets and painters, and Taoist monks were to play a leading part in the development of Chinese medicine.

*Meditating sage* A 12th-century statue of Laozi, seeking through meditation the inner power known as de. Some Taoists used magic rituals as a short cut to de.

*Hoofs of history* Cavalry horses, drawn from the plains of Mongolia, played a major role in the expansion of the Han empire.

## New heights under the Tang

The Han expanded China's boundaries, but it was the peasants who paid the price in forced labour and crippling taxes. Weakened by a peasant revolt, the dynasty collapsed in AD 220, and was followed by three and a half centuries of chaos and civil war. The empire split up into the Three Kingdoms, and at one stage into the Sixteen. The Sui Dynasty (589-618) restored unity and built a canal linking north and south China, but such ambitious schemes added to the misery of the peasants.

A new revolt swept aside the Sui and brought to power a dynasty that wrote a glorious chapter in China's story – the Tang (618-907). They reorganised the administration, dividing the empire into ten regions. Law and order returned, irrigation schemes opened new areas to rice-growing, industries thrived and trade expanded. The arts entered a brilliant period, reaching a pinnacle under the emperor, Xuanzong (712-56), himself a poet. Chang'an, the Tang capital, was the greatest city in the world, with more than a million inhabitants. For all their culture, the Tang were brutal realists abroad, overreaching themselves with conquests that stretched into central Asia, Korea and Vietnam.

*At war   A battle scene from the Chinese tale* **The Romance of the Three Kingdoms.**

The Tang empire collapsed, following mutiny, nomad incursions and a peasant revolt. Under the Song, who came to power in 960, unity was restored, society was run on Confucian principles and the arts flourished again. But in 1126 the Song court fled to the south, under attack by barbarians from the north-east, the Jurcheds.

## Korea's debt to China

Unity was slow in coming to Korea. As late as the 7th century AD, the peninsula was split into three kingdoms: Koguryo in the north, Silla and Paekche in the south. All three looked to China for much of their culture. Buddhism was introduced in 372 by a Chinese monk, and Korea in turn became a conduit through which Chinese culture reached Japan. Admiration for Chinese culture did not imply a welcome for

Chinese rule. The three kingdoms fiercely resisted China's attempts to turn them into colonies. Following a war between the kingdoms, Silla made an alliance with Koguryo that drove out the Chinese. Korea now entered a golden age. Imposing palaces and tranquil pleasure gardens made life pleasant for the rich, but a rigid system of ranks meant that privileges were reserved for the nobility. Only their sons, for instance, could take the examinations to become mandarins, the top rank in the civil service. Resentment seethed among the 'have-nots' and in 935 General Wang Kon founded the Koryo dynasty, from which comes the country's name.

### Buddha's message reaches China

Buddhist missionaries were sent out into the world in the 3rd century BC by Emperor Asoka of India. The Himalayas proved an impassable barrier, and it was not until the 1st century AD that monks, begging their way along the Silk Road, brought Buddhism to China. The early Buddhist communities were persecuted, but the more they suffered, the more adherents they gathered. By the 6th century, north China had some 30 000 Buddhist temples. Accused under the Tang Dynasty of being a foreign import, Buddhism adapted itself and penetrated deep into Chinese life.

**Horseman from the tomb** *China under the Tang Dynasty was renowned for the quality of its pottery. This finely crafted horse and rider was made as a funeral offering, to accompany a man on his journey into the afterlife.*

**Carved in the mind**   *This colossal statue of a reclining Buddha is sculpted into the rock at Daodingshan, Sichuan, China. The statue measures nearly 102 ft (31 m) in length and is (18 ft) (5.5 m) high. It represents the Buddha Shakyamuni entering Nirvana, the ideal state of enlightenment. Below it are statues of Buddhist masters and bodhisattvas, who have renounced their own hope of Nirvana to save others.*

**On the path of enlightenment** *Foot-weary monks, living on charity, spread Buddhism along the Silk Road to China, then on to Korea, land of the tiger. Korean monks carried it to Japan.*

***The crown that united Korea*** *The royal crown of Silla, the kingdom that unified Korea by imposing its authority over the entire peninsula.*

## Buddhism takes over in Tibet

Buddhism was slow to take root in the soil of Tibet, whose early inhabitants revered the natural powers of shamans. It was introduced from India and Nepal in the 7th century, and became the state religion in 780. In the 16th century, Tibet became the most devout Buddhist nation in the world, ruled by the Dalai Lamas.

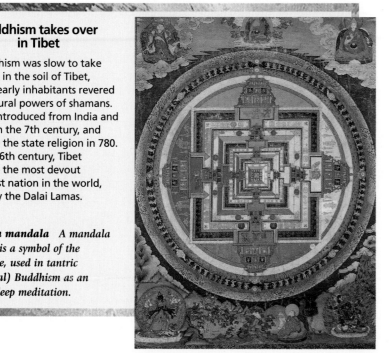

***Tibetan mandala*** *A mandala (right) is a symbol of the Universe, used in tantric (mystical) Buddhism as an aid to deep meditation.*

## Buddhism, Japanese-style

Korean monks carried the Buddha's teachings to Japan in the 6th century, but they were not the first. Chinese Buddhists, refugees from persecution by Taoists, had already landed on Japan's shores. Along with Buddhism, the Koreans brought the Chinese architectural styles that had influenced their own country. The Japanese capital, Nara, was laid out on a chessboard pattern, inspired by the Tang capital, Chang'an. The Buddhist temples of Nara are the best surviving examples of Tang architecture. An even more splendid capital was built at present-day Kyoto in 794, again modelled on Chang'an. Buddhism helped unite a nation in which the Shinto tradition stressed the importance of local shrines. It suited the Japanese temperament and gave birth to many schools. Zen, the main Japanese form of Buddhism, had an impact on all the arts, from ink-brush painting to the tea ceremony.

***Sacred footprints*** *Footprints carved into a stone in a Kyoto temple represent the holy presence of the Buddha.*

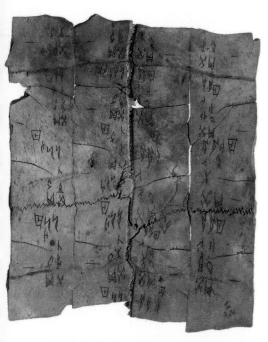

*Looking ahead* Early Chinese picture-writing inscribed on a tortoise shell. Sages used such 'oracle bones' to tell the future.

*One language, four scripts* The Japanese use four scripts, one of them based on Chinese.

## Tangled origins of the spoken word

Despite using different scripts, Chinese and Tibetan can trace their roots to the same language family, the group known as Sino-Tibetan. Japan and Korea, on the other hand, although their earliest scripts were borrowed from China, belong to entirely different language families. Korean is part of the Altaic group, which originated in the Altai Mountains of Central Asia and is related to Turkish and Mongolian – possibly even to Finnish and Hungarian. The origins of Japanese are obscure, though some scholars believe that it, too, may eventually be traceable to the Altaic family.

*Easy as ABC* Korean is syllable-based, making it easier to learn than Chinese.

## The written word

The earliest-known examples of Chinese writing are symbols inscribed in the 14th century BC on tortoise shells and the shoulder blades of cattle. These 'oracle bones' were used under the Shang Dynasty to foretell the future. Over the centuries, Chinese script has developed some 40 000 ideograms, or characters, though fewer than 4000 will serve for most purposes. Learning to read and write up to the standard required by the examinations for the imperial civil service took years of expensive study, so in effect only the sons of the rich could hope to become mandarins. The launch of Pinyin ('spell as it sounds') in 1954 was a modern attempt to simplify written Chinese, using the Roman alphabet.

When Korea and Japan first became interested in Taoism, Confucianism and Buddhism they had no script of their own,

*Words from the past* Tibetan script has not changed since the 7th century.

## Writing in pictures

Simple pictures work well enough as symbols of solid objects, but are less effective at conveying emotions and shades of meaning. To make new words, Chinese scholars hit on the idea of combining symbols. The word 'peace', for instance, is made from the characters for a roof and a woman. In a further advance, characters were used for syllables, just as an outline of waves ('sea') in a child's picture puzzle might stand for 'see'. In a country with many spoken dialects, the traditional script has the advantage that once learned it can be understood anywhere.

so they turned to China. Their scholars and monks had to master Chinese characters in order to transcribe the sacred texts. Both countries later developed their own forms of writing. Korea adopted a phonetic system, *hangul*, in the 15th century. It has 24 letters, supplemented by some 1800 ideograms. Japanese writing, the result of a long process of development, is a complex mix of Chinese characters known as *kanji*, two syllable-based systems that use 46 characters each, and a fourth system based on the Roman alphabet. Tibetan writing is modelled on Indian. The written language has remained unchanged since it was introduced in the 7th century, although the spoken language has changed considerably over the intervening centuries.

## Genghis Khan

The barbarian Jurched tribes, who forced the Song court to flee to Hangzhou in the south of China, were subjugated by an even more terrible foe – the Mongols. The fierce tribes of Mongolia, united under Genghis Khan, set out in 1206 to conquer the world. Their empire was to stretch from eastern Europe to the China Sea. The Mongols swept into northern China in 1209, subdued the Korean peninsula ten years later and by 1279 had China in their grasp.

### Marco Polo at the court of Kublai Khan

The Venetian merchant Marco Polo was only 17 when he set out in 1271 with his father and uncle in search of the fabled wealth of the Orient. They travelled on the Silk Road, a 4000 mile (6400 km) route pioneered by Chinese traders in the 2nd century BC. They arrived at the court of Kublai, the 'Great Khan', in 1275 and Marco Polo was to stay in his service for 17 years. After returning to Venice he was captured by the Genoese, and while in prison dictated *The Description of the World*. Its account of the wonders he had seen – a dazzling court, splendid cities and such marvels as paper money and coal – seemed so fantastic that at first he was taken as a madman, or at best an outrageous liar.

*Traveller   A Chinese statue of Marco Polo.*

Kublai Khan, grandson of Genghis, moved the capital to Beijing and announced a new dynasty, the Yuan. He seized land both from the peasants and from wealthy Chinese to give to his adherents, and extended his rule into Tibet, where land grants won the support of the Buddhist lamas. Kublai made two attempts to invade Japan. The first was repulsed by samurai warriors and the second, in 1271, ended in disaster for the Mongols when a 'divine wind', the *kamikaze*, wrecked their fleet. The Chinese response to alien rule, with its high taxes and discrimination, was to form secret societies and mount insurrections. The Yuan Dynasty was overthrown in 1368 by a peasant general who established a new native dynasty, the Ming. Many of the Mongols were by this time steeped in Chinese culture, but the new emperor, Taizu, banished them from Beijing. He set up his own court at Nanjing, but a later emperor returned it to Beijing.

*The Silk Road*

The Ming reduced taxes, encouraged trade and planted Chinese colonies abroad. To contend with opponents inside China they set up a police state, with spies and informers. They had enemies on the frontier, too: the constant menace of the Mongols.

***The Conqueror***
*A Persian illustration of Genghis Khan on his throne. In 1227 his empire reached from the China Sea to the Caspian.*

***Beating the Mongols***
*Alone in East Asia, Japan resisted the Mongol tide. Here, Mongols surrender to samurai after a failed invasion bid.*

## Japan's first shogun

By the end of the 8th century, Buddhism had put down deep roots in Japan; but for all the religion's striving for peace, there was a long period of feudal government, punctuated by blood-steeped civil war and peasant uprisings. Step by step, the emperor lost contact with the nation and was drawn ever deeper into the ceremonial aspects of life at court. As his real power waned, a new group of warrior clans came to the fore. The most prominent among them, the Minamoto and the Taira, fought a vicious civil war that ended in 1185 with victory for Minamoto Yoritomo. Leaving the emperor in Kyoto, Yoritomo established a new capital at Kamakura, far from what he saw as the decadence of the court. In 1192, he secured the title of shogun, or military governor. The local nobility still held influence in the countryside, but took their orders from a military council set up by Yoritomo. For the next 700 years the country was ruled by the system of military feudalism started by Japan's first shogun.

*Fairy-tale fortress  With its tier upon tier of curving roofs, the castle of Himeji, built in 1606, west of Osaka, is a remarkable work of art. It was also a formidable fortress.*

## The strategic insights of Sun Tzu, philosopher and general

Sun Tzu, a general with the insights of a philosopher, lived during some of China's most tumultuous years. During the period of the Warring Kingdoms, in the 6th century BC, warlords from rival petty states were laying waste to entire regions. Many things were changing in society, including the nature of war itself. For Sun Tzu, war was no longer a question of risking thousands of lives in pitched battles, but rather of defeating the enemy by the use of manoeuvre, deception and strategy. The lessons that Sun Tzu learned during those hectic years were distilled in writings that became a classic text: *The Art of War.* Sun Tzu's insights have been studied in military academies all over the world, and have recently enjoyed a new lease of life in management training schools, because of his emphasis on winning by strategy rather than by force. He laid down guidelines for guerrilla warfare, giving full value to surprise and deception, stressed the value of psychological warfare, and advised the use of spies and counter-intelligence. Sun Tzu's approach was based on the Taoist philosophy of his day: an army, he said, should be at one with nature, and become fluid to the point of melting into its surroundings. The path to victory lay in the rule: 'Embrace the Taoist ways of the past and you will master the present.'

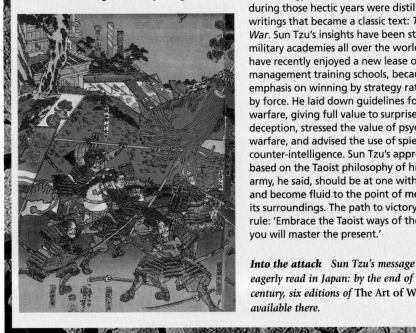

*Into the attack  Sun Tzu's message was eagerly read in Japan: by the end of the 9th century, six editions of* The Art of War *were available there.*

## The samurai: living by the code of the warrior

The soul of a samurai was lodged in his sword, a razor-sharp weapon with which he could slice an enemy in two. Emerging as mercenaries in the service of local lords, the samurai became a force in the 12th century, when warrior clans such as the Minamoto used them to climb to power. A samurai ('one who serves') lived by a code of courage and honour that was formalised in the 17th century as *bushido,* 'the way of the warrior'. Under the Tokugawa shoguns (1603-1867) they were made a hereditary caste; but their days were numbered when feudalism was abolished in Japan in 1871. Five years later, the samurai lost their right to carry swords. Some turned to business, others to government service. The samurai as a caste disappeared, but their prestige was to live on.

*Man-at-arms
After seven centuries of power, the samurai lost even their right to wear swords when, in 1876, Japan introduced military service for all.*

## The 'long-nosed barbarians' reach China

Thanks to a powerful navy and its intrepid commander, the eunuch Zheng He, China under the Ming prospered from trade links throughout South-east Asia. Its junks sailed as far as the coasts of Arabia and Madagascar, into the South Pacific and the Indian Ocean. When delegations from abroad came to China, they were treated as lesser breeds, come to pay homage. But far to the west there were other trading nations whose self-esteem in every way matched that of the Chinese. The Portuguese arrived in 1517, to be followed by the Spaniards, the Dutch and the English. The Chinese looked on them as 'long-nosed barbarians' and did not realise that China's technology was destined to be overtaken by that of the newcomers. With Europe's merchants came its missionaries: the Jesuits Matteo Ricci and Adam Schall made few converts, despite immersing themselves in Chinese culture. In Rome, the pope dismissed Chinese religion as nothing more than 'superstitious practices'.

## The iron rule of the Manchu

The last years of the Ming Dynasty were marked by intrigues at court, banditry and famine in the country at large and the breakdown of authority. Manchu rebels, who had conquered vast territories in the north, swarmed into Beijing in 1644. The last Ming emperor hanged himself, and the Manchu, or Qing Dynasty, imposed a rule of iron. Opposition to the Manchus was mainly from the trading ports, so the Qing burned merchant fleets and forcibly resettled entire coastal villages. The majority Han Chinese were forced to wear pigtails. Emigration, the only hope for a starving peasantry, was banned: the 450 million subjects of the Middle Kingdom were penned in behind the Great Wall. Only a dozen merchants had

### A Jesuit at the Imperial court

In their mission to convert the Chinese to Christianity, the Jesuits took a long view. They took meticulous care not to offend imperial sensitivities, and they put their vast knowledge of astronomy and mathematics at the disposal of their hosts. So impressed was the Manchu emperor with the Jesuit father Adam Schall (below) that he appointed him head of the imperial observatory.

*Beauty from Korea* Celadon vases, with a pale green glaze, were a speciality of Korean potters. This one dates from the 17th or 18th century.

*China's secret* A porcelain vase from the Ming Dynasty, decorated in cobalt blue. Porcelain became highly prized in Europe, but the Chinese jealously guarded the secret of its manufacture.

*The newcomers* Detail of a Japanese folding screen, depicting the Portuguese arrival in the middle of the 16th century.

permission to trade with the barbarians from Europe, and that trade was limited to a single port – Canton.

## Japan turns its back on the world

In 1543 Portuguese navigators landed in Japan and found an outward-looking nation that welcomed trade. They were soon followed by the Jesuit Francis Xavier, who stayed for more than two years and founded several Christian communities. In the 17th century, Japan turned in on itself. Portuguese and Spanish missionaries and merchants were seen as potentially

*Pride in craftsmanship* Japanese craftsmen took pride in showing off their skill, as in this 17th-century portable medicine box, known as an inro. Its fine lacquerwork is decorated with gold and mother-of-pearl.

subversive, and were expelled, while the Dutch were confined on a small island off Nagasaki. Korea, too, went into a period of isolation, in reaction to the harsh terms imposed after defeat in a war with China. In 1636, when 36 Dutch sailors were shipwrecked on its shores, they were cast into prison. Some escaped after 13 years and reached Japan. They were the first Europeans to give an account of Korea.

**Victors and vanquished** *Chinese captives look on in dismay as the Japanese take over their fortress in the Sino-Japanese War.*

**Foreign trade** *Trading posts of foreign companies in Canton during the 18th century. Trade was limited to a few coastal towns.*

## The Opium Wars

The demand in 19th-century Europe, and above all in Britain, for tea, silk and porcelain was insatiable. China was a prime source of all three, but the imperial court had no taste either for Western goods or for Western merchants. Many of the emperor's subjects, though, had a taste for opium – so many that the drug was seen as a threat to social harmony. In 1799, imports of the 'foreign filth' were banned by imperial decree. But opium, carried from India in the holds of British ships, was all that Western traders could offer in exchange for imports from China. The tension snapped in 1839, when the Chinese seized 20 000 chests of opium that had been smuggled into Canton. London reacted by sending in gunboats. After a blockade, China was forced to open a number of ports and to cede Hong Kong to

**The Orient, Western style** *Two ladies of Shanghai, which was to become the most Westernised city in China.*

Britain. The Qing empire was already in danger of being destabilised by revolts in the interior when, in 1856, the search of a British-registered ship by Chinese officials was taken as an excuse for British and French troops to take Canton and Tianjin. China's humiliation was complete: she had to open still more ports and allow in Western merchants and Christian missionaries.

## Japan enters the modern era

Japan was jolted into modern times in 1853, when a US naval squadron under Commodore Matthew Perry arrived in Tokyo Bay. Returning the following year, he forced Japan to accept trade with the USA, opening the door for other Western powers. Contact with the West was a profound shock for a feudal society, resulting in 1868 in a coup that overthrew the Tokugawa shogunate and restored power to the boy emperor Meiji. He was determined to modernise Japan's industry and armed forces, taking Western countries as a model. His success became evident when Japan invaded Formosa (Taiwan) in 1874, won a foothold in Manchuria at China's expense in 1894-5 and crushed the tsar's army and navy in the Russo-Japanese War (1904-5) to gain control of Korea, which it annexed in 1910.

**A shock for the tsar** *Japan's victory in the Russo-Japanese War took Russia by surprise.*

*Grim fate* *With the Boxer cause lost, their empress turned against them.*

## From the Boxer Rising to the last emperor

Resentment against foreigners, secretly encouraged by the Manchu Empress Cixi, lay at the root of a rebellion in 1899 by the Boxers, a Chinese secret society. The rebels slaughtered Westerners and Chinese Christians and besieged the foreign legations in Beijing. An international relief force broke the siege and went on to loot the city and the treasures of the imperial palace. Power was oozing away from the Qing Dynasty, and the regime was overthrown by a popular rising in 1911. Sun Yat-sen, a lifelong nationalist, returned from exile to take charge of the revolution he had orchestrated. He proclaimed a republic in 1912 and forced the boy emperor, Pu Yi, to abdicate, ending China's last imperial dynasty.

*Nationalist leader* *In 1912 Sun Yat-sen proclaimed China a republic.*

## The birth of the Chinese Communist Party

Sun Yat-sen led a Nationalist government in Canton, but bandits and warlords ruled the provinces. On May 4, 1919, students demonstrated in Beijing against foreign influence and the anarchy that was crippling China. In the ranks of the 'May Fourthers' was a young man who had already taken part in the revolution of 1911 – Mao Ze-dong. The son of a rich peasant from Hunan, Mao was one of the original members of the Chinese Communist Party, founded at a secret meeting in Shanghai in 1921. A new political force had appeared, at a time when traditional values were collapsing and every day seemed to bring a new outrage. The new party had no more than a dozen members, but its ideas fell on fertile ground, for Mao had founded the Society for the Study of Marxism. The man who was to be his most formidable foe, Chiang Kai-shek, at first accepted communist help to defeat the warlords. As commandant of a military academy near Canton, he turned to Moscow for aid to reorganise the establishment on Bolshevik lines, and allowed communists to join the Guomindang Nationalist Party, which he took over after Sun Yat-sen's death in 1925.

### The decline and fall of the Mongol Empire

In the Middle Ages, the civilised world trembled as the Mongols beat out a path of conquest that ranged from China to southern Austria. Such frantic energy could not be sustained, and in the 17th century, following defeat by the Manchus, Mongolia became a province of China. In 1911, when the Qing Dynasty was toppled, Outer Mongolia declared its independence, under Russian protection. After a period of reoccupation by the Chinese (1920-2) the Outer Mongolians rose against their masters and declared a People's Republic, closely linked to the Soviet Union. Inner Mongolia remained part of China and, like China in the 1920s, suffered all the agonies of a land in which rival warlords fought for power.

## Civil war and the Long March

To Chiang, the communists were dangerous rivals, and in 1928 he struck, executing a number of their leaders and crushing their trade unions. China faced yet another civil war. In 1934, when Chiang's troops encircled the communist base in southern China, Mao and 100 000 followers broke out and embarked on the Long March – a journey of 6000 miles (9600 km) that lasted just over a year. Only 10 000 of Mao's tattered forces survived to reach safety in

*Captured on canvas* *A revolutionary painting celebrates the Long March.*

*Atrocity in Nanking   Some 200 000 Chinese civilians were killed by Japanese troops, in a frenzy of rape and looting when they sacked Nanking in 1937.*

Japan and America's General MacArthur gave the country its first democratic constitution: women won the right to vote and the emperor renounced his divinity.

### Mao's triumph

Mao and the Chinese Red Army won China's civil war because they had the support of the peasant masses. Chiang fled

the north. The Long March, a great semi-circular sweep across deserts, mountains and raging rivers, became the most potent legend in the annals of Chinese communism, and established Mao's reputation as an outstanding leader.

### Japan's last challenge

The militarist party in Japan, driven by a remorseless will to expand, saw an easy victim in a China that was divided by civil war. Annexing Manchuria, in 1931, gave Japan a base from which to invade the rest of the country. China's civil war was temporarily put aside when Chiang and Mao formed a united front against the invaders. But the Japanese juggernaut rolled on. The sack of Nanking, in 1937, was an orgy of rape and slaughter that shocked the world. Short of oil to feed its industries and wage war, Japan decided on a desperate strategy:

*A god no longer   For the first time in his life Emperor Hirohito leaves the Imperial Palace as a mortal man, not a god. This change of status was ordained in a new constitution, given to Japan by America's General MacArthur. Announcing Japan's surrender, Hirohito had told the nation: 'The war situation has developed not necessarily to our advantage.'*

to win an empire of its own in the Pacific. A surprise attack on the US base at Pearl Harbor, on December 7, 1941, was followed by a string of dazzling victories against Western empires and outposts. But aggression brought retribution: the Western allies recovered, and US planes pounded the Japanese mainland. When atomic bombs were dropped on Hiroshima and Nagasaki, on August 6 and 9, 1945, the war was over. American troops occupied

#### The Korean War

The Cold War saw Korea divided between a communist North and a pro-Western South. On June 25, 1950, Cold War became hot war, when the communist leader, Kim Il Sung, sent tanks across the 38th Parallel to invade the South. China entered the war when the USA, with United Nations' support, pushed back the invaders almost to the Chinese frontier. An armistice was agreed after three years of struggle which left more than four million dead or wounded, both Koreas in ruins, and a warning that America was prepared to resist communism.

*Day of judgment   Bound, kneeling and under armed guard, a landlord is interrogated by a people's tribunal. Mao Ze-dong's Land Reform Law of 1950 is about to claim another victim. At the end of the 1980s, Mao's successor Deng Xiao-ping restored private property rights.*

with his Nationalists to Formosa (Taiwan), and on October 1, 1949, Mao announced in Beijing the birth of the Chinese People's Republic. The 'Great Helmsman' then set out to re-create China. He gave land to 300 million poor peasants and executed 2 million rich ones. He encouraged public criticism of 'anti-revolutionaries' and had children denouncing their parents. Then he declared: 'Let a hundred flowers bloom, and a hundred schools of thought contend.' Those who took him at his word and offered real criticism suffered for it. In 1958 Mao's 'Great Leap Forward', intended to

send production soaring, was a disaster, helping to create a famine in which up to 30 million died. To destroy opponents within the party he created the 'Cultural Revolution', using the zeal of young Red Guards to keep China in a permanent state of revolutionary excitement. Brandishing copies of the *Little Red Book* that contained Mao's thoughts, they marched around the

*Tibet under the yoke   China invaded Tibet in 1950, and nine years later the country rose in a revolt that failed. Here, monks lay down their arms. The Dalai Lama escaped to India.*

country, killing, terrorising and humiliating suspects. Intellectuals were condemned to 're-education' through menial work. With China falling yet again into chaos, and Red Guards clashing with the Red Army, Mao decided the Cultural Revolution had gone too far and abruptly called it to a halt.

## Into modern times

After Mao died in 1976, Deng Xiao-ping emerged as China's new leader. His policy was modernisation: of industry, agriculture, the army and technology. This approach aroused long-pent-up demands for political freedom, but Deng was not prepared to slacken the Communist Party's grip. When students demonstrated in Beijing's Tiananmen Square in 1989, Deng crushed the protest with troops and tanks. Up to 2000 demonstrators were killed as the tanks bulldozed barricades in front of the TV cameras of a horrified world. After the massacre, Deng continued to encourage economic growth and to seek better relations with the West. And as the events in Tiananmen Square became part of history, China was viewed increasingly in the West as a huge potential market and a valuable trading partner. In the new millennium, a major question for China and other nations of East Asia is: can they maintain their economic dynamism and throw off the torments of the political past?

*Mao's army of youth   Schoolchildren, waving copies of Mao's Little Red Book, bring chaos to the streets during China's Cultural Revolution. They were pawns in his game of creating a climate of perpetual revolution in order to eliminate opposition within the Communist Party.*

*Mending bridges   Deng Xiao-ping (front row, second from left) seeks to repair relations with the USA after Tiananmen Square.*

# THE PLACE
## AND ITS
# PEOPLE

The closing decades of the 20th century witnessed some remarkable success stories in East Asia. The 'Asian tigers' of Japan, Hong Kong, Taiwan and South Korea showed what could be done by resilient, enterprising people. The economic whirlwind they unleashed put to the test traditions that dated back for thousands of years. In a single generation, the children and grandchildren of poor peasants had to adjust to life as city-dwellers. But traditions are resilient too, and the special gift of East Asia is its ability to combine the very old with the very new.

# CHAPTER 1
# THE SPLENDOURS AND POWERS OF NATURE

The Taoist tradition that began in China gave human life its place in the natural order. Nature's system was a complex network that linked the five elements – water, fire, wood, metal and earth – with the seasons, the points of the compass, animals, plants, the organs of the body, colours, tastes and sounds. In Taoism, philosophy and religion presented a single vision of the world and everything in it. Mountains, so dominant in the landscape of East Asia, were invested with a spirituality sensed by all who contemplated them. In Japan, where Mount Fuji with its perfect cone was held sacred, volcanoes were proof that the Earth was a living thing. Nature demonstrates its power to excess in winds that scour the Mongolian plains, typhoons that lash the tropical coasts, drenching monsoons, devastating floods and earthquakes – all seeming to show how fragile by comparison are the works of mankind.

*Clouds of steam rise from volcanic springs in the Bepu region of Japan.*

# The mountains: refuges of minorities and ghosts

*According to a Taoist saying, a mountain is 'a space void of people, but full of emptiness'. The words begin to make sense in an awesome expanse of mountains that were created 40 million years ago, in a cataclysmic collision between two of the vast plates that make up the surface of the Earth.*

A quick glance at a relief map of China will show at once how large a part is played in the country's physical make-up by mountains. Eighty-five per cent of these mountains and plateaus are more than 1650 ft (500 m) high. As for Korea, it is three-quarters covered by mountains.

## Realms of mystery

Their rugged landscape has had a profound effect on the way of life of both the Chinese and the Koreans. Essentially farmers and peasants, they have settled in low-lying areas with rich soil that is suitable for growing rice and other cereal crops. The high lands, with poorer soil, have been occupied by smaller ethnic groups: Tibetans from the high plateaus, who raise yaks and grow barley; Mongols from the grassy northern steppes, who raise sheep and horses; nomadic Turks from Xinjiang, who herd sheep. The ethnic majorities in both countries, the Han Chinese and the Koreans, traditionally had mixed views about mountains. They were remote, mysterious, and even dangerous places, associated with avalanches, savage beasts and fierce tribesmen. Their sheer rock faces seemed terrifying and their forests were impenetrable. There were also rich treasures to be found in the mountains: mineral

wealth and rare medicinal plants such as ginseng, widely believed to hold the secret of longevity. Moreover, mountains were touched by magic, for nymphs, ghosts and genies lived in their caves.

## Temples and monasteries

Buddhist monks in China built temples among the heights. Wutai Shan, Emei Shan, Putuo Shan and Jiuhua Shan became sacred mountains and attracted pilgrims. The Taoists chose Tai Shan, Hua Shan, Song Shan and the two Heng Shans as lofty locations for their monasteries. In Korea, even before the Buddhists arrived, tribal shamans held the summits of Ch'wiri and Paektu to be sacred places. Monks, hermits and other seekers after truth found the peace needed for meditation and contemplation in the mountains.

Despite the modern emphasis on materialism, the gods and spirits of the mountains linger in the folk memories of China and of Korea. Processions of pilgrims still wind their way to a world that lies halfway between heaven and earth.

***Monastery in the sky***
*Residents of a 1400-year-old hanging monastery on Hengshan, China, are reminded every day of the precarious nature of existence.*

***Stone forest*** *Limestone pinnacles in China's Yunnan Province have been sculpted by rain and wind.*

# Islands born of fire

*Japan had a violent birth, when two of the gigantic crustal plates that carry the Earth's continents crashed into each other, buckling the surface of the land to form mountains and spewing out molten rock to form volcanoes. Small wonder that Mount Fuji, with its near-perfect volcanic cone, is an icon of the nation.*

Millions of years ago, Earth's Pacific plate, adrift on a sea of molten rock, collided with the Eurasian plate, squeezing up the sea-bed to form the Japanese archipelago, a sweeping arc of islands sprinkled with more than 160 volcanoes, some 60 of them still active. Located in a region where continents not only collide but also grind against each other, Japan is prone to earth-

**Nature's bounty** *Open-air bathing, beneath an invigorating waterfall on Mount Yudono.*

quakes and tsunamis, the towering and destructive waves caused by underwater earthquakes and volcanic eruptions. The highest ever recorded was off the Ryukyu Islands in 1971. It reached a stagger-ing 280 ft (85 m).

## Crowded plains and empty mountains

With the seventh largest population in the world (126 million), Japan crowds the vast bulk of its people into coastal plains, narrow river valleys and land reclaimed from the sea. Only in such places is the land flat enough for settlement, sustained agriculture and industry. The largest flat area, around Tokyo on the main island of Honshu, is only 5800 sq miles (15 000 km²) – three-quarters the size of Wales.

About 62 miles (100 km) from Tokyo stands the grace-ful, snow-clad cone of Mount Fuji, a volcano that has been dormant since early in the 18th century. At 12 389 ft (3776 m) Mount Fuji – called *Fujisan* by the Japanese – is the country's highest mountain and most celebrated landmark.

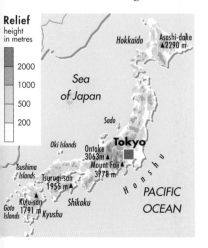

**Relief**
height in metres

2000
1000
500
200

Sea of Japan

Hokkaido
Asashi-dake ▲2290 m

Sado

Oki Islands

Ontake 3063m ▲
**Tokyo**
Tsushima Islands
Mount Fuji ▲ 3778 m
Tsurugi-san 1955 m ▲
Honshu
Shikoku
PACIFIC OCEAN
Kyu-san 1791 m ▲
Goto Islands
Kyushu

*A mountain landscape Jagged, steep-sided mountains cover more than 70 per cent of Japan. These peaks are in the Seto-Naikai National Park.*

Other peaks that rise above 10 000 ft (3000 m) lie in the 'Japanese Alps' in central Honshu. From the sky, the most striking aspect of these mountains is their sheer emptiness. After the outskirts of Nagano, there is not a village to be seen – only endless forests and the streams that tumble down steep mountain slopes.

Attempts at the economic development of Japan's mountains have met with limited success. Only a few workable deposits of minerals have so far been discovered, and the only effective way of exploiting these untamed wildernesses is through tourism, espe-cially skiing. Good centres for this sport are the cities of Nagano and Morioka, the north terminus of the *shinkansen*, the 'bullet train', which whisks passengers from Tokyo, 285 miles (460 km) away at 130 mph (210 km/h).

The mountains have another attraction to offer: the magma, or molten rock, that seethes in the bowels of the Earth can burst out in a volcanic explosion, or it can have a gentler effect, creating hot sulphur springs, known as *onsen*, There are well over 2000 such springs, and the Japanese flock to them to seek cures for their ail-ments, or simply to reduce stress.

**Under the volcano** *The menacing crater of an active volcano near Kagoshima. When it erupts, the citizens carry umbrellas as protection against the fine ash that falls.*

# Desert wastes that cradled lost civilisations

*Two vast deserts, sparsely peopled by ethnic minorities, lay long forgotten in the centre of the Asian continent. But today there is renewed interest in them because of the mineral riches beneath their sands.*

Between the frozen swamps of northern Siberia and the jagged peaks of the Himalayas lie the two driest regions in East Asia – the Gobi Desert and the desert of Taklimakan. Until the Jurassic era, about 190 million to 135 million years ago, when dinosaurs were the dominant form of life on Earth, both these vast areas were covered by sea.

## Treasures in the wilderness

The Gobi and Taklimakan are trackless, arid wastelands, blocked off from the moisture-bearing summer monsoon by the Himalayas and other mountain bastions, exposed to the winter winds blowing dry polar air south from Siberia. Winter temperatures in the Gobi can fall to as low as –40°C (–40°F), while in summer they can soar to 45°C (113°F).

The Gobi was the home of the Mongol horsemen who were led by Genghis Khan on a path of terror and conquest in the 13th century. It extends for some 500 000 sq miles (1 295 000 km²) and covers half of Mongolia. The desert is fringed by grassland, and not completely without rivers, for there are occasional cloudbursts – though most of the streams run away into the sand or into a desolation of storm-battered, flint-strewn gravel plains. The discovery of coal and oil deposits in the Gobi has led to a search for further mineral treasures beneath the sands.

## A sea of sand

In the language of the Uighurs, the name Taklimakan means 'once you enter, there is no escape'. This vast sea of sand in China's Xinjiang Province covers some 135 000 sq miles (350 000 km²). Dunes driven by the winds reach up to 1000 ft (300 m) in height. Staking out the edges of the desert are a few oases where fruits and cereals can be grown. China's first contacts with the West were made along the caravan routes that have linked these oases since ancient times.

In more modern times, Lop Nor ('the Filthy Lake'), in the east of Xinjiang Province, became a centre for China's nuclear testing in 1964.

*A wandering life   The Tajiks of China's Xinjiang Province have a nomadic lifestyle.*

### The lost cities of Taklimakan

In the late 1970s an intriguing find was made in the Taklimakan Desert: the mummified bodies of a fair-haired people. About 100 of them had lain in the sands for more than 3000 years, preserved by the extreme dryness of the climate. Archaeologists are almost certain that they were of Indo-European stock. The Taklamakan was far less hostile then than it is today. Rains refreshed the soil and rivers flowed. The vanished people of this once fertile land were farmers and shepherds, and they had a form of writing that drew on an ancient Indian alphabet. Their main city, Niya, seems to have prospered for 500 years before disaster struck.

Whether suddenly or gradually, the climate changed: rivers dried up, crops withered and pastures vanished. Along with other cities in ancient Taklimakan, Niya was abandoned to the remorseless advance of the sands.

*Restless sands   Constantly resculpted, continuously on the move, the great dunes of the Taklimakan Desert are slaves to the wind.*

# The magic of Huang Shan

*Poets and painters have long celebrated the splendours of the Yellow Mountains, and monks, hermits and philosophers have found spiritual nourishment in a landscape that seems to have been designed for those seeking quiet contemplation.*

**Art on a rock** *So compelling are the Yellow Mountains to artists that calligraphy adorns their rocks.*

Since the days of antiquity, the Chinese have looked on mountains as places of spiritual intensity, the abode of the gods and a refuge for those who venerate them. It is no accident that, to write the words 'divinity' and 'hermit', Chinese script makes use of ideograms based on the shape of a mountain.

### Earth's 'most perfect' mountains

In terms of height above sea level, there is nothing out of the ordinary about the Huang Shan, or Yellow Mountains, in China's Anhui Province: Mount Everest stands nearly five times higher than their highest peak, the 6039 ft (1841 m) Linhua Feng ('Peak of the Opening Lotus'). But to many Chinese, the Huang Shan are the most perfect mountains on Earth. The range, roughly parallel to the course of the Yangtze, but 62 miles (100 km) south of the river, attracts thousands of tourists every year. What they see as they ascend is a dreamlike vision: swirling mists roll away to reveal granite pinnacles, with the contorted roots of pine trees clinging to crags and dizzying ledges. Bamboo forests spread below their feet, and in the distance more summits rise triumphantly above the clouds. Colours change according to the season, as thousands of trees play variations on the themes of green, yellow, red, brown and gold.

### Temples in the mist

Xuanzong, an emperor of the Tang Dynasty (618-907), gave the Huang Shan their name, and both emperors and commoners have ascended their slopes – though the emperors were carried on palanquins, while lesser men had to use their legs. The names given to favourite sites and scenes speak eloquently of the love the Chinese feel for Huang Shan: 'Welcoming

Pine', 'Western Ocean of Clouds', 'Temple of Merciful Light', 'Jade-screen House', 'House of Clouds Cave', 'Purple Cloud Peak', 'Celestial City Peak' and 'Peach Flower Summit'. Still today, artists and poets find inspiration in scenes that were immortalised by painters of the Ming period (1368-1644), and by celebrated poets such as Li Bai, who lived in the Tang period.

Paths of steep stone steps on the eastern and western slopes of Huang Shan make it easier for tourists, pilgrims, painters and poets alike to ascend. The climb is best in autumn for its spectacular colours, or in winter for its invigorating air. It takes about ten hours to reach the top, but when a Buddhist temple or a Taoist monastery looms out of a receding wall of mist, the effort is more than worth while.

**Homage at sunset** *Pilgrims gather to watch one of the sunsets for which Huang Shan is renowned.*

**Above the clouds** *Summits pierce the cloud banks, pine trees perching improbably on their steep sides.*

# The mighty Yangtze, China's powerhouse

*For millennia, the Yangtze River has been a vital link between China's interior and its coast. Today, it is no less vital: its prodigious hydroelectric potential is the key to the future of a region with 300 million inhabitants.*

An unbelievable turbulence of thrashing brown waters that becomes a main artery of inland trade, the Chang Jiang, or 'Long River', as the Chinese call the Yangtze, is the third longest river in the world, after the Amazon and the Nile. It begins life on the Tibetan plateau and, swollen by 700 tributaries, is notorious for bursting its banks. The river crosses ten provinces on a winding, 3716 mile (5980 km) journey to its delta at Shanghai.

**The three gorges** *The gorges are spectacular passes where the furious waters of the Yangtze are forced into passages that narrow to 300 ft (100 m) wide.*

**Taking a chance** *The might of the Yangtze is challenged (right) on a flimsy-looking raft. Experience shows that the ramshackle design works.*

36

### Hauling against the rapids

During the 1970s a system of cables was installed to allow boats to make headway against the currents that surge through the Yangtze's gorges. In earlier centuries, boats were hauled against the rapids by teams of up to 100 'trackers', bent double as they strained against their ropes on perilously narrow cliff ledges. Today, the Yangtze carries around two-thirds of the total river water of China. The riverside towns and cities awaken each day to an almost theatrical bustle of barges, ferries, pleasure cruisers, passengers, porters, stevedores and cargoes. Every summer, this major commercial artery is threatened by the monsoon. Already swollen by melting snows from the mountains, the river and its tributaries become rushing channels for the monsoon's downpour. Vast deposits of mud and silt clog up the river bed, and its waters overflow into the surrounding plain. Lakes both upstream and downstream of Hunan

#### The waterways of China

China's inland trade moves along a web of 37 500 miles (60 000 km) of navigable waterways, crisscrossing the country like veins. Today, bulky goods such as wood and bamboo are carried in powered barges, but in ancient times cargoes moved at the pace of the buffalo or humans that pulled them. The 1125 mile (1800 km) Grand Canal, dug in the 7th century on the orders of Emperor Yang Di to carry rice from the fertile south to the more heavily populated north, was the engineering wonder of its day. The canal linked the Yangtze with the Yellow River and three other major river systems, and was dug by millions of conscripts. On sections that have been cleared of silt, it still carries foodstuffs and consumer goods from the south to the north. The Yangtze is the main artery of central China, and Chongqing, lying some 1400 miles (2250 km) from the sea, is its heart. This capital of the Yangtze basin was heavily bombed by the Japanese during the Second World War. Now it is preparing for the future by remodelling the city centre. The office blocks and traffic highways of a modern city are replacing the labyrinth of overcrowded streets that once were filled with the cries of stallholders and wandering traders.

take up some of the overflow, but in 1931, 1954, and more recently 1998, exceptionally heavy floods brought death and desolation when thousands of square miles were inundated.

The other serious problem is that progress comes at a price. As fast as hydroelectric projects such as the Three Gorges Dam turn the Yangtze into central China's economic dynamo, so does the river risk pollution from the growing industries and cities along its banks. On the credit side, two of the world's most endangered species, the Yangtze River dolphin and the Chinese alligator, are protected in riverside sanctuaries.

***Building for tomorrow*** *The Three Gorges Dam on the Yangtze is a colossal hydroelectric project, not due to be completed until 2009.*

## The Three Gorges Dam

The plan to build a dam across the Yangtze has been hotly debated since the 1920s. The Three Gorges – Qutang, Wu and Xiling – begin 280 miles (450 km) downstream from Chongqing and confine the river between towering cliffs for 75 miles (120 km). Modernists see a shining future in harnessing the Yangtze's hydroelectric potential, while conservationists worry about the impact of reshaping nature on such a colossal scale. So far, the modernists are winning: in 1992 the government decided to build a dam below the third gorge, at an estimated cost of 50 billion dollars. When completed, in 2009, it will be more than 0.6 mile (1 km) wide and house 26 giant turbines. Opponents argue for a series of smaller dams on tributary rivers: the big dam, though it will help flood control and turn the Yangtze into a super-highway into the interior, will displace some 1 200 000 people from their homes and dramatically raise the level of the river through the gorges. The battle is not yet over: resettlement has been slowed down by local corruption and by one of the most powerful forces in China – the stubbornness of the peasants, who refuse to leave their homes.

***Boom city*** *Trade on the Yangtze has grown at a phenomenal rate. Wuhan, 680 miles (1100 km) from the sea, can be reached by ocean-going ships.*

# From the frozen north to the tropical south

*The coastline of China, stretching more than 5350 miles (8600 km) from north to south, has a climate that varies from the near-Siberian cold of the largely landlocked Yellow Sea to the tropical heat of Hainan Island in the country's far south.*

***A natural paradise*** *Beautiful beaches with tropical vegetation line the coast of Hainan Island, in southern China.*

Looked at in profile, China slopes from west to east, descending towards the coast like a gigantic staircase. In the north, the peninsulas of Liaoning and Shandong thrust into the Yellow Sea, stretching protective arms around the delta of the Yellow River. In the centre, the Yangtze delta is the focal point of a great plain, while in the south the coast is rocky and studded with islands.

## Even the sea freezes

Beijing, on a line of latitude that puts it south of Naples, is as cold as the Baltic in winter, when winds blow in from Central Asia. Just as in the Baltic, the Yellow Sea, 125 miles (200 km) to the north-east of the capital, can freeze over. Beijing has an average temperature of –4.5°C (24°F) in January, but the thermometer reading can climb above 35°C (95°F) in July – as hot as Singapore, which is less than 125 miles (200 km) from the Equator.

Moving south, the coastal provinces of Jiangsu, Zhejiang, Fujian and Guangdong swell out into the East and South China Seas like a pot belly. Jiangsu is one of China's most prosperous provinces, producing rice and cotton, and developing new industries. Mountain forests of pine, spruce and bamboo cover most of Zhejiang, giving it a flourishing paper and timber industry. Fujian, too, is mountainous and well-forested, but fishing is the main industry. There are still more mountains in Guangdong, which lies partly in the tropics. The climate is so benign that farmers in some areas can grow three rice crops a year. Mangrove forests flourish on the southern coasts, their tangled roots forming an all but impenetrable wall when the tide goes out. These coasts, once the haunt of fearsome pirates, have always borne the brunt of the storms when the summer monsoon bursts – a blessing for thirsty crops, but a source of peril if the rains cause serious flooding.

### Monsoons and typhoons

A monsoon, from the Arabic word meaning 'season', is a wind that blows cold and dry from the land in winter, but warm and wet from the sea in summer. The summer monsoon affects much of eastern China, bringing rains from April to September or even October. From July to September, updraughts of hot, moist air over tropical seas can develop into broad, spinning spirals that suck in the energy of yet more heat and moisture from the sea, creating winds that can reach up to 200 mph (320 km/h). In the North Atlantic such phenomena are known as hurricanes; over the Indian Ocean they are called cyclones; and in the western Pacific and the China Sea they are called typhoons. When a typhoon hits the coast, it can completely devastate both towns and the countryside, flooding streets and homes, drowning crops in the fields, tearing the roofs off buildings and sweeping away cars, livestock and people.

***After the typhoon*** *On August 23, 1999, Typhoon Sam hit the New Territories and Hong Kong. Its aftermath was a devastating flood that brought chaos to the entire region.*

***Winter wonderland*** *Winter has come to Manchuria in north-east China, and ice sculptures transform Stalin Park in Harbin, the capital, into a glittering fairyland.*

# The Japanese islands and the Korean peninsula

*More than 10 000 years ago, two narrow strips of land joined Japan to the mainland of continental Asia. Then, as the Ice Age ended and sea levels rose, the waters of the Pacific surged through breaches in both land bridges. Japan was left as a scattered chain of islands on the eastern rim of the Asian continent.*

The 3900 islands that make up Japan are the peaks of mountains that were submerged at the end of the last Ice Age. The four main islands, Honshu, Hokkaido, Kyushu and Shikoku, are particularly rugged. Hokkaido, the northernmost, has an almost Siberian climate: it is so inhospitable that until the end of the 19th century its wild interior was left to the native Ainu, a race of Siberian origin, until Japanese colonists moved in. Japan's second largest island, it still has fewer than 6 million people.

**Onion planters** *Peasant women in Hokkaido take advantage of a warm spell to plant out onions.*

## A mega-city around Tokyo

Honshu, the largest island, is divided by a mountainous backbone. On the side facing the Sea of Japan, it can be howlingly cold in winter. On the Pacific side, where the summers are hot, two extensive plains contain the heaviest concentration of population in the archipelago. One city runs into another on the plain of Kanto, and the Tokyo-Kawasaki-Yokohama-Chiba conurbation is home to one in four Japanese. This mega-city, powerhouse of a dynamic nation, has 30 million inhabitants. The other plain, Kansai, was the cradle of Japanese civilisation. Within it lie two ancient capitals, Nara and Kyoto, and a major port, Osaka. From the Yamato lowlands, between Osaka and Kyoto, the first imperial dynasty extended its authority over the whole of Japan.

Shikoku, across the Inland Sea from western Honshu, has a mountainous interior. Winds from the Pacific drop their burden of moisture on the south coast in summer, making it possible to grow two crops of rice a year. Further south, Kyushu was the gateway through which Chinese culture entered Japan. It is now 'silicon island', centre of the electronics industry.

Some 310 miles (500 km) away, in the East China Sea, lies Okinawa, main island of the Ryukyu group. The island saw some of bloodiest fighting in the Second World War, when US troops drove Japanese defenders from their caves and strongholds. The defeated Japanese general committed hara-kiri and many of his troops also killed themselves rather than be taken prisoner.

## Between two giants

Across the Sea of Japan lies the mountainous peninsula of South Korea. The 38th Parallel, meant to be a temporary division between Soviet and American zones of occupation after the Second World War, was cemented as the frontier between North and South Korea by the armistice that ended the Korean War. The Communist North occupies 55 per cent of the peninsula and has important resources of coal and iron. But good agricultural land is scarce there and the regime had few solutions when famine struck recently. Although classed as one of the 'Asian tigers', South Korea suffered a severe setback in the economic crisis of 1997. The Koreans, wedged between powerful neighbours, have kept their identity and stubbornly survived invasions by China and Japan.

**Unspoilt coast** *Shikoku, smallest of Japan's four main islands, has so far been bypassed by industrialisation.*

# The Earth trembles

*The threat of a catastrophic earthquake, Daishin or 'The Big One', is ever-present in Japan, for the country lies on the 'Ring of Fire' that encircles the Pacific. In a maelstrom of seismic activity some 30 000 ft (10 000 m) beneath the ocean, the crustal plate carrying the western Pacific is sliding under the plate carrying Japan. The result, on the surface, can be devastating.*

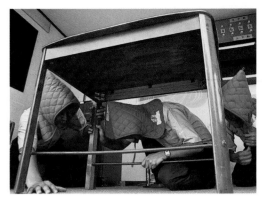

**Preparing for the worst** *Japanese citizens learn at a training centre how to cope with disaster.*

On September 1, 1923, the most destructive earthquake ever recorded in Japan hit Tokyo and the port of Yokohama. Its toll was 140 000 known dead, 45 000 reported missing, 103 000 seriously injured and 255 000 homes destroyed. Some 37 miles (60 km) from Tokyo, the shock was violent enough to kill fish off the peninsula of Miurato to a depth of 3000 ft (1000 m).

The islands of Japan are hit, on average, by 1000 earthquakes a year, though many are too weak to register on any but the most sensitive instruments. Stronger tremors are part of everyday life. Not a month passes without people being startled out of their sleep somewhere, and every household has its survival kit, containing, among other things, money and identity papers. People are told by the local authorities where to assemble, usually

**Devastated city** *Aftermath of the 1923 Tokyo earthquake.*

in a park, if disaster strikes. Every year, on the anniversary of the 1923 earthquake, the entire nation takes part in survival training.

On the beaches of the east coast it is not unusual to see defences against tsunamis, giant waves set in motion by undersea earthquakes. The largest known tsunami, 280 ft (85 m) high, raced past the Ryukyu Islands in April, 1971, dissipating its energy at sea. More deadly was a tsunami of the 1960s, which was started by an earth tremor near Chile. The wave gathered height as it crossed the Pacific and smashed into Japan with titanic force, wrecking 5000 homes.

## The power of earthquakes

On the Richter scale of earthquake magnitude, any tremor with a reading higher than 5 can cause damage, and one with a reading of more

## The earthquake they tried to keep secret

Tangshan, 95 miles (150 km) east of Beijing, was all but wiped off the map on July 28, 1976, when it was at the epicentre of an earthquake registering 7.8 on the Richter scale. Nearly a quarter of a million people were killed, and thousands left homeless. Western seismologists picked up traces of the shock, but not a word leaked out from the Chinese authorities. They had decided to keep the calamity secret and rely on their own resources, drafting in 100 000 soldiers and 50 000 volunteers to help the victims and rebuild the ravaged city. It was two years before they broke their silence. Today, the numerous earthquakes that hit China are made public immediately.

**Helping hands** *Volunteers and Red Army soldiers help to clear up after the Tangshan earthquake.*

than 8 can result in total destruction. In the 1970s, 15 earthquakes with a Richter reading of more than 5.5 were recorded in Japan. The most severe, both with magnitudes of 7.4, were at Nemuro in 1973 and Miyagi in 1978.

In cities built largely of wood, fire can be the deadliest hazard, but modern building techniques have gone some way towards mitigating the ravages of earthquakes. When an earthquake shook Kobe, on January 17, 1995, claiming more than 6000 victims, the nearby Kansai international airport emerged practically unharmed. It had been built on an artificial island in Osaka Bay, and the sea had acted as a shock absorber.

## *Waiting for disaster*

Earthquakes of the future are of more pressing concern than those of the past. The inhabitants of Tokyo and the entire Kanto plain live with the terrifying knowledge that another major tremor is statistically overdue. The 1923 earthquake, which had its source in a fault that runs under the bay of Sagami some 50 miles (80 km) from the capital, was predicted to the exact year by Imamura Akitsune, professor of seismology at Tokyo University. Today's leading seismologists say that, on average, the region is likely to suffer an earthquake of similar magnitude every 69 years – which suggests that a major tremor was due in 1992.

***Kobe in ruins*** *The earthquake that shook Kobe in January 1995 measured 7.2 on the Richter scale. It was Japan's worst earthquake disaster since the one to hit Tokyo in 1923.*

### Omens of violent change?

In the modern world we turn to science to explain the workings of nature, and we know that earthquakes occur when sections of the Earth's crust slide against each other. We know, too, about the subterranean turmoil that causes such movements. In Asia, the crustal plate that carries India has been forcing its way beneath the Eurasian plate for 40 million years. In ancient China, people

explained natural calamities in ways that accorded with their own perceptions of the world. If the Earth trembled, it could be an omen announcing a sudden and brutal change in leadership of the Empire. Old traditions die hard: a rumour spread in China that the Tangshan earthquake of July 1976 was a prediction of the death, in September of that year, of Mao Ze-dong, the 'Red Emperor'.

In the Japanese psychological make-up there appears to be a fascination with terror. The same nature that has enchanted priests, poets and painters, can be terrible in its wrath. According to legend, earthquakes are caused when a giant catfish, the Namazu, which lives deep under the ground, shakes its tail. In modern times, disaster movies and novels have drawn on the mixture of dread and fascination that apocalyptic events seem to have for the Japanese. In 1974, *Japan Under the Sea*, a film based on a best-selling book by Kumatsu Sakyo, was a runaway box office hit. It told how, with volcanic eruptions raining destruction, and Japan swamped by tsunamis, the government had to evacuate the entire population. Nor is such speculation confined to films and novels. In 1989, the respected Tokai Bank published *Tokyo Trembles*, a study of the future that predicted a world economic meltdown should there be another major earthquake in Tokyo, which ranked at the time as the world's sixth economic power in terms of production.

# China's wildlife under threat

*Despite the immensity of China's landmass, and the diversity of its climate and habitats, from parched deserts to steamy rain forests, many species of wild animals are threatened with extinction. Their misfortune is to be in competition with the most successful animal on the planet – man.*

**Prized plumage** *The crested ibis, reduced to a handful in Japan, now breeds in captivity.*

The major threat to China's wildlife comes from the remorseless advance into their habitats of an ever-expanding human population. Alive to this peril, the Chinese government has set aside 300 nature reserves where endangered species are protected. Such havens cover 1.8 per cent of the country – some 67 000 sq miles (173 000 km²) in total, an area that is more than twice the size of Scotland.

## The threat of poachers

Loss of habitat is not the only threat to wildlife: poachers take their toll, too. Monkeys, snakes, giant salamanders and freshwater turtles are some of the species appreciated by the Chinese in the south of the country as a source of protein. Despite an official ban on eating certain kinds of animals, they can still be found on restaurant menus. It is difficult for the government to call a halt to long-established traditions: bear's paw, for example, is a dish that enjoys the prestige of having appeared on the emperor's menu at the imperial court.

Hats made out of the pelt of the snow leopard, an animal that lives on the high Tibetan plateau, sell for phenomenal prices, as do tiger skins – even though tigers are on their way to extinction – and there is a growing curio trade in skins, claws and teeth. The tiger's body parts are used in traditional Chinese medicine.

Hardly 100 tigers survive in South China, and experts estimate that while there may be a world total of about 500 Siberian tigers, as few as 30 may remain in the forests on the borders of Russia and North Korea.

**The hunter hunted** *The Siberian tiger, a highly efficient forest hunter, is falling victim to poachers. Some of its body parts are used in medicines that are claimed to have aphrodisiac properties.*

### The giant panda

Also under threat, mainly through the destruction of bamboo forests, is the giant panda. This solitary animal lives almost exclusively on a diet of bamboo, chomping its way through 30 lb (15 kg) a day. Once, giant pandas were distributed throughout South China, Vietnam and Burma, but now there may be fewer than 1000 of them left. Outside zoos, they are found in only half a dozen mountain chains in south-west China. The panda moves from one area to another to find food, and as the bamboo forests become more and more fragmented by the activities of man, such mobility grows more difficult. In an attempt to preserve the species,

33 nature reserves have been set aside for the panda and, as it is slow at breeding, international efforts have been set on course to study its way of life and its breeding habits. Its appealing face, allied to the very real threats to its survival, have made the giant panda a symbol for other endangered species.

*Future uncertain* *Wildlife reserves have been set aside for the giant panda, but efforts to save it in the wild may have come too late. As it seems reluctant to breed in captivity, some Chinese naturalists have had the idea of showing zoo animals video films of other pandas mating.*

*'Little brother'* *The red panda, only 2 ft (61 cm) long compared with the 5 ft (1.5 m) giant panda, has a range that overlaps that of its 'big brother' in the bamboo forests. With its long striped tail it resembles a racoon.*

*Under threat* *Inroads have been made on China's bamboo forests (left) for scaffolding material. The numbers of the elegant Japanese crane (inset) have been reduced by hunting.*

CHAPTER 2

# PROGRESS VERSUS TRADITION

For the greater part of 3000 years, the emperors, shoguns and other rulers of the lands of East Asia feared change. In China, Korea and Japan there were long periods when contact with the West was prohibited or severely restricted. Convinced that their own civilisations were unshakably superior to those of the 'barbarians' beyond their frontiers, these ruling forces devoted their energies to preserving them. When they did face reality in the 19th century, they found themselves overtaken, and were forced to open their borders to the Western powers. Japan was the first to embrace the cause of its humiliation – Western know-how and Western ways. A disciplined and well-educated workforce took Japan out of a feudal past to become, by the second half of the 20th century, the first of the 'Asian tigers' to burst into the front rank of economic powers. Taiwan and South Korea followed, and made dazzling progress within a few decades.

*Freshly caught tuna is auctioned at a wholsesale market in Tsukiji, Japan.*

# China's population explosion strains food resources

*It is no accident that the Chinese word for 'population' is formed from the characters for a man and a mouth. China's Environmental Protection Commission has calculated that the country has the resources to feed around 700 million people – the problem is that the actual population figure is 1.25 billion.*

Like other early civilisations, China began by producing a food surplus. More than 3000 years ago, under the Shang Dynasty, peasants toiling on fertile land produced enough food not just for themselves, but also for craftsmen and for an upper class of aristocrats and priests. Conditions were favourable for the population to expand, and by the year AD 2, when the first official census was taken, there were some 57 million Chinese. Over the centuries, war, famine, disease, and to a lesser extent emigration, played their traditional roles in holding back population growth – but even so the population of China had reached 432 million by the 18th century.

During the 19th century population growth was steady but not spectacular. However, the communist revolution of 1949 prepared the ground for a sharp increase. The population total rose from 582 million in 1953 to more than a billion in 1982 – a rate of increase in less than 30 years that had previously taken more than 17 centuries. Against figures like these, the millions who died in the famine caused by the Mao Ze-dong-inspired Great Leap Forward of 1958 represented little more than an outsized blip on the demographic screen.

## Overcrowded cities

China is mountainous and settlement is spread unevenly. Some 90 per cent of the people live in 40 per cent of the country, concentrated in the east and along the coast. Millions of peasants have been enticed into the cities. There are approaching 14 million people living in the greater Shanghai area, and over 11 million in and around Beijing. Even so, only 30 per cent of the population is urban, though that is likely to change by 2025. Industrialisation is turning China into an economic superstate, but feeding its people is still a concern.

**Crowded beach** *The space available per person is strictly limited on a Chinese beach.*

### Looking for work

The economic advances of the 1970s improved conditions for the vast majority of Chinese, but also provoked a massive exodus from the countryside. Tempted by the prospect of higher pay and a better way of life, the peasants abandoned farms and villages to find work in the cities and in the new 'Special Economic Zones' set up along the coast. But this huge influx of manual labour could not be entirely absorbed, and more than 100 million peasants were left to wander from city to city, seeking any job they could find.

**Hope in their hearts** *Migrant workers arrive at Shanghai, hoping to find jobs in the building trade.*

**Teeming streets** *At least 20 Chinese cities contain more than 5 million inhabitants.*

# The single child policy

*One of Mao Ze-dong's sayings was: 'A great nation needs people.' For him, the bigger the population, the more powerful the state, and while he was in charge, China's demographic time bomb ticked at a furious rate. He left behind a problem that has not yet been solved.*

Towards the end of the 1970s, the population of China passed the 1 billion mark, and every year brought well over 10 million more mouths to feed. The new regime, reaching desperately for a solution, decreed that only one child was to be allowed to each married couple. But this policy, first applied in 1979, three years after Mao's death, had unwanted social consequences, both for the age profile of the nation and for the balance between the sexes.

## The reign of the 'little emperors'

Under the single child policy, families with more than one child faced fines and could lose their privileges of access to state schools and to state-funded apartments. Strictly applied in the cities, where communities were easier to control, the policy was always harder to enforce in the countryside. The wishes of the planners collided with the natural desire to have children, above all sons, to carry on the family name and look after parents when they grew old. Baby boys, in both town and country, were so pampered, over-protected and overfed (and sometimes overweight) that they came to be known as 'little emperors.'

The policy nevertheless bore fruit, and the birthrate dropped from 3.4 per 100 in 1969, to 1 per 100 today. But in the past ten years there has been a relaxation of the rules, coinciding with a rise in numbers of the comfortably off middle classes. They can afford their own apartments, can pay the fines when a second child is born, and do not need to send their children to state schools.

## Girls not wanted

One tragic consequence of the single child policy was a rise in female infanticide, especially in the countryside. In a male-dominated society, where sons were preferred to daughters, if only one child was permitted, it had to be a boy. The government has banned non-essential medical scanning of pregnant women because the procedure allows them to know the gender of the child in the womb, and so tempts those carrying female babies to consider abortion. One

alarming social consequence of the preference for male children was a shortfall in female births, with 114 boys born for every 100 girls. The lack of balance between the sexes caused a surplus of single men, which is a source of serious problems. The kidnapping of young girls has become more and more frequent in recent years. Another factor is that people are living longer as a result of better hygiene and improved medical care. This means that the average age of the population is rising. It is in part for these reasons that the state has decided to be more flexible. Between now and 2005, the one-child-only rule is being relaxed for people of child-bearing age who were single children themselves. In the meantime, every minute that passes sees another 20 babies born in China.

**Public propaganda** *The highway to happiness: one child only.*

**An ageing nation** *With fewer babies born, and people living longer, the number of sexagenarians in China (8.6 per cent of the population in 1999) is set to double by 2010.*

**The ideal family** *Couples who could not follow this role model, and have only one child, faced an array of penalties, including fines, sterilisation and enforced abortion.*

# A mosaic of peoples in the Middle Kingdom

*To the outside world, China can seem like a monolithic, mass-produced society whose citizens lead drab, uniform lives. The true picture is different: the nation contains 55 ethnic minorities, some of them fiercely independent.*

More than 90 per cent of the 1.25 billion Chinese are descended from the Han, a people who came from the valley of the Yellow River and founded the country's first centralised state. The remainder of the population are made up of no fewer than 55 different ethnic groups.

### Trouble in the frontier provinces

Many of the minority ethnic groups cling fiercely to their own traditions, and while this can give them a certain colourful appeal, it can also cause serious annoyance to the authorities. Antagonism against Beijing is most marked in the frontier provinces of the north and west – Xinjiang, Inner Mongolia and Tibet.

Xinjiang is home to more than 8 million Muslim Uigurs, along with Kazakhs, Tajiks and Kirgiz. Renowned for their horsemanship, these peoples are Turkic in origin, and so more European-looking than other ethnic groups. During the Cultural Revolution, Red Guards wrecked mosques and forced Muslims to eat pork, but nowadays religion is tolerated and the main threat to native cultures comes from the influx of Han Chinese – well over one-third of Xinjiang's population today. Uigur children have to learn Chinese at school.

North China is home to 6 million Mongols and 11 million Manchus, two ethnic groups who must find it hard to forget that their ancestors once ruled all of China. In the past 50 years, the government has tried with limited success to force the Mongols away from their old herding life and into communal farms.

The ethnic groups of the south are more closely related to the Burmese, Thais and Vietnamese than to the Han. The Zhuang of Guangxi, China's largest minority, number more than 15 million. They build their houses on stilts, with livestock living beneath. The peasant tradition is for wealth to be easily portable, and the Dong, Bai, Yi and Yao carry it on their backs, in the form of sumptuous national costumes. The hill-dwelling Yi are also renowned for their expertise in herbal medicines. The Hmong make elaborate silver jewellery, as well as fine embroidery.

**Beauty in colour** *A woman of the Yi, in her finely embroidered national dress.*

**Inside a yurt** *A Kirgiz family in their yurt – a warm, circular tent made of felt.*

**Baby carrier** *A mother of the Dong minority, on her way to work in the fields, takes her babies with her.*

### Resistance in Tibet

The Chinese seizure of Tibet in 1950 was represented not as an invasion but as a reclamation of lost territory, which liberated the Tibetans from a feudal, priest-ridden society. A popular revolt in 1959, and widespread support for the Dalai Lama, who fled to India, showed how the Tibetans welcomed the 'liberators'. Tibet suffered further blows in the Cultural Revolution of the 1960s, when Buddhist monasteries were destroyed and thousands killed. The hardy nomads of Tibet still wander the plains with their yaks, as their forefathers did, but their culture is threatened by Chinese immigration.

# The 'little Chinas' that lie beyond the homeland

*China, with its teeming millions, has for centuries been known for an export even more valuable than porcelain or silk – manpower. Chinese emigrated to North America to build the railways that opened up a continent; to South-east Asia to work on plantations; to Britain, France and a score of other lands to open restaurants and establish prosperous communities. But they never forgot their homeland.*

Every vibrant city in Europe and America has its Chinatown, a jumble of restaurants, exotic supermarkets, travel agencies, banks and community associations. Some 50 million people of Chinese descent have been scattered to the far corners of the world in an exodus that dates from the growth of industrialisation in the West during the 19th century.

### A labour force for the West

The Chinese have brought many benefits to the countries where they settled – not only by providing a labour force and expanding the taste horizons of diners from Sydney to San Francisco, but also by helping to build the future. Lee Kuan Yew, for example, who came from the Chinese community in Singapore, became the country's first prime minister in 1969 and did more than any other politician to build the former British Colony into one of the most successful economies in the world.

The Western world's near-insatiable demand for labour coincided with China's surplus of manpower. Chinese peasants streamed in their millions to hire themselves out in new lands. The provinces of Guangzhou (Canton) and Fujian lost more than

**Lending a hand**  *Chinese workers in a munitions factory take over the jobs of young men who have gone to fight in the trenches in the First World War.*

one-tenth of their populations – but not always permanently, for it was the custom for exiles to return to their home village to choose a bride and establish a line of descendants. During the First World War, France and Britain opened their doors to nearly 150 000 Chinese to work in the factories. Among the Chinese student-workers in Paris was Deng Xiao-ping, who later became the most powerful man in China.

Numerous opponents of the communist regime fled to Taiwan and Hong Kong after Mao Ze-dong's victory in 1949, and many Chinese who had settled in Vietnam and Cambodia swelled the ranks of the 'boat people' who fled those countries after the communist takeover of South Vietnam in 1975. Mao's successors lifted the Bamboo Curtain, and emigration began again. In the regions of Fuzhou and Wenzhou alone, an estimated half million people left between 1970 and 1995. Many of those who sought a better life in the West had to turn to criminal gangs, who smuggled them to the other side of the world as illegal would-be immigrants. Not all of them survived the journey, and those who did faced a lifetime of debt to the smuggling gangs.

**Chinatown, Los Angeles**  *Chinese workers flocked to the USA in the 19th century to build railway lines and work in the stockyards. Those who stayed created their own colourful communities.*

# Rice, a cereal and a symbol

*Growing rice calls for three things, all of which are available in abundance in south and central China and in parts of Japan: warmth, water and sheer hard work. In both countries, rice has long been both a staple food and a national symbol. In China, old people are cared for after they cease working under a pension policy known as the 'iron rice bowl'.*

**Harvest time in the rice fields** *Rice is ready for harvesting from three to six months after sowing, according to the variety. This means that two crops can be grown in a year.*

Rice, developed from a wild grass of tropical marshlands, is the staple food of one-third of mankind. Records of its cultivation in China, where annual production reaches 200 million tons, go back for 4000 years. A single ear, containing 400-500 grains, is densely packed with nourishment. This means that it can be grown profitably on small parcels of land: family plots in the countryside are frequently 5 acres (2 ha) or less.

### Labour-intensive cultivation

Rice is a demanding plant, but no complicated tools are needed to produce it – though mechanisation has been introduced in some areas. The paddy fields are ploughed (often using water buffalo), fertilised and smoothed over. Seedlings are started in special beds, then planted out in the fields after 30-50 days. Dykes and irrigation canals have to be dug, for the plants need to be covered by 2-4 in (5-10 cm) of water during the growing season. The fields are drained before harvesting, which is followed by threshing to loosen the husks and winnowing to remove the chaff.

Since the 11th century it has been possible to grow two crops a year, thanks to a variety of rice known as champa, introduced from Vietnam. In modern times high-yielding varieties of 'miracle rice' have been developed. Polished or white rice, widely eaten in the West, has been milled to remove both husk and bran, while brown rice, more common in the East, is higher in protein and food value.

*Planting out   Rice seedlings are set out in the paddy fields.*

*Irrigating the crop   Terraces, flooded during the growing season, shape the hillsides of China's Yunnan Province.*

### North Korea's famine dilemma: food or guns?

Torrential rain, followed by heavy floods, ruined North Korea's rice and maize harvests in 1995 and 1996. At first, communist leader Kim Chong Il tried to divert attention from the problem by making menacing military moves, such as sending troops into the demilitarised zone between the two Koreas. Aid programmes were mounted by a number of countries, including South Korea, and by private charities, but there were suspicions that the regime was stockpiling rice, rather than distributing it. In March 2000, a French humanitarian team withdrew its services because food meant for children was being diverted to the army and to state officials. The government admitted that, by 1998, 220 000 people had died in the famine, but an American aid team put the number of dead at 1.5 million.

## The world's most expensive rice

In the Land of the Rising Sun, the diet of most peasants was for centuries restricted to a simple bowl of rice, a handful of roots pickled in brine, and soup. Those who lived on the coast could add to their protein intake by catching fish. So important was rice as a staple food that it became a symbol of power. In the Middle Ages, taxes were calculated according to the amount of rice that could be produced by each individual family.

Many aspects of life in Japan have become increasingly Westernised in recent years and this has included the national diet. In 1965, well over half the food intake of Japanese people consisted of rice, whereas today the figure is barely one-third. The Japanese cook their rice to the point where it becomes slightly sticky, making it easier to scoop up with chopsticks than if individual grains have to be chased around the bowl. Oddly, perhaps, given that vitamins and minerals are lost with the bran during the polishing process, the Japanese prefer white rice and regard the brown variety as somewhat inferior.

But it is not changing tastes alone that have led to the decline in rice consumption: cost is a factor, too. Rice may still be served at any meal in Japan, and at special meals it may be accompanied by warm sake, a drink high in alcohol that is made from the fermented grain. But Japanese rice is easily the most expensive in the world. The home-grown grain costs five times as much as rice bought at world prices, yet the Japanese are reluctant to import it from overseas.

*Big industry on a small scale*  The rice crop is cut and set out for drying (right and below). Rice takes up more than half of Japan's cultivable land, but is grown in pockets of land that average only 3.2 acres (1.3 ha).

## A state monopoly

When the country was being reconstructed following the Second World War, the Japanese government declared that the marketing of rice was to be a state monopoly and it began to support the price of rice with subsidies. This strategy was introduced mainly for political reasons – though it was also important to encourage rice production because it was such a powerful symbol of national identity. The Liberal Democratic Party, which has been in power almost without interruption since it was formed in 1955 from a merger of conservative parties, relies significantly on the countryside vote, so it is in the party's interest to apply a protectionist policy to home-grown rice.

After many years of closing the door to imported rice, Japan finally allowed it to enter the country – but only on payment of extremely high customs duties. Tokyo took a firm stance on this position in 1999 at the world trade talks in Seattle, USA.

*No space wasted*  *So precious is rice in Japan that it is grown even along Tokyo railway tracks.*

### A dish for all seasons

The rice eaten in Japan, round-grained and slightly sticky, forms the basis for many meals. *Bento*, a kind of packed lunch that is especially popular with schoolchildren, almost always contains rice, either with vegetables or with pork covered in breadcrumbs, when it is known as *tonkatsu*. The dish called *onigiri* consists of rice wrapped in paper-thin seaweed. On special days, such as the festival held to celebrate the arrival of the New Year, most families eat *mochi* – cakes of ground rice that can be grilled or eaten with a clear soup.

*Good fortune!*
*China's god of wealth.*

# Triumphs and setbacks for Asia's 'mini tigers'

*In the closing decades of the 20th century, Hong Kong, South Korea and Taiwan brought the heady smell of success to a part of the globe more used to hardship and penury. Their dazzling progress into the ranks of the world's leading industrial powers was all the more remarkable because of their small size.*

Only a few years ago, the rest of the world looked on with admiration – and perhaps with a tinge of envy – as three 'mini tigers' of the Far East gave a textbook lesson in how to create prosperity from a standing start. Like many other countries, Hong Kong, Taiwan and South Korea suffered a setback in the world economic crisis of the late 1990s, but one of their strong points is resilience in the face of a challenge.

## Before the economic miracle

Hong Hong was little more than a barren rock in the South China Sea when it was ceded to Britain after China's defeat in the Opium War of 1842. Taiwan (then Formosa) was one of the poorest islands in the world at the end of the Second World War, after 50 years as a Japanese colony. South Korea was a land of rubble and ruins at the end of the Korean War in 1953. All three were to flourish in the complex political and economic climate of the Cold War.

Under easy-going British colonial rule, Hong Kong enjoyed freedom in its economic affairs, if not in its political life. Even in the days of Mao Ze-dong, the colony was the sole corridor of trade between China and the outside world, and it had the capital, the contacts and the commercial know-how to take full advantage of the 'Open Door' policy announced by Mao's successors in 1978. By 1987, Hong Kong was the world's busiest container port, and in the mid 1990s it ranked as the seventh or eighth largest trading nation.

Taiwan had the advantage of being at a crossroads of sea routes between the Asian mainland and Japan. Chiang Kai-shek's Chinese Nationalist forces fled there after the communist victory in 1949 and were joined by capitalists from Shanghai. The USA saw Taiwan and South Korea as bulwarks against communism, and US aid helped to build military and economic strength.

*Busy by night   Hong Kong, the world's biggest container port.*

### The secret of economic success

The prosperity of Asia's 'mini tigers' was based on the productive energy of thousands of family workshops. Entrepreneurs met big orders from Western firms by subcontracting them to small units, then collecting the finished products. It was common for families to live and work in the same place, sleeping on straw palliasses alongside machines that moulded plastic or stitched clothing. The top priority was to meet an order on time or sooner. Families worked for 12 hours or more a day. It was also essential to adapt quickly to changing fashions and to the needs of the market.

## Prosperity from plastics

Plastics and textiles were the two products that pumped vitality into the economies of the future 'mini tigers'. Lacking an abundance of raw materials, they concentrated on manufacturing and technology. Hong Kong exported a stream of consumer goods including toys, ready-made clothing, radios, TV components, cameras, hi-fi and optical equipment. It also developed into a financial centre, with the fifth biggest concentration of banks in the world. Taiwan launched itself into textiles, then into radios and electronic components. South Korea found markets for textiles, shipbuilding, automobiles and electronic products. All three thrived on supplying the needs of the information age.

*Rest period   Macao incense factory.*

Region, a haven of economic freedom. The Chinese leaders promised to leave the economic system untouched for the next 50 years. This promise was taken at face value, and the mass exodus of Hong Kong Chinese that had been anticipated in Britain did not happen. Around 90 per cent of Hong Kong's trade is with mainland China, but it is now internal trade. At the 1997 handover, the former Chinese Premier Li Peng announced that Hong Kong's future would be 'even more splendid' than its past. Nobody can guarantee what will happen tomorrow, but China needs Hong Kong as much as Hong Kong needs China.

## Meeting new challenges

Cheap labour and low costs were powerful arguments deployed by the region's manufacturers seeking to sell their goods in the West, but once China had opened her borders, there was a source of even cheaper labour just across frontiers. Workshops and factories were moved to Asia's fast-developing colossus. Hong Kong in particular, knowing that it was due to be returned to China, integrated its economy closely with that of its neighbour. The handover came on July 1, 1997, and China began the process of absorbing an economy that had been a shining example of freewheeling entrepreneurship into a society that had been reared on communism and a powerful bureaucracy. Under the slogan of 'One country, two systems', Hong Kong became a Special Administrative

*Money makes money Batteries of computers and eager traders inside the Hong Kong stock exchange. While still a British colony, Hong Kong became an international centre for trade and finance.*

*Happier days   Car workers 'on parade' at Daewoo's Inchon factory, South Korea. The economic crisis of the late 1990s hit the company hard and sent it towards bankruptcy.*

# Vanishing horsemen of the steppes

*Mongolia, a land of steppe and desert, is traditionally the home of nomadic herdsmen. But the modern world is forcing more and more Mongols into giving up the old ways and moving into permanent settlements.*

**Mobile homes** *Motorbikes, not ponies, are drawn up in front of these yurts – a reflection of the changing times.*

The world of the Mongols is a world in transition, uneasily placed somewhere between modern times and the days when nomad tribes followed the banners of Genghis Khan and struck terror into the civilised world. Communist theory, both in Soviet-dominated Mongolia and in Chinese-ruled Inner Mongolia, dictated that families should raise livestock on cooperative ranches, rather than tend their own herds. In recent years there has been a strong drift into the towns: in Mongolia to work in mining; in Inner Mongolia following the influx of Han Chinese, who now greatly outnumber the native Mongols. The past is recalled in the sports and pastimes of a warrior race: wrestling, archery and fiercely contested horse-racing. The future is indicated by the fact that even the Mongol yurts – portable tents made of felt – have been invaded by the flickering light of the television screen.

## A way of life in retreat

For the dwindling numbers who follow the old ways, life is still centred around the need to find pasture for their horses, sheep, camels and goats. Mongolian soils are so thin that they provide only subsistence grazing. But in several regions the nomads no longer move between summer and winter camps.

In the camps, the day's tasks revolve around looking after the herds and making milk products – curds, clotted cream and *airag*, a fermented liquor made from mare's milk. The produce is bartered for some of the commodities of modern life. However, the barter system is unsuited to a society that is beginning to show signs of consumerism: television has introduced a new world, with new images, new dreams and new desires.

### A close partnership

A nomadic way of life depends on a close understanding between horse and man. Small and hardy, the Mongol pony can gallop for up to 20 miles (30 km) over rough terrain. It provides milk, hide for clothing and hair for making rope. The skills of herding, breaking and raising horses are handed down by practical instruction and by observation. Nomad children are raised for a life in the saddle, and by the age of six take part in races, the most famous of which take place in the capital, Ulan Bator, during the Nadaam festival.

**Wealth on the hoof** *For centuries, the main wealth of Mongolia lay in its flocks and herds. Even today, when mining vies with herding as a source of national income, more than 400 000 Mongol herdsmen look after some 30 million animals.*

# The menacing power of China's rivers

*In a country whose rapid industrial growth has led to a soaring demand for new sources of energy, the rivers of China hold an enormous potential for hydroelectric power. But at the very moment when the government is embarking on works of a scale rarely seen since the time of the pharaohs, the poor quality of many dams is causing concern.*

**Coping with disaster**
*Floods near Hubei, 1998.*

China has more than 50 000 rivers and streams, most of which, like the Chang Jiang (Yangtze) and the Huang He (Yellow River), cross the country from west to east and empty their waters into the Pacific. They have been both a blessing and a curse. It was in the valley of the Yellow River that civilisation put down its first roots in the country, and rivers have been mighty avenues of trade down the centuries. But they have also, when swollen and enraged, flooded the plains, leaving a trail of ruin and death.

## A ravenous appetite for energy

China's hydroelectric potential is unevenly distributed, not only because of the terrain, but also because of the diversity of climate. The rivers in the north are in full flow during the summer, but their waters are reduced during the dry winter months. In the south, the situation is reversed: swollen by melting snow and glaciers, and by the monsoon rains, the rivers can overflow their banks. In past centuries, dykes were built to reduce the misery caused by floods. Today, there is a pressing need for dams to produce hydroelectric power. China's breakneck pace of industrial growth cannot be sustained with coal as the dominant energy source, and its oilfields are expensive to develop.

It was in the north-west, during the Japanese occupation, that the country's first hydroelectric schemes were undertaken. In the early decades of the communist regime, under the impetus of such programmes as Mao's 'Great Leap Forward', hundreds of dams were hastily thrown up. But the enormous hydroelectric potential of the industrially underdeveloped south-east has long been neglected. By the end of the 1990s, only a quarter of China's energy needs were being generated by water power. With the booming central and coastal regions developing an appetite for energy, those in charge of China's future look to dam-building as the solution.

### Controversy over the superdams

More than 3000 dams have burst in China since 1949. Some 200 000 people were drowned in two such disasters in 1975 – catastrophes that were not revealed to the world until 20 years later. During the Mao Ze-dong years, all that mattered was to set targets and announce their achievement. Many dams built then are of poor quality, and engineers are worried about their condition – at a time when China is throwing herself into the construction of superdams to harness the waters of the Yangtze (the Three Gorges Dam) and the Yellow River. These vast undertakings are opposed by environmentalists and by those who object to the uprooting of more than a million people.

**Under construction**  *A dam being built on the upper Mekong.*

**Fisherman's house**  *One of the last houseboats on the Yellow River.*

**In full fury**  *The Yellow River is called 'the scourge of the children of Han', because of the frequent raging floods.*

# Empire of the sea

*The scattered islands of the Japanese archipelago can muster between them a staggering 17 000 miles (27 000 km) of coastline. Small wonder that Japan, with few natural resources on land, has always considered the sea a natural extension of its living space. But today, this dependence on the sea and its products is bringing the nation into conflict with conservationists in many lands.*

**On the menu**   *Octopus at Tsukiji market.*

Japan's debt to the sea is incalculable. Along maritime trade routes have come a host of influences as well as cargoes – the principles of Buddhism and rice cultivation as well as Chinese crafts. It was by sea, too, that Commodore Perry arrived in the middle of the 19th century, bringing the modernising influence of the USA.

### A Japanese lake

In the Middle Ages, the seas that separate Japan from China and the Korean peninsula brought to the Land of the Rising Sun precious silks, coins and copper, books and porcelain, as well as monks, merchants and men of letters. In return, Japan exported pearls, gold, wood and mother-of-pearl. From the 15th century onwards, the Japanese took over from the Koreans as leader in the region's seaborne trade; by the 16th century the East China Sea was almost a Japanese lake. There was still room, however, for fortune-seekers from China and Korea, even from Spain and Portugal. The merchants of that time had few scruples, and sometimes mixed a little piracy or smuggling with their legitimate trade. But it was thanks to them that Japan opened trading stations in far-flung parts of Asia – places as distant as the Philippines and the Kingdom of Siam.

The decision of the third Tokugawa shogun, around 1640, to close the country to outside influences came as a heavy blow to the overseas merchants. Only the Dutch were authorised to trade with

Japan, through a trading post at Nagasaki. But the decision greatly benefited the country's internal trade. Thousands of junks carried their cargoes across the Inner Sea between Honshu and Shikoku and established regular routes between Edo, the new capital, and other Japanese ports.

### Into the modern world

Two hundred years after closing its ports to the outside world, Japan was forced to re-open them, and once again the impetus for change came from the sea. In 1853, the American Commodore Matthew Perry, with a flotilla of four warships, dropped anchor in what is now Tokyo Bay, demanding the opening of trade. He returned with a bigger fleet the following year, to enforce the demand. Japan had entered into the modern era, and by 1858 had commercial treaties with the USA, Britain, France and Russia.

**Harvest of the sea**   *Landing tuna at the port of Shizuoka, in central Honshu. The Japanese consume about 10 million tons of fish a year.*

**Brisk bidding**   *Restaurateurs and sushi vendors make their auction bids at Tokyo's huge Tsukiji fish market. In January 2001 a world record £120 000 was paid for a single blue fin tuna. It weighed 444 lb (201 kg).*

Coastal fishing, most often a family business, could not keep pace with the demands of a rising population. One recourse has been to turn to fish-farming. Around the islands and in the Inland Sea, a new industry has developed to supply the home market with farmed salmon, sea bream, chinchard, oysters, cockles and seaweed. But still the market demands more, so Japan has launched herself on all the seas of the world. These days Japanese trawlers and factory ships scour the world's oceans for a steadily dwindling stock of fish, competing with other major fishing nations.

***Where fish is favourite*** *Every year, the Japanese eat an average of 200 lb (90 kg) of fish per person.*

## Threats to the world's whales

Japan has the biggest deep-sea fishing fleet in the world, and the country's determination to regard the seas as its own preserve has led to a barrage of international criticism. After centuries of being intensively hunted, several species of whale were so close to extinction that in 1985 the International Whaling Conference (IWC) declared a moratorium on commercial whaling, allowing only a limited number to be taken for scientific purposes. Japan's flexible interpretation of the word 'scientific' outraged conservationists. In 1999, Japan was accused of bribing countries in need of aid to join the IWC and support the Japanese demand for the moratorium to be lifted. The following year, President Clinton said that Japan would not even be considered as a candidate to fish within the 200 mile (320 km) limit around US waters, because of her record on whaling.

Two factors are helping to set limits to Japan's appetite for whale meat. One is that it can be robbed of much of its taste by being frozen at sea, on ships equipped with modern refrigeration plant. The other is that it is very expensive. Japan has also been accused of adding to the perils of overfishing by trawling the ocean with drift nets that are several miles long, and trap not just fish but also sea birds and mammals such as dolphins. Yet still Japan's demand for the harvest of the sea is not satisfied. With shrimps, octopus, squid and tuna coming mainly from the USA, Korea, Taiwan and Indonesia, Japan is today the world's leading importer of sea produce.

### The bounty of the seas comes up for auction

The islands of Japan may be poorly endowed with natural resources, but this is certainly not the case in the seas that surround them. The Pacific coast north of the main island of Honshu, where warm and cold ocean currents meet, is one of the richest fishing grounds in the world. Japan has around 3000 ports and 750 major fish auctions through which the daily catch reaches shops, restaurants and sushi bars in the big urban centres. The Tsukiji market in Tokyo is one of the world's biggest fish auctions. Every day is a hubbub of activity as millions of tons of fish and shellfish come under the auctioneer's hammer.

***Caught and sold*** *Tuna at Tsukiji are marked with buyers' names.*

# Progress puts the planet in peril

*When Mao Ze-dong came to power in 1949, he tried to catch up with the industrial development of the West in a single generation, at a terrible cost to his people and to the environment. Other nations of East Asia, in a similar headlong rush to join the economic giants of tomorrow, have also paid a high price.*

***Frustration at feeding time*** *Two babies in Beijing learn how to use chopsticks – but their heads are entirely covered in netting, to keep out dust-laden air.*

The creeping fingers of the desert turning vast expanses of China into a wasteland; rivers in Taiwan facing biological death from their burden of untreated sewage; smoke pollution and greenhouse gases contributing to global warming – the nations of East Asia face an ecological catastrophe. When a nation is in a hurry to catch up, concern for the environment is not usually high on its list of priorities. Only in recent years have the voices of conservationists begun to make themselves heard over the hum of machines and the noise of chainsaws cutting down the forests.

### Shattered harmony

The traditional image of the Chinese countryside is a land of yellow earth and brown mud walls in the north, gradually giving way to green paddy fields towards the centre of the country. Silhouetted against this background, peasants harness their bullocks or stoop to tend their crops, following the rhythm of the seasons. Man and nature seem to have reached a lasting harmony. The reality is quite different. Mao's China had so many enemies, and so many mouths to feed, that he had little choice but to embark on an industrial revolution: a 'Five Year Plan' that more than tripled steel production,

and the so-called 'Great Leap Forward' of the late 1950s, grandiose in its concept but pitiful in its results. His programme had the same consequences for the environment as the industrial revolution in the West two centuries earlier. Moreover, China's population began to outstrip its food supply. With 10 million more mouths to feed every year, the problem was not brought entirely under control by the 'one child per family' policy launched by Mao's successors. Even so, it has been calculated that without it, another 300 million Chinese would have been born.

Only 10 per cent of China's land surface is cultivable, and when collective farms were broken up in the 1980s, those peasants who stayed on the land began chopping down forests to extend their

**A hostile land** *Poor farmers enjoy few comforts in the northern province of Shaanxi. Equipment is primitive and the land is prone to drought. Yet, with hard work, wheat and millet can be coaxed out of the reluctant earth.*

**Homes for new workers** *China's rapid industrial expansion caused millions of people from the countryside to flock to the cities in search of better-paid jobs – and cities to grow at an unchecked rate.*

*A beach made to order*   *With natural havens becoming scarce in Japan, Miyazaki has created its own artificial beach, with waves.*

*Death of a beauty spot*   *A dramatic illustration of the price China pays for progress: toxic smoke chokes a valley in Sichuan Province.*

fields. In the pursuit of profit, new industries were set up in the countryside, where labour was cheap. Such changes had a disastrous impact on the environment: assembly plants, working seven days a week, turned the rice-fields of the Pearl River delta into one of the most polluted regions in the country. The coal burned to generate electricity was 'dirty' coal, with a high sulphur content. The once legendary blue skies of Manchuria in the north were streaked by smoke belched out by a thousand factory chimneys.

### Japan's plan to create a New Earth

The atomic bombs dropped on Hiroshima and Nagasaki in 1945 left the Japanese suspicious of nuclear power. But Japan has to import 80 per cent of its energy, and demand is so pressing that the country has built more than 50 nuclear power plants. In 1990 the government announced its 'New Earth 21' programme, with the aim, over the next 100 years, of restoring the land to the state it was in before the industrial revolution. Deserts would be reclaimed, forests replanted, and new sources of energy developed. The vision included building dams for hydroelectric schemes, using geothermal energy from molten rocks below Earth's surface, sending heat-gathering platforms into orbit around the sun, and creating 'clean' nuclear energy from fusion, rather than fission.

### Japan's permanent war on pollution

Rapid industrialisation after the Second World War left Japan with serious pollution problems. In the early 1950s, 200 people died after eating fish poisoned by mercury wastes discharged into the sea at Minamata, a fishing port on the western side of Kyushu Island. Japan has won praise for its efficiency in the use of energy, but its record on environmental protection has, until recently, been poor. In the 1970s, victims of pollution began for the first time to win compensation in the courts, and today the government sets aside 1.6 per cent of its GDP (Gross Domestic Product) for environmental protection. Japan is committed in principle to reducing the output of greenhouse gases that are believed to cause global warming, but the country has a love affair with the car, and pollution in the cities is so bad that people wear masks. There is also the issue of 50 million tons of household waste produced annually. The capital has solved that problem, at least for the time being, by dumping landfill waste into Tokyo Bay, where it has formed the basis of several man-made islands.

*After the blast*   *On September 30, 1999, three workers were injured when an explosion shook a Japanese nuclear plant near Tokai-Mura. Here, doctors check a young employee for radiation levels.*

CHAPTER 3

# THE SHOCK OF THE NEW

No society in East Asia has escaped the changes and progress that have overthrown the old, traditional ways of living that date back for millennia. Japan offers some prime examples of the contradictions embedded in a society in the throes of change. The emperor was revered as a living god until the country's defeat in the Second World War; now he has been stripped of his divinity and authority, yet the world's second-ranking industrial power still accepts him as a unique symbol of the nation. Japanese women may lag behind their sisters in the West, but they are beginning to assert themselves and raise questions about the dominant position of men in society. Even Sumo wrestling is losing its hold to baseball and football in the mass-media age. China, too, is finding that moving from a world impregnated with traditional values into the 21st century world of tower blocks and modern technology is fraught with problems.

*The twinkling lights of floating restaurants in Hong Kong harbour.*

# The long struggle for religious freedom

*Taoism, Confucianism, Buddhism and Islam are enjoying a revival in China, after surviving Mao Ze-dong's attempt to wipe out belief in any faith other than communism – but his successors do not extend their toleration to new sects. Japan, the home of nature-worshipping Shinto, has also seen the rise of new cults.*

**Study time**   *A South Korean Catholic.*

In China, raising a skyscraper requires the skills not only of architects, entrepreneurs and builders, but also those of a geomancer – a master of the art of feng shui. This tradition of orientating a building so that it is in harmony with nature arises out of Taoist beliefs. In a land where cold winds tend to blow from one direction – the north – it also has a practical basis. If the laws of feng shui (literally 'wind and water') are followed, a building will be protected from demons, ghosts and other evil spirits, and it will fall under kindly influences, including those of revered ancestors. Belief in the power of ritual is deeply ingrained among the more traditionally minded Chinese, who recognise no sharp line of distinction between the human world and the world of the spirits.

### Shamans and their rituals survive in South Korea

Despite all the changes that modern times have brought to South Korea, the ancestral belief in the power of shamans has not been erased. The word shaman means 'holy man', although most shamans in South Korea today are women. The belief, which probably reached Korea from Siberia, is based on the notion that people in the living world are surrounded by invisible spirits, which can affect their lives for good or ill. A shaman passes on requests to the spirits by offering sacrifices and going into a self-induced trance. The authorities frown on shamanism, and altars and rituals have disappeared from many public places. But shamans continue to enjoy immense prestige in both town and country, and the rituals continue – in the privacy of the shamans' own homes.

**Ritual**   *A South Korean shaman tries to make contact with the spirits, invoking their aid to protect a client.*

## Three ancient faiths

At funerals, for example, the dead are furnished with an array of objects made of paper that will help them in the next world: a paper house, a paper carriage, make-believe paper money, and so on. The living and the dead belong to a single harmonious universe. Three ancient faiths have contributed to this unity: from Taoism comes the importance of being in harmony with nature; Confucianism emphasises the importance of social order; Buddhism has contributed its doctrine of rebirth and the cycle of life. Buddhism is flourishing in modern China, and life for monks in some of the most celebrated temples is even verging on opulence since they began selling statues and incense and charging for admission or for prayers of intercession.

Buddhism in Tibet is a different matter. Temples have been rebuilt following destruction by Chinese Red Guards during the Cultural Revolution, but many nuns and priests still languish in prison and the Dalai Lama, who fled to India in 1959, is still regarded as a threat. In December 1999, his lead was followed when the 14-year-old Karmapa Lama, the third holiest figure in Tibet, also fled to India.

The Cultural Revolution also brought persecution to China's 30 million Muslims, who live mainly in the Western provinces. But in the new China, mosques have been rebuilt and going on pilgrimage to Mecca is now officially permitted.

Religious toleration does not extend to those faiths or sects which, in the view of the authorities, represent a challenge. Christianity is approved only in an official, state-sponsored version. New sects find fertile ground among people wracked with anxieties about the future, but the authorities are highly suspicious of them.

**The way ahead**   *Pilgrims plod up the steep sides of Huashan, a Chinese mountain that is sacred to Taoists.*

## A persecuted cult

The Falungong cult, which claims 70 million members, is regarded as a particular threat because it has made converts among officers in the armed forces, and even in the ranks of the Communist Party itself. The cult, which was founded by Li Hongzhi, a Chinese living in exile in America, teaches that meditation and exercises known as *qigong* can cure illnesses, and promises salvation in a world that is on the brink of destruction. The Chinese government has outlawed meetings of cult members, burned its books, destroyed its videos and jailed its leaders. It has accused the cult of 'advocating superstition and jeopardising public stability'.

Falungong members responded to persecution with silent sit-down protests in public places, including Beijing's Tiananmen Square, which has special significance in the struggle for human rights in China following the June 1989 massacre of protestors there.

*Homage to Buddha   A moment of reverence in a Buddhist temple in the heart of Canton.*

### Christianity and Islam

Roman Catholicism is not tolerated in China, where the Church has been driven underground. The government supports the rival Chinese Patriotic Catholic Association, and is trying to stamp out allegiance to the Pope. In November 1998 more than 70 Protestant missionaries were arrested and the international Press reported that one woman was so badly beaten that she suffered brain damage. Islam is based in western China but is also strong in southern ports that had links with Arab traders as early as the 7th century. It enjoys toleration.

*A sage remembered   Ritual to celebrate the 2545th anniversary of the birth of Confucius.*

*Islam recovers   Around half the population of the province of Xinjiang are Muslims.*

*Starting young   Novice monks in a Buddhist monastery in the Chinese province of Yunnan. They start to study the faith at the age of eight.*

*Home of the gods*  Twisted cords of rice straw, weighing six tons, mark out the purification zone in the 2000-year-old Shinto shrine at Izumo, on Honshu, Japan. The gods are said to gather there each October.

## The many Shinto gods of Japan

Until defeat in the Second World War, both political and religious power in Japan stemmed from the same source – the living god who ruled as the nation's emperor. The constitution drawn up by the victorious Americans in 1946 abolished both the emperor's divinity and the special status of the state religion, Shinto, which had placed that divinity at its heart. But the Shintoism survived. It is a faith grounded in village life and has its origins in nature worship, but it has many adherents in towns and cities as well as in the countryside. Shinto means 'the way of the gods' and the traditional form includes a belief in *kamis*, the gods that inhabit trees, rocks, rivers, mountains, animals, even household items such as the

*Hands of destiny*  The hands of the colossal Buddha of Kamakura, near Tokyo, in the classic position required for meditation.

kitchen stove. Modern Shintoism, however, tends to lay more emphasis on rituals, shrines, pilgrimages and the veneration of ancestors than on such beliefs.

Shinto is one of two major religions recognised in Japan: the other is Buddhism. It is customary to consult a *kami* on occasions such as a birth or a marriage, but it is to the Buddhist faith that most Japanese turn when somebody dies. There are three important Buddhist universities in the country, and 60 per cent of Japanese families have a Buddhist altar in their homes. Zen Buddhism, one of several strands of the faith, teaches that enlightenment depends on contemplation and intuition rather

*Shinto priest*  From 1868 to 1945, Shinto was in effect the state religion of Japan.

than on learning. It is popular in the West for its searching questions such as: 'What is the sound of one hand clapping?' The Soka Gakkai is a society of Buddhist laymen that founded its own political party in 1964 and has built an empire based on finance and real estate.

In recent years, thousands of Japanese have joined sects formed around the personality and teachings of a charismatic leader, and some of these groups represent a very real danger to society. In March 1995, ten commuters died and more than 5000 were injured when the Aum Shinrikyo cult released the deadly nerve gas Sarin on the Tokyo underground system. Their motive for the attack was never revealed, but they believed that the world would end in 1997. In January 2000, the cult admitted that their leader, Shoko Asahara, had been responsible for the outrage, and said they were renouncing violence and changing their name.

*Cleansing flames*  Purification rite at a Shinto shrine in Kyoto.

# One people, one emperor

*The Japanese royal family renounced its divinity and was stripped of all political authority after the country's defeat in the Second World War. The present emperor, Akihito, is closer to the people than any of his ancestors, yet he is no ordinary citizen: he is a potent symbol of the nation's unity.*

***Coronation Day*** *In Tokyo, on November 12, 1990, Akihito is crowned the 125th Emperor of Japan.*

When Emperor Hirohito announced Japan's surrender over the radio in 1945, he spoke in an archaic, courtly language that few of his subjects had ever heard before. The war situation, he said, had developed 'not necessarily to Japan's advantage.'

### From a god to a mortal man

Hirohito was a remote, inaccessible figure, usually photographed in uniform on a white horse. Even his closest advisers dared not look him in the face, out of fear and respect. Schoolchildren had to bow if they passed his portrait, for the emperor was a living god, the descendant of the sun goddess Ameratsu. His position was clearly set out in the constitution of 1889: the emperor was 'sacred and inviolable.'

The constitution dictated to Japan by the victorious Americans, 57 years later, buried for ever the notion of the emperor's divinity. Not only was the emperor no more than a mortal man, but Article 4 of the 1946 constitution laid down clearly that he had no power to govern. He could represent the nation as a figurehead, and reign as its symbol, but he could no longer rule. The atom bombs that fell on Hiroshima and Nagasaki in 1945, bringing the war to an end, had smashed the mystique of Japan's line of god-emperors.

Hirohito, the 124th Japanese emperor in direct lineage, died in 1989, and during his lifetime there always hung over him a question about his personal involvement in the aggressive policies that led Japan into war. He was at the head of both the military and the civil government, but his presumed divinity put him on a level far removed from day-to-day decision-taking. His son and successor, Akihito, carried no such awkward baggage. He was educated at a school for commoners, and in 1959 he became the first member of the imperial family to choose a bride from outside the ranks of the aristocracy – Michiko Shoda, daughter of a flour company president. Their children were brought up at home, instead of being exiled to a separate residence. Akihito, like his father, is a keen amateur marine biologist, who has written several monographs on the subject. The Japanese royal family has turned its back on many of the trappings of the past, but it still holds the loyalty of the second most commercially powerful nation in the world.

***The cautious bridegroom*** *Prince Naruhito, and his future princess, Masako, announcing their wedding plans in 1993, after a courtship that lasted for six years. Naruhito carried on the new tradition started by his father of marrying a commoner. Masako, a graduate of Oxford University, is the daughter of a Japanese diplomat.*

***Restored residence*** *The Imperial Palace, a haven of calm in the heart of Tokyo's business district. Much of the palace was destroyed by American bombing, but it was reconstructed after the war.*

# Chinese medicine: the quest for harmony

*Traditional Chinese medicine is holistic – that is, it treats the patient, not the symptoms, and it looks at the patient as a rounded human being, with emotions and worries, as well as physical manifestations of illness. Two people with the same problem may be given entirely different courses of treatment.*

In the early morning, before the day's work begins, parks and avenues all over China are filled with people, alone or in groups, stretching to the gentle rhythms of taiji quan. The slow-motion, dance-like movements aim to encourage good health by helping participants to reach a state of internal harmony. Taiji, which loosely translates as 'wholeness', focuses on the emotional and mental state, as well as on the body. It is part of a traditional system of medicine that sees illness as the result of a blockage in the body's subtle system of circulating energies, or of an imbalance between two opposing energies, the feminine yin and the masculine yang.

## Vital energies in the body

The principles of Chinese medicine were set out in the *Nei Jing*, a manual on acupuncture that was composed at around the beginning of the first century AD. It describes how the vital energy *qi* (pronounced 'chi') flows through the body along 12 major pathways, called meridians. Some of this energy is yin and some is yang, and their correct balance can be restored by the insertion of fine needles at 365 acupuncture points located along the meridians. Another means of restoring the balance is by moxibustion – setting fire to powdered leaves of the mugwort plant, placed on the patient's body along a meridian.

***When modesty forbids*** *Ivory statuettes allowed women to indicate the site of their illness to a doctor without feeling embarrassed.*

## Yin and Yang

The first-known reference to the energy forces yin and yang is in a medical treatise of around AD 200, but the concepts were worked out by philosophers centuries earlier. Yin is the feminine force: passive, dark, receptive and cool. Yang is masculine: bright, thrusting and active. They are both opposing and complementary, and illness is a sign that they are out of balance. Health is restored by re-creating harmony between them, using acupuncture or other techniques.

The human body is perceived as a whole, with pathways linking the different organs – the heart, lungs, liver, and so on. Health is regulated by a system of interactions, not just between yin and yang, but also between the five elements of which everything is composed: earth, fire, water, wood and metal. Traditional Chinese doctors diagnose the state of health of a patient by checking 12 pulses, six on each wrist.

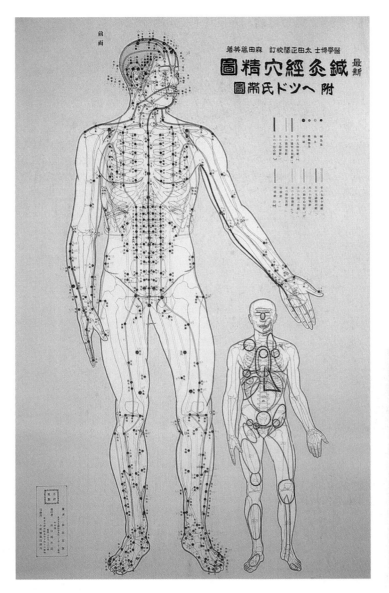

**Pathways for energy** *Meridian lines and acupuncture points on a chart of the body, from a version of the* **Nei Jing.**

***Roadside repairs*** *A citizen has his medical problem treated in the street. The Chinese are used to living their lives in public.*

In Europe, medical science had to wait until 1628 before the Englishman William Harvey published his discovery that the blood circulates around the body. Chinese scholars knew about the circulation of the blood in the 3rd century, and knew that the bloodstream takes part in a constant interchange with the circulation of air in the lungs, carried in channels so small as to be invisible to the naked eye.

## Cures by the thousand

An array of remedies forms part of the armoury of Chinese medicine. The walls of a traditional chemist's shop are lined with hundreds of little drawers, full of powders and decoctions of animal, herbal or mineral origin. The Chinese medicine chest contains some 16 000 remedies, among them powdered sea horse, which is believed to be good for goitre, and octopus ink and vinegar, which are used for heart disease. But such remedies are not prescribed automatically: for each patient, the chemist will recommend a personal course of medication. Diet, too, can be an essential part of the treatment. The link between certain illnesses and the diets which seemed to be beneficial in treating them was established as long ago as the 2nd century BC, possibly as the outcome of trial and error, coupled with observation of the patient.

Operations such as brain surgery or dental surgery, which in the West would call for anaesthesia, are carried out, seemingly without distress to the patient, according to the traditional principles. Nevertheless, modern China does not turn its back on Western advances. In 1912 the young Chinese Republic, which was attempting to bring China into the modern era in every possible way, even tried to abolish traditional medicine altogether. It did not succeed: the ancient ways are still taught in specialist institutes, and still practised in some hospitals.

The training of a traditional medical practitioner, however, now includes a grounding in Western techniques. Thousands of people, especially in the countryside, still turn to a traditional healer when they fall ill, and this is not just because no alternative is available: it is because they know that the ancient cures work. In the cities, where Western-style treatment is becoming more available, patients are increasingly able to choose between the two systems. And, as in the Western world, some doctors are trying to build bridges between the two different approaches.

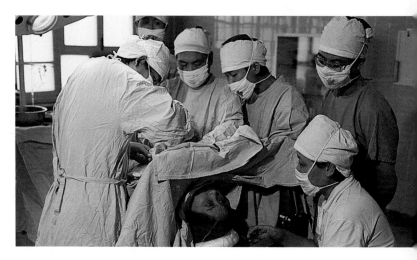

***Free, but not for all*** *About half of town dwellers and 10 per cent of those living in the country benefit from a health service that is free for officials and state employees.*

### Organ grafts from the condemned

China executes more people than the rest of the world put together. The death penalty has been meted out for crimes ranging from murder, rape and kidnapping to drunken driving, smuggling and tax fraud. The high rate of executions was even turned into a profitable trade. The world was horrified when it was revealed that wealthy patients in need of a new liver or new kidneys had travelled to China for operations that gave them the healthy organs of condemned criminals.

***Cures for sale*** *A seller of herbal medicines lays out her wares in Gaungxi Province.*

# China's controlling party

*In theory, China's Communist Party is separate from its government. In reality, all power resides in the party, and it still reaches into every aspect of the nation's life.*

**Party badge** *The emblem of China's Communist Party.*

On the flag of the People's Republic of China – five gold stars on a red background – the biggest star represents the Chinese Communist Party. The other stars are the four social classes of the nation: peasants, industrial workers, white collar workers and managers. It is a fitting symbol of the dominance of a party that fought its way to power in a hard school. It learned ruthlessness in a civil war against Chiang Kai-shek and his Nationalists, that was set aside, but only temporarily, during the struggle against Japanese aggression. In those days, too, it learned that its greatest strength lay in the support of the peasants. Mao Ze-dong, the communist leader, promised them land reform, and swept the Nationalists off the mainland into Taiwan. Proclaiming the birth of the People's Republic, on October 1, 1949, the victor announced in Beijing's Tiananmen Square: 'The Chinese people has risen'.

## The Red Emperors

The first Red Emperor opened a new era in the long story of the Middle Kingdom. He imposed party rule and revolutionised Chinese society by a policy of systematic terror. Theoretically, Mao's China was a classless society. But party members enjoyed special privileges, and there were grades within the Party: only upper grades, for example, could stay in a hotel with a private bath. Membership applications swelled, and by 1955 there were 10 million card-carrying members of the party.

Mao died in 1976 and the second Red Emperor, Deng Xiao-ping, realised that in order to survive the party had to give the Chinese people some realistic hope for a better life. He set about the enormous task of introducing the profit motive into a society that had been used to central planning and economic control. 'To get rich is glorious,' he proclaimed. But although prepared to offer a limited degree of economic freedom, the regime was not yet ready to give up its control of ideas and grant political freedom. This was made brutally clear in 1989, when Deng's troops and tanks crushed a demonstration by pro-democracy students, killing an estimated 1000 demonstrators.

At the start of the new millennium, the Communist Party can claim some 50 million members. Its third Red Emperor, Jiang Zemin, has had to fight corruption, and he has also had to accept that the people know it is possible to succeed in life without being a member of the party or even without sharing its ideas – so long as they are not openly questioned. That would still be dangerous heresy.

**A nation reborn** *In Beijing, on October 1, 1949, Mao Ze-dong proclaims a communist victory and the foundation of the People's Republic of China.*

**Power in appearance only** *The opening of the 8th National Congress of the People, in a Beijing palace. But real power lies with the Communist Party.*

### The *laogai*, China's gulag

In 1998, three founders of a new prodemocracy party in China were sentenced to a total of 36 years in prison. Their destination: one of the hundreds of labour camps in China's gulag, the *laogai*. China has signed the United Nations' Covenant on Civil and Political Rights, but an estimated 10-20 million prisoners are held in the camps, surrounded by watchtowers and barbed wire. Some are criminals, but many are political prisoners accused by the Party of threatening the stability of the regime.

**Brief dawn of freedom** *In 1989, students calling for a more democratic China raised 'The Goddess of Democracy' based on America's Statue of Liberty in Tiananmen Square. The government's response was to send in tanks.*

# The Red Army on trial

*The Chinese army, more than 2.5 million strong, is the biggest in the world, but its equipment lags behind that of the West, and some of its higher ranks have developed a taste for doing business, rather than fighting.*

**Arms parade**
*A display of Chinese military strength.*

China's Red Army was forged in the heat of civil war and created its own legend on the Long March of 1934-5. Hounded by Nationalist foes, and faced with 6000 miles (9600 km) of rivers, mountains and ravines to cross, only 10 000 of the 100 000 soldiers who had begun the march survived. In those days, the army chiefs and the Communist Party leaders were one and the same, and Mao Ze-dong, the supreme leader, learned the lesson that 'power comes out of the barrel of a gun'.

## A fighting record

The Red Army, officially the People's Liberation Army (PLA), fought in the Korean War of 1950-3, invaded Tibet in 1950, crushed a rebellion there in 1959, defeated India in an unofficial war on the Himalayan border in 1962, and supported the North Vietnamese in their war with the USA. Inside China, the Red Army brought the over-zealous Red Guards to order when Mao decided that the Cultural Revolution was leading to chaos. In 1989 students staged a demonstration in Tiananmen Square, Beijing, and more than 1000 were killed when the Red Army obeyed the order to disperse them with tanks. Today, the Army's duties include keeping order in Tibet and fighting Uigur separatists in western China.

The technical equipment of the PLA is vastly inferior to that of the West. In 1998 President Jiang Zemin announced that its manpower would be cut from 3 million to 2.5 million over the next three years, as part of a programme of modernisation. This still leaves the PLA as the biggest army in the world. Fighter planes, bombers, warships, missiles and advanced radar defences have been bought from Russia and Israel. China is a nuclear power, and has tested a ground-to-ground missile that is capable of reaching North America. The reason for this build-up of military might goes beyond national security. China has never made a secret of the fact that it regards Taiwan as part of the motherland. It has the weapons to launch a devastating strike, but the consequences make it unlikely.

**Power at sea**  *The Chinese navy on exercises in November 1995.*

### China's generals go into business

Everyone in China benefited from the economic reforms that Deng Xiao-ping set in motion in the 1980s – but the generals of the Red Army more than most. They built up a business empire that included hotels, mines, toy factories, farms, organised smuggling, even brothels. They ran 15 000 to 20 000 enterprises, across all sectors of the economy, making an estimated $7 billion profit. Their activities became such a national scandal that in 1998 President Jiang Zemin cracked down with the order: 'Get out of business and spend more time defending the country!' He set up a special police force to deal with smuggling and the generals promised to hand over their private enterprise empire, but little has changed since then.

**Stepping out**  *Female soldiers train for the Chinese national parade.*

# Taiwan: living in the shadow of a giant

*Only 120 miles (200 km) from the mainland of China, Taiwan was a place of refuge for the defeated Chinese Nationalists in 1949. The island has managed to prosper and preserve its independence during more than half a century of sabre rattling by its giant neighbour.*

**Long-term leader** *Chiang Kai-shek took power in 1949, and was re-elected up until his death in 1975.*

When the Portuguese arrived off Taiwan in 1620, they were so taken with its forested mountains that they named it *Ilha Formosa*, the 'beautiful island'. The Portuguese were followed by the Dutch, who were expelled in 1662 by a Chinese general fleeing from the Manchus. In 1683, Taiwan became part of the Manchu empire, but in 1895 it was annexed by Japan, as part of the spoils of war.

## Towards democracy

After being defeated by the communists in 1949, Chiang Kai-shek and his Nationalist army fled to Taiwan and set up a new state, the Republic of China, insisting that they were the legitimate government of all China. Mao Ze-dong thought otherwise, and a noisy propaganda war broke out. Despite its unreality, Taiwan's claim was accepted by other nations to the extent that Taiwan was the sole representative of China in the United Nations until 1971, when it was expelled. The People's Republic of China, which took over the UN seat, saw Taiwan as a lost province that ought to be restored – by force if necessary. In 1958, force was attempted. Quemoy and Matsu, two Nationalist-held groups of islands just off the coast of China, were heavily shelled from the mainland. The USA, which had a defence treaty with Taiwan, sent its mighty 7th Fleet to the Taiwan Strait and the invasion threat subsided.

With US economic and military support, and with an influx of entrepreneurially minded Chinese who had escaped from the mainland, Taiwan embarked on a course of economic development that dazzled the world. With amazing speed, an island of only 22 million people transformed itself into the 14th most powerful trading nation in the world. This 'tiger' of the Pacific rim enjoyed a spectacular growth rate of more than 8 per cent a year for 20 years, falling to around 5 per cent in the past few years. Prosperity went hand-in-hand with the advance of political freedom. Under Lee Teng-hui, elected president in 1988, Taiwan became a fully fledged democracy.

Chen Shui-bian, who won the presidential election in 2000, declared: 'Taiwan's sovereignty must not be treated as a subject for negotiations.' One of the highlights of his inauguration celebrations was the singing of Taiwan's national anthem by the popular Chang Huei-mei. She had many fans on the mainland, too – until that day. For the pained response of the Chinese government was to ban her from its airwaves.

**Thorn in the side of China** *Downtown Taipei, Taiwan's capital, contains all the trappings of Western capitalism.*

**Election fever** *During the elections of March 2000, promotional material for Chen Shui-bian dominates the streets of Taipei.*

# Korea: divided by a war and the results of peace

*Laid waste by civil war in the 1950s, the Korean peninsula contains two worlds that are radically opposed. From authoritarian beginnings, the South has evolved towards democracy and prosperity, but the North remains a Stalinist society, frozen in a Cold War stance.*

Before South Korea showed the world a new face, at the 1988 Seoul Olympic Games, the image of the country was not a flattering one. It was based on memories of the civil war of 1950-3, and of the brutal and corrupt dictatorship of President Syngman Rhee. The image of North Korea was even worse. Its communist leader, Kim Il Sung, had started the civil war with a surprise attack across the 38th Parallel in June 1950. America and the UN sprang to the defence of the South; China backed Kim.

### Kim's personality cult

After the war ended, in 1953, at the cost of some four million killed or wounded, the 'Beloved Leader' Kim continued his military dictatorship, crushing all dissent and building up a shameless personality cult by filling the streets with gigantic statues and portraits of himself. On his death in 1995, he was succeeded by his son, Kim Jong Il.

In South Korea, student unrest in 1987 began a shift towards democracy. Without much in the way of basic raw materials, but with American aid and Japanese investment, the South Koreans set their sights on industrial growth. A string of success stories in textiles, clothing, electronics, shipbuilding, steel and car-making put South Korea among the ranks of the 'Asian tigers'. For years they enjoyed an uninterrupted growth rate of 10 per cent a year. Today, even with a downturn in the economy, the 46 million South Koreans enjoy a standard of living around 14 times higher than that in the North.

Ignored by the old allies, China and Russia, life in North Korea remains bleak. Kim Jong Il runs a paranoiac regime that devotes more than three-quarters of its meagre revenues to armaments, building up reserves of nuclear warheads, nerve gas and missiles. After heavy floods in 1995 and 1996 ruined harvests, the people starved while humanitarian supplies sent by other countries were diverted to feed the army. South Korea, with its capital, Seoul, less than 38 miles (60 km) from the border, lives under a military and nuclear threat. But despite the disparity between the two Koreas, the dream of re-unification haunts Korean minds. The South's president, Kim Daeyung, has adopted a 'Sunshine policy' in an attempt to thaw his communist neighbour, and trade talks between the two Koreas opened in the spring of 2000.

*Mascot  Boy with a tiger, Korea's national animal.*

*The powerhouse  Seoul, capital of South Korea, has grown rapidly in the past 50 years.*

### Panmunjon, a hot spot left over from the Cold War

Panmunjon, where the armistice ending the Korean War was signed in 1953, is a village close to the 38th Parallel, which marks the frontier between North and South Korea. For 1.25 miles (2km) on either side of the line is the demilitarised zone, a no-man's-land that nobody enters, or they risk becoming target practice for armed guards. Thousands of soldiers are on watch all along the frontier, a potential hotspot left over from the Cold War. Since the armistice, 35 000 American GIs have been stationed in South Korea, as insurance against another surprise attack.

*Uneasy border  Sentries and a pagoda-shaped watchtower at Panmunjon, on the armistice line between the two Koreas.*

71

# A passion for games of chance

*Wherever they go, the Chinese have a reputation for gambling. It may be in the elegant cocktail bar at the Hong Kong racecourse, or amid the clamour and frenzy of a cock-fighting den – but a Chinese man is always ready to back his judgment ... or his luck.*

***The hustler*** *A makeshift pool table at Suzhou.*

In China, you must have family connections to do well in life, but you must also have luck. Being lucky means that the world beyond this one – the world of the spirits – has singled you out for favour. After years of rigid control under communism, gambling fever has broken out once more in China.

## Risking all

The Chinese have always wagered, risked everything and backed their hunches with a rare passion. Sometimes they win, sometimes they lose, but always they return. Their taste for gambling is as strong as their taste for doing business – so strong that sometimes it can lead them into

crime. Gambling is also a strong element in the lives of the yuppies, who 'play' the stock exchanges of Shanghai and Shenzhen.

Macao, the casino capital of Asia, attracts thousands of gamblers every day, some of them high rollers, from Hong Kong, where casinos are illegal. Fortunes are won and lost as, at each throw of the dice, the gamblers put their destiny in the hands of the god of fortune. Money changes hands even at mah-jong: undercover mahjong gambling saloons, protected by the triads, the Chinese mafia, have flourished both in the cities and in the countryside.

Not all games, of course, have been taken over by gambling fever. Some are played just for the joy of the game. *Weiqi*, which was called 'go' when it was taken to Japan in around AD 500, is played with counters called stones and is based on military strategy: the objective is to capture the opponent's territory and stones by surrounding them. Another popular game often played for its own sake is the Chinese version of 'scissors, paper, stone'. The players shout out numbers as they jab fingers into the air, and the loser is the one whose number, added to those already called, makes ten.

***At the day's end*** *Work over for the day, the serious business of cards or dominoes can begin.*

### Mad about *pachinko*, Japan's pinball game

Every Japanese town or city has its bright, neon-lit halls packed with scores – even hundreds – of vertical pinball tables. The game is *pachinko*, and the players stand as if mesmerised in front of the machines. Hundreds of silver balls are propelled into the air at the touch of a button, hitting contact points and liberating other balls as they fall in a metallic cacophony, made even more exciting by flashing lights and electronic buzzings. The game, which was invented in the 1950s, rapidly became a craze. It is cheap to play and is supposed to be for amusement only, but Japanese gangsters, the *yakusa*, rake in profits from more than 15 000 *pachinko* parlours, and any balls won can be illegally exchanged for cash.

***Spot the winner*** *Greyhounds at Macao stadium.*

# Tentacles of the Chinese Triads

*Born out of rebellion against China's Manchu conquerors, China's Triads set foot on a slippery slope when they started raising funds by extortion and evolved into a gangster organisation, ruling a drugs and vice empire that reaches into Chinatowns all over the world.*

**Big city mobster**  *A Triad member in Macao hides his face as he is picked up by police.*

Secret societies have flourished in China and have fostered rebellion against the ruling powers at least since the time of the oddly named Red Eyebrows Society in 9 BC. The Triads, a byword today for criminality, were politically motivated at the start. They claim to have been founded by Buddhist monks in the late 17th century, when the Manchus were extending their rule over the whole of China. One monastery held out for three weeks against an entire Manchu army, and the handful who escaped after it fell organised a secret society pledged to restore the Ming Dynasty.

## Oaths and rituals

New recruits were initiated with oaths and complex rituals that still exist in a simplified form today. The word 'Triad' means an equilateral triangle, whose sides represent heaven, earth and man, and every Triad member is assigned a number that is divisible by three. Under the corrupt rule of the Manchus, the Triads became 'godfathers' to the ordinary people, meting out their own justice and their own punishments. In the 19th century they turned to extortion and made fortunes by dealing in opium, prostitution and gambling. They extended their 'protection' to the communities of Chinese workers overseas.

In the 20th century, Chiang Kai-shek used the Green Gang Triad to massacre communist trade unionists in Shanghai, and on his defeat, in 1949, they moved into Hong Kong. According to the Hong Kong police some 50 criminal secret societies, with a total of 100 000 members, set up there after the communists took over on the mainland. Their numbers have swollen since. By the 1970s, the Sun Yee Triad alone had nearly 45 000 members. When the police arrested the top man in 1987, Hong Kong discovered with horror that he was a respectable-looking solicitor's clerk.

Today, the main source of money for the Triads is the heroin trade, based on opium supplies from the 'Golden Triangle' area of Laos, Thailand and Burma. In the USA they have even moved into the territory of the Sicilian Mafia. But their profits are so astronomical that they are now laundering their money by moving into legitimate business enterprises.

### From drugs to illegal immigrants

One consequence of the return of Hong Kong to China in 1997 was to send the Triads in search of lucrative new markets. In the USA, they battled with the Mafia for control of the narcotics trade. In China, they established a foothold by smuggling out peasants who wanted to make a new start overseas, working as labourers or washing dishes in a Chinatown restaurant. On June 19, 2000, customs officers at Dover found 58 Chinese illegal immigrants who had suffocated to death inside a truck. They had undertaken to pay the gang that smuggled them to Britain the equivalent of five years' wages.

**Last respects**  *Triads muster at a funeral of a top leader in Taiwan.*

73

# Perils of the race to the top

*Schooldays are supposed to be the happiest of one's life, but in Japan they can be days of constant strain. From an early age, children are pressurised by parents and teachers to do well in competitive examinations and to accept that those who fail in school have failed in life.*

**Morning assembly** *Earnest young pupils listen respectfully to their headmaster's morning address.*

Wearing a sailor suit, complete with round hat held firmly in place by a strap under the chin, a six-year-old Japanese boy joins the crowds of 'salarymen' catching the morning tube train in Tokyo. They are on their way to work and he is on his way to school – and it is a moot point which of them will find the day's tasks the more demanding.

### The importance of a diploma

Japanese children learn early in life that the world is a competitive place. Even before they enter the school system, ambitious parents will have dug deep into their pockets to send them to a good nursery school. A flying start is a great help in a system based on the idea that the object of education is to pass examinations. For Japan is a meritocracy, where the only way to land a good job, either in the business world or in government service, is by possessing a diploma or degree.

The race begins in primary school, entered at the age of six. At 12, the children move on to *chugakko*, or secondary school, where the pace quickens. Although they already attend school on Saturday mornings, most children take extra tuition at the end of the day, or even on Sundays, at a *juku*, or cramming school. The most prestigious of these can be cripplingly expensive. At 15, if they pass the demanding examination, the children go on to high school, or *kotogakko*. Nine out of ten Japanese children have a diploma, but some give up school before the next hurdle, the university entrance examinations. Nervous breakdowns have been suffered preparing for this ordeal, and suicide is not unknown, for failure can be seen as letting down one's family, as well as oneself. Some observers cite unbearable pressure to succeed at school alongside the breakdown of traditional family life as possible causes of a recent spate of violent crime among Japanese teenagers.

Oddly enough, once in university the pace slackens and students can enjoy themselves for the next four years, knowing a degree will be their passport to the future. Some girls go on to university, although it is not generally expected of them. Instead, there is a two-year college course that will probably lead to a clerical or secretarial job. The government is planning to reform the system but any major change will come, perhaps, from big business – which, faced with a crisis, is looking for recruits who are creative thinkers, rather than simply memorisers of facts.

**High hopes** *A young Japanese girl makes an offering at examination time before the shrine of a Shinto god.*

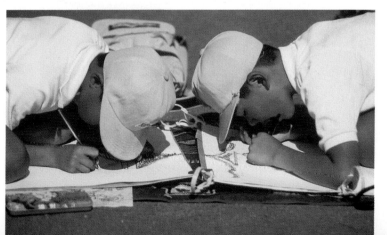

**Friends and rivals** *Japan's educational system is meritocratic, inculcating a competitive spirit early in life.*

**Breaktime** *Schoolchildren eat lunch beneath Osaka castle.*

# The growing power of Japanese women

*Strangely, perhaps, for a nation whose emperors until recently derived their authority from the belief that they were descended from a goddess, Japan has always been a male-dominated society. But in today's rapidly changing world, some Japanese women are beginning to question traditional roles.*

**The pioneer** *Fusae Ota, the first female governor of Osaka.*

At the age of 48, Fusae Ota became a pioneer: she was appointed governor of Osaka, the second biggest city in Japan, and its surrounding region. The nation had to wait until the beginning of the 21st century for a woman to reach such an important position. More usually the place for a woman in politics is in the shadows, playing the role of the loyal wife while her husband makes the speeches and wins the votes. So far, women have won only 8 per cent of the seats in the Japanese Diet (parliament), though they have fared better in local politics.

## The glass ceiling

In the world of work, the situation for women is not much better. More than half of Japanese women go out to work, but when it comes to executive responsibility only one post in ten is held by a woman, and a glass ceiling operates as a block to promotion. Some 40 per cent of working women are part-timers, which means that in hard times they are relatively easy to sack. Even when the economy is buoyant, part-timers do not enjoy the benefits of full-time employment, such as twice-yearly bonuses and pensions.

**Learning to sell** *Some of the 1300 salesgirls recently recruited by a large chainstore learn sign language so that they can give good service to any customers who are deaf.*

Despite being under-represented in politics and overlooked at work, Japanese women are beginning to occupy a more important place in society. The country is going through an economic crisis and its dominant males seem to have lost some of their confidence. Finance minister Kiichi Miyazawa went so far as to say in March 2001 that the nation's finances were 'quite close to collapse'. Women, who are used to being on the margins of society, are becoming more assertive and independent. In the old days the wife's role was to stay at home and bring up the children. Her duty was to hide her emotions and be pleasing to men. At a Shinto wedding ceremony, the bride still wears a large white headdress whose symbolic function is to conceal the horns of jealousy. In the event of divorce, which was easy for men, the home and children belonged to the husband, not to the wife. After work, Japanese salarymen still tend to carouse with their friends rather than go straight home – but now, women are getting out of the house, too.

Women's Lib may not have made quite the same impact on Japan's tradition-steeped society that it has made in the West, but the new generation of women are making their voices heard by joining societies. More and more of them are becoming involved in movements for such causes as civil rights, education, and the protection of the environment.

Inside the home, women often take charge of the family finances. Younger women in particular are becoming aware of their power as consumers, and although raising a family is still the ambition of many they have woken up to a realisation that the years before marriage are freedom years. The average age of marriage for a Japanese woman has risen in a few decades from 24 to 28 – and when they do marry these days, it is more likely to be for love than the result of an arrangement between two sets of parents.

**The new generation** *Young Japanese girls have rejected the constraints put upon them by tradition and demonstrate their new-found independence in their fashions and lifestyles.*

# The traditional Chinese house

*As long ago as the time of Confucius the principles of Chinese building were laid down. A house should be 'round above and square below' so as to symbolise both heaven and earth.*

***Imposing entrance*** *A gateway in Yunnan Province.*

Continuity and harmony are the hallmarks of the traditional Chinese building style. Down the centuries, princes and peasants have built their homes on the four-square base that became the model under the Zhou Dynasty in the time of Confucius (551-479 BC). The finest examples of the style are in the Forbidden City in Beijing. The Hall of Middle Harmony is a 52 ft (16 m) square chamber, raised on a triple terrace, in which the emperor would inspect seeds for next year's crop. The Temple of Heaven and Earth is a circular building within a square courtyard.

### Four generations under the same roof

Apart from size, luxury and number of rooms, there was no major difference between the palace, the temple and the ordinary home in ancient China. All followed the same basic pattern, and their openings faced south in accordance with the principles of feng shui – for evil things such as freezing winds and merciless invaders came from the north. The traditional house, intended to shelter four generations of a family under the same roof, is an

***Shared courtyard*** *Rice is laid out to dry in a courtyard shared by several homes.*

***New house, old style*** *A new traditional home goes up near the borders of Sichuan.*

assembly of gardens and square-based buildings surrounded by a circular wall. The classic design has three courtyards, each entered through a gate, which helps to deter evil spirits and gives the house the intimacy of a closed world. Houses in north China are usually of one storey, and in the south they have two. The wooden walls are often painted red, and the heavy tile roofs are green or yellow. The eaves turn up with a graceful, pagoda-like curve at the corners.

The display of wealth was frowned on during the Mao years, and an elegant courtyard might be used for storing coal. Today, the houses of the rich have pleasure gardens, while the poor must content themselves with a shared courtyard. The basic model had many variations, but all were designed for calm and harmony.

### Homes of the rich and poor

The houses of rich people were built with courtyards and wings, and the layout always followed the same pattern. The central bay, which had the best aspect and the best rooms, was for the master of the house. It also contained the shrine to his ancestors. The wings were for the women and for junior members of the family. The kitchen was in the basement, where the servants were housed. The homes of the poor, clustered around a common courtyard, were noisy and overcrowded.

# The Japanese home: a protected inner space

*However much Japanese houses may be changing on the outside, the inner space still preserves many reminders of the past.*

A modern Japanese house is not built to last. Within a few years – 40 at the most, but sometimes as few as ten – it will be pulled down and a new one built in its place. Every year, more than a million new homes are built in this land of 126.8 million people. But not all of them are houses: in the cities especially, land prices are so high that individual houses are disappearing before the advance of apartment blocks, six or seven storeys high.

### Built to withstand earthquakes

In the older sections of Tokyo or Osaka it is still possible to find ancient wooden houses, but modern homes are more likely to be faced with concrete or composite materials. They still have a framework of posts and beams, which means that in all but the most severe earthquakes they may tremble but will not collapse.

Whatever the outside appearance, the interior arrangement has hardly changed. A Japanese home is still entered through the *genkan*, a threshold at which guests remove their shoes and put on slippers. To Western eyes, the rooms look small and practically bare of furniture. In the main room, flat covers known as *zabutons* are arranged around a low table where tea is served. In winter the family lights the *kotatsu*, a heater beneath the table, fitted with a cover that will

**Golden mile** *The price of land per square yard in Tokyo is the highest in the world.*

gently warm cold feet. During the day, *futons* (Japanese mattresses that also have an appeal in the West) are rolled up and stored away behind the sliding doors of a closet, alongside family papers and documents. The floors are covered with *tatami*, mats of woven rice straw, measuring about 6 ft by 3 ft (1.8 m by 1 m). Dividing one room from another are *shoji*, thin, sliding wood partitions.

The traditional home was surrounded by a gallery covered by projecting eaves, which provided a transition space between the inside and the outside world. Screens around these galleries could be moved to vary the play of light and shade coming into the house. The orientation of a Japanese house is of great importance – not so much to take advantage of the sunshine, for a glaring light is not admired, but to placate the 1001 gods of Shinto. If it is possible, architects like to place the entrance door on the south side, facing roughly in the direction of the land of Buddha.

**A style for all times** *The traditional interior of a modern Japanese house.*

### Zori and tatami

Cleanliness is very close to godliness in the Shinto religion – which is why the Japanese do not bring the dirt of the outside world into their homes. They remove their shoes at the threshold and slip on *zori*, light cloth or straw slippers. Whether the home is a house or an apartment makes no difference. When apartments are sold, their size is given in *tatamis*, rice-straw mats on which families and visitors sit. A six *tatami* flat is a one-roomed studio; a 12 *tatami* is a two-roomed apartment.

**Minimalist** *The clutter-free main room of a Japanese house.*

# The Mongol yurt

*From Manchuria to Afghanistan, the conically shaped yurt has played a vital role in the lives of nomads following their herds across the steppes of Asia. Even as the old nomadic ways disappear – a quarter of Mongolia's population now live in the capital, Ulan Bator – the yurt still represents a cherished way of life.*

**Instant house** *It takes only two hours to put up a yurt.*

The yurt may well be the world's first mobile home, and certainly it is the longest-lasting. Around half of the 2.5 million inhabitants of Mongolia still live in these huge tents that were used by their ancestors millennia ago. They consist of a framework of long strips of wood and crisscrossing battens, bound together with strips of leather, and covered with several layers of felt, wool and animal skins.

A yurt is big enough to provide a home for up to 20 people. It is designed to conserve heat during the cruel months of winter on the high plains, so it has no windows, but a hole is left at the top of the roof to let out smoke and fumes. There is only one door, made of painted wood, and it is always placed on the south side of the yurt, to protect those inside from the piercing north wind.

### The yurt and family life

The yurt plays an important role in the life stages of a nomad. When a boy enters adult life, after his military service, his parents build him a new yurt. The same thing happens when a couple get married. Tradition calls for the parents of the young man to ask the parents of his intended bride for their blessing and to agree on the day of the wedding. When the young people move out, the oldest members of the family move with them, and it is common in the yurt encampments to find several generations living under the same roof.

**Window on the world** *Children learn English from the television.*

### Motorbikes parked with the ponies

When dismantled, a yurt is taken to its next site on the backs of pack animals. Its contents and furnishings are sparse, for they have to be carried, too. Inside the yurt, they are usually arranged in a time-honoured way. At the central point is a stove, for warmth and cooking. Beds – and, if there are children, wooden cradles – are set on either side of the entrance door. The northern side of the yurt is often taken up with chests and sideboards, decorated in traditional motifs. For those yurt-dwellers who live near towns, this area is now likely to be the place for the radio or the television, which gives them access to an exciting new world.

Long resistant to new trends, the Mongolians are beginning to be tempted by modern technology. It is not unusual these days to see motorcycles outside a yurt, parked close to where tough little Mongol ponies are tethered. Tradition dies hard in Mongolia, however: even when nomads turn to the urban life, in permanent settlements, the design of their houses of mud or clay recalls the familiar conical shape of the yurt, home of their forefathers.

**Home-makers** *Women stitch together the roof of a yurt.*

**Isolation** *A yurt in the steppes of Mongolia.*

# Breaking with the past, in China's high-rise cities

*For centuries, the typical Chinese home was a hovel that crammed four generations under one roof. In today's China, it is increasingly likely to be an apartment in a new tower block, which may be shared with another family rather than relatives.*

Mao Ze-dong made many mistakes when he set out to force China into the modern world, and the most disastrous was the so-called 'Great Leap Forward', launched in 1958. It led to a famine in which an estimated 30 million lost their lives. But his ruthlessness was the price China paid in a process that was to transform the country. Peasants seeking work in the new factories began to drift from the countryside in Mao's time. By 1980, four years after his death, 192 million Chinese out of a population of 981 million lived in towns and cities. The drift became a torrent, and by 1997 the figure had more than doubled, to 390 million. To house them, the planners abandoned tradition and erected Soviet-style tower blocks – drab, uniform and with few concessions to comfort.

## Boom times for real estate

The end of the Maoist era and the move towards a mixture of socialism and the market economy preached by Deng Xiao-ping and his successors in the 1980s led to a boom in real estate. It was fuelled by a heady mixture of foreign investment and Chinese capital, both government and private. Beijing, Shanghai, Canton and other great cities grew into sprawling conurbations with 10 million inhabitants, or even more. Brand new towns such as Pudong near Shanghai and Shenzhen near Hong Kong were born. The ancient quarters of some cities were bulldozed to the ground, then leased to developers. Industry dictated where homes should be sited, and the architects of new banks and offices began to create skyscraper cities of concrete and glass.

In the wake of the Chinese-American I.M. Pei, designer of the Louvre pyramid in Paris and the breathtaking Bank of China in Hong Kong, creative young architects such as Peng Yigang, Liu Li and Cui Kai turned entire districts into futuristic showcases for their talents. The standards they set were comparable to those of fashionable architects in the West. They were building a new China, whose cities should stand comparison with San Francisco or Tokyo. But while the planners could point with pride to expensive real estate, the ordinary city-dwelling worker was a poorly housed exile in surroundings sadly lacking in infrastructure and social amenities. He could not afford a car, and the bus services were ancient and decrepit. All too often, the landings and walkways of the new cities became breeding grounds for crime.

**Model shoppers**  *A young family select their flat from a model in a supermarket.*

**All together**  *Apartments are so much in demand that families must sometimes share.*

**Magnet for business**  *Shenzhen, near Hong Kong, is in a Special Economic Zone, set up to attract overseas investment.*

# The infinite variety of Chinese food

*Chinese cuisine plays cleverly on contrasts between tastes, odours, colours, shapes and textures of food. From the hearty mutton stews of Inner Mongolia to the delicate blending of flavours in an iced fruit salad it offers an endless gastronomic adventure.*

**Tea and thanks**   *A newly married Chinese couple serve tea to their wedding guests.*

A Chinese meal is not meant to be eaten alone. It consists of many tiny but tempting dishes that demand to be shared with other people. Throughout all the turbulent events of their long history, the Chinese people have shown a passion for the art of cooking – and for enjoying the results at family meals, or at noisily convivial banquets. Anybody who wanted to eat on their own in China would be hard-pressed to find a table at a good restaurant. A single diner would have to seek out one of the cheaper eating establishments, or buy a bowl of tasty noodles from a hawker selling them in the street.

### The range of flavours

In China, etiquette demands that as many dishes should be served as there are diners – so giving everybody at the meal the chance to taste everything on the table. Diners are offered a delicate combination of colours, flavours and scents, placed on a large plate in the centre of a round table. Chopsticks are used to dip into one dish then another, then to scoop up little mouthfuls of rice – providing the neutral flavour that the taste buds need to recover from sensations of sharp and dry, sweet and sour, fatty and crisp, fresh and fragrantly perfumed.

A good Chinese cook knows how to balance and contrast flavours, and also how to appeal to the eye. He is skilled at cutting narrow strips and thin slices: vegetables, which add colour, are sometimes carved into miniature sculptures. He is an expert in marinading dishes so that they soak up subtle flavours; in adding the right sprinkling of salty soya sauce or the right hint of ginger. He can roast, smoke or steam, simmer a dish for hours or stir-fry it rapidly in a wok in sizzlingly hot oil.

### Four great schools of cooking

The principles of Chinese cooking are health and harmony, and there are four great schools. In the south, the Cantonese style is renowned for its lightness and creativity. Among its specialities are

### Canton's food market: anything that flies, walks or crawls

If Adam and Eve had been Cantonese, so an old story goes, they would not have been thrown out of the Garden of Eden, for they would have ignored the apple and eaten the snake. The huge market of Guangzhou (formerly Canton) is crammed with stalls selling not only snakes but anything that flies, walks or crawls. To the Cantonese, every animal is edible, and for this they are regarded as uncouth by people in the capital, Beijing. The market comes alive at five in the morning and the accent is on fresh food – so fresh that it is sold live. Among the rabbits, crabs, eels and fish are food items that would horrify a Western shopper: cats, monkeys and dogs. In the special section devoted to medicines and cures there is octopus, jellyfish, dried hippopotamus, powdered deer antlers or stag's testicles, which are reputed to have aphrodisiac powers, and turtles with soft shells for couples wanting a male child.

**Korean treat**   *Preparing* kimchi, *fermented cabbage.*

**Late snack**   *Night market in Shanghai.*

**Family meal**   *At a Chinese dinner, cooked dishes are placed in the centre of the table and people reach out with chopsticks for tasty mouthfuls. Soup is served at the end of the meal.*

**Going Western** *An American-style fast-food restaurant in Shenzhen.*

roast meat and dim sum – dumplings and other small delicacies that are served at breakfast or lunchtime. Contrasting flavours, such as sweet and sour sauce, preserve the yin-yang balance of a meal. The flavours of Shanghai cuisine are far stronger. Here there are a number of delicious ways of serving fish, both salt and freshwater varieties, and salty dishes are served in the heat of summer.

Sichuan cooking, from central China, is highly spiced, with a generous use of fiery chillies. Among its specialities are stockpots and spicy broths into which strips of meat or vegetables are plunged. Dry-frying and smoking are traditional cooking methods, and smoked duck sprinkled with tea leaves is a favourite dish.

In the north, the Beijing style has inherited some of the lavishness and extravagance of the days when cooks had to please the palates of the emperor and his court. It is unlikely, though, that even a state occasion in modern times will rise to the 300 separate dishes that were served at an imperial Manchu banquet. Peking duck is eaten in an almost ceremonial way, beginning with mouthfuls of crusty skin, then eating slices of the meat wrapped with spring onion in a wheaten pancake and dipped in a sweet-sour sauce, and finishing with a soup prepared from the duck's carcass. Body and soul are fortified against the harsh winter climate with cabbage and forced wheat pancakes, cooked in steam.

The Mongols brought to China hotpots and meats that were roasted or grilled, while the Muslim population brought a taste for lamb. There is a choice of drinks to wash down the meal: tea, the yellow wine of Shaoxing, which has a liquorice taste, a glass of Chinese beer, or French brandy.

**Oodles of noodles** *Rice noodles in preparation. In some provinces they are preferred to the rice grains.*

**Soup kitchen** *A restaurant cook prepares dinner, a meal served late in China, at about 11 pm.*

### Korea's national dish: an acquired taste

Korea's national dish, *kimchi*, is not to the taste of many visitors, particularly those from the West. It consists of cabbage and turnip, fermented over a long period in sour vinegar, garlic, ginger and sweet red pepper. It is served as a main course or a side dish at any meal of the day, even breakfast. *Kimchi* owes its origin to the Portuguese, who introduced pimento, the red pepper, in the 16th century. More to Western tastes is *pulgogi*, beef marinated in soya sauce, garlic and chilli, grilled at the table.

81

# Japanese food: a cuisine based on the bounty of the sea

**Fish dish** *Assorted* sushi.

*With little pasture land available for raising cattle or sheep, Japan dips into the surrounding seas and into the world's oceans to produce a cuisine of astonishing variety that is presented on the plate with panache and artistry.*

Walk into a *sushi* bar in Japan, and after being greeted with a warm *Irrashaimasse!* (Welcome!) you take your place at the counter ready to admire the skill of the chef as he prepares the raw fish in front of your eyes. You can order *sashimi*, thinly sliced fish that you dip into a soya sauce spiced with *wasabi*, a sharp green horseradish paste; or you can opt for *sushi*, slices of raw tuna or other fish presented on a bed of rice. Raw fish is an essential element of the Japanese diet, but it is not the only way of preparing the produce of the sea.

## Portugal's gift to Japanese cooking

In winter, the Japanese keep out the cold with *nabemono*, fish boiled with horseradish, carrots and Chinese cabbage. Or there is *tempura* – shrimps, crayfish, chunks of white fish, and sometimes lotus root or vegetables, soaked in soya sauce, dipped in batter and deep-fried. The idea of cooking fish in this way was borrowed from the Portuguese after they arrived in

Japan in the 16th century. From seaweed served as a side salad or as a soup, to a bewildering variety of fish and shellfish, Japanese food is endlessly inventive and always elegantly presented. Rice, cooked until it becomes slightly sticky so that it is easy to pick up with chopsticks, features in many meals, but noodles are also popular. Swallowed quickly on a station platform, or at the counter of a *ramen* shop, they are slurped down noisily and appreciatively.

Japan is one of the few countries in the world where it is possible to order whale meat. These giant mammals, ostensibly caught for scientific purposes, can end up in restaurants as *sashimi* or fritters of *tempura*. Happily for the survival chances of the whale, its meat is becoming increasingly expensive. All meat is costly in Japan, but there is still a good demand for *sukiyaki*, cooked at the table with mushrooms, tofu and soya sauce, and for *teriyaki*, marinated in soya sauce and then grilled.

Different regions of Japan have their own styles of cuisine. *Kaiseki ryori* is from the ancient capital, Kyoto. Developed to accompany the tea ceremony, it consists of many small dishes, beautifully presented. In smart restaurants, a kimono-wearing waitress will offer each course on gleaming china or lacquer-ware. The meal will be priced beyond the reach of ordinary Japanese families, but salarymen can console themselves with a cheaper version in a *bento*, or packed lunch.

### Taking a risk with *fugu*

Between October and the end of March, *fugu* appears on the menu of a few specialist Japanese restaurants. Also called moonfish, it is prized for its delicate flesh, but has to be prepared with meticulous care because its liver and ovaries contain a deadly poison. One slip of the chef's knife and the poison can leak out. A *fugu* chef needs a special licence before being allowed to prepare moonfish. Clients have been known to die from eating it, and when this happens the restaurant loses its reputation and the chef will lose his job.

**Balanced meal** *A chef prepares food to be presented in bowls that harmonise in size and colour with the food itself.*

**Bonding after work** *Japanese office workers unwind with their colleagues after work and discuss the day's events over a fish meal in a traditional bistro.*

# Tea, the leaf that made history

*Native to India, China and possibly Japan, tea is a plant that helped to change the world. Its popularity in the West opened up trade with the Orient, and the Boston Tea Party was a milepost along the drama-filled journey to independence of Britain's American colonies.*

In *The Rules of Tea*, a classic work of the Tang Dynasty (618-907), Lu Yu praised the ability of tea to refresh and reinvigorate: 'If anybody is suffering from dehydration, melancholy, headache, dry eyes, pain in the arms or legs, or stiffness in the joints, let him take four or five swallows.' Tea has been widely appreciated in China at least since the 4th century. It is taken without milk or sugar: a glass pot, a few leaves, perfumed perhaps with jasmine or with chrysanthemum petals, and boiling

**Harvest time**   *Gathering tea in China.*

water are all that are needed. When taken as an aperitif, to stir the gastric juices, this bitter-sweet infusion is served in tiny cups that hold perhaps three mouthfuls. When a lump of yak butter is added to a generously sized cup or bowl, the tea becomes an invigorating drink for the Tibetan, camping beneath the snow-clad peaks of the Himalayas.

## The race to be first

Tea pressed into bricks for ease of transport was used as a form of currency during the Song Dynasty (960-1279). It reached Russia along the caravan routes and its Chinese name, *cha*, became the Russian *tchaï*. The English word 'char' is even closer. Early in the 17th century, the Dutch East India Company introduced tea to Western Europe, and in Britain it became so highly prized – and highly taxed – that a single pound of tea cost the equivalent of £300 in today's money. It was a tax on tea that led to a major event

in the American Revolution – the Boston Tea Party of 1773, when a group of angry colonials threw tea from British ships into Boston harbour.

In the following century, China's tea crop was so valuable that it led to the development of the fastest sailing ships ever built, the clippers, which raced each other to the ports of Fuzhou and Xiamen to buy the best crops at the best price. A clipper could make the 16 000 mile (25 700 km) trip back from China to London in 99 days. Most famous of these ocean greyhounds was the British clipper *Cutty Sark*.

**Labour intensive**   *In this factory in the province of Fujian, 700 women sort the tea by hand.*

## The tea ceremony in Japan

Buddhist monks from China introduced the tea ceremony to Japan as a part-religious, part-social ritual. It has been elaborated by the Japanese into a set of formal rules that spell out, down to the most minor gesture, the correct way to receive guests. The bowls and other utensils must be shining, the flowers arranged, and the cakes and powdered green tea ready before the guests arrive. During the ritual, conversation is exquisitely polite: the objective is to create harmony and calm.

**An elaborate ritual**   *It is customary to wash your hands and remove your shoes before entering the place reserved for the tea ceremony.*

# Karaoke: an escape valve for a nation hemmed in by tradition

*Through karaoke, an introvert can turn into an extrovert; a young man with a voice that is normally best confined to the privacy of the bathroom can become Frank Sinatra.*

Invented in 1971, karaoke has reached bars all over the world and has become one of the best-known exports of Japanese popular culture. The word is made up from *kara*, meaning 'empty' and *oke*, a Japanese abbreviation of the English word 'orchestra'.

## A chance to break free

With a karaoke machine, the voice of the original singer is removed from the sound track of a song, leaving the orchestra playing the melody. Anybody with the nerve to stand in front of an audience can give their version of, for example, Frank Sinatra singing 'My Way'. The rules, written and unwritten, of traditional

*Quiet so far...   Karaoke bar in Tokyo.*

Japanese society do not encourage the uninhibited expression of emotions: respect is gained by showing restraint and control. In such a society, permission to break out in the right context is gladly taken. A salaryman, after a few drinks with his friends, will feel emboldened to take the microphone in a karaoke bar. The main clientele, however, is young people. To win their loyalty, competing establishments equip themselves with the lastest technology and offer a selection of songs that is almost inexhaustible.

After three decades of runaway success, the karaoke boom shows signs of slowing down. Two rival forms of entertainment are moving in on karaoke territory, both of them products of the electronic age and the craze for novelty. The first is the mushrooming growth of brightly lit saloons where video games can be played; the second is dancing. Standing on a moving platform, young men dance in synchronisation with a virtual partner, who appears on a large screen. Their feet and bodies move to the rhythm of an electronic tango or paso doble. Karaoke has not yet been dethroned, but its golden age seems to be over, in a society where any young man can now be not just his own Frank Sinatra, but his own Fred Astaire.

## Stars for a night

Karaoke began in big city bars that were open late at night: for hard-pressured salarymen it was a good way of relaxing and throwing off inhibitions. Then the craze moved out to the provinces and to rural areas. In 1988 it penetrated still deeper when the first karaoke studios were opened. People who did not normally go into bars or clubs found that they, too, could enjoy the thrill of standing in for a star. Students and office workers who could not afford bar prices could slip into a karaoke studio and sing in a sound-proofed booth. Today, there are some 12 000 studios throughout Japan, hiring out space and machines for 1000 yen (about £5) an hour.

*Anyone can play   Karaoke studio run by a Tokyo company.*

*A song for everyone   More than 10 000 tunes are available at this karaoke bar.*

# The manga phenomenon: a hero for everyone

*The newsstands and street kiosks of Japan have been taken over by a publishing sensation – mangas. These illustrated magazines tell cliff-hanging stories about heroes and heroines created to appeal to every type of reader.*

A foreigner travelling by train in Japan cannot help but notice the manga phenomenon. These comics, for grown-ups as well as for children, are piled high on the platform newsstands, their brightly coloured covers competing for attention. A manga can be leafed through during the course of the journey, then thrown away into a wastepaper basket specially designed for the purpose. Discarded, but not forgotten – for the manga stories are serials designed, like the old Saturday morning movies, to end with a cliff-hanging climax that leaves the audience on the edge of its seats waiting to know what will happen next.

## Selling by the million

The themes of the manga stories range from science fiction to crime thrillers and adventure stories – even to cooking. The love stories woven into many of the plots are often spiced with eroticism. The characters are designed to fit the fantasy lives of the potential buyers: the manga hero or heroine may be a salaryman white-collar worker, a car enthusiast, a golfer, a rock'n' roller, an office receptionist, or a civil servant. Mangas are big business, and big business knows its market: the comics have captured one-third of the reading market in Japan. Shonen Jump, the biggest manga publisher in the country, sells 3.5 million copies every week. An author-artist with a break-through concept may achieve total sales of more than 250 million.

**Manga heroine** *Kamiya Kaoru, a character in the* **manga The Vagabond.**
© Nobuhiro Watsuki, "RUROUNI KENSHIN", SHUEISHA INC.

**Fantasy world** *Japanese youngsters dress up as manga heroes and heroines.*

One of the most famous authors is Osamu Tezuka, creator of the robot *Astroboy*, and known as the Walt Disney of Japan. *Dragonball Z*, by Toriyama Akira, has sold 50 million copies, while the adventures of *Doraeman*, the robot cat, have filled 44 volumes since 1974, and sold around 70 million copies to enthusiastic young readers.

The manga artists have a sure finger on the pulse of their readers. To follow their stories is to keep in touch with a society in the throes of change. For example, one of the most popular characters these days, because so many readers can identify with him, is Kintaro the Salaryman, who exposes corruption in the company he works for and denounces unsavoury connections between people in high places in business and in the government. The manga that features Kintaro has reached a sale of 16 million copies.

## Mangas on the big screen

The most popular serials are reprinted and bound together to be sold as books. But the phenomenon has not stopped there: it has spawned a whole range of spin-offs, including toys, video games and animated cartoons, shown both on television and in movie houses. In the cinema, full-length cartoon features such as *Princess Mononoke* have won a new public for a popular art form that draws its inspiration from Walt Disney, America's *Superman* or *Captain Marvel* comics, and traditional Japanese painting.

**Easy buy, easy read** *Mangas, which sell phenomenally well, cost only £1 to £1.50.*

*Mangas for sale* *Manga comics account for a third of Japan's publishing market.*

# Empire of the Japanese media barons

*The Japanese are the most avid newspaper readers in the world: their biggest daily has a circulation that reaches 10 million. And the press barons are extending their empires by forging links with television.*

Three-quarters of the Japanese population read a daily newspaper, and many, in their eagerness to find out what is happening in the world, read more than one. The *Yomiuri Shimbun* has the largest circulation in the world, selling a staggering 10 million copies of its morning edition and 4.5 million in the evening.

## Massive circulation figures

Apart from the five big national dailies available to a news-hungry readership, each region or major city has its own provincial newspaper, some with a circulation that would be the envy of a national newspaper in the West. The *Chunichi Shimbun*, for example, sells more than 2 million copies a day in the Osaka region. Most Japanese newspapers, which are fairly serious in tone, are delivered to readers' homes through a network of distribution units affiliated to the great printing houses, rather than picked up on newsstands. There are also a number of evening newspapers, more in the style of British tabloids, which cover sport, the lives and activities of celebrities, and human interest stories.

Despite their massive readership figures, the dailies keep news separate from comment and report the facts neutrally, rather than trying to put a political spin on them, as has become the habit in many British newspapers. And they hardly ever report scandals – that is left to the weekly magazines.

## The advance of television

For several years, the big press groups have been forging links with independent television companies. There could be a cultural gap to bridge, for Japanese television is best known in the West for its frenetic game shows, in which contestants endure extremes of discomfort and humiliation for the entertainment of laughing audiences, both in the studio and in front of the television set at home. In 1999, Japan had 126 television networks and 97 radio compa-

*Leisure pursuits* *Japanese salarymen (top) unwind at the end of a hard day with a drink and a newspaper. In yet another popular Japanese game show, young unmarried men have to choose a soul mate.*

---

### The big dailies: patrons of the arts

Japan's big daily newspapers are like medieval dukedoms or principalities in the way they have extended their activities into the nation's cultural life. As well as publishing newspapers, books and magazines, they run sports teams and theatre groups. The *Yomiuri Shimbun* owns a famous orchestra as well as a baseball team, while *Nikkei*, a leading business daily, has opened its own business school.

nies. The five biggest television groups – TBS, Fuji, Nippon, Asahi, Tokyo – have developed nationwide coverage. Cable television, too, has made rapid inroads. In 1997 it had 15 million subscribers, an increase of 15 per cent on the previous year.

Public television is controlled by NHK, the biggest media empire in the world. The group owns two chains of terrestrial television stations as well as two chains that broadcast via

satellites. On top of that, it controls a score of companies that produce programmes and publish books. Financed largely by public money, NHK does not need to take advertising, but is continually seeking new sources of income – an attitude that alarms its competitors in independent television. NHK led the way into satellite broadcasting in 1989, but in 1998 SkyPerfectTV became the pace-setter in digital television, offering a choice of some 300 television stations and radio wavelengths. MITI, the Japanese Ministry of Trade and Industry, is backing the digital revolution.

# The information revolution sweeps through China

*The enormous strides made by television in China in the past 20 years have made life difficult for the authorities, who like to keep all communications under strict control. Now, censorship faces an even more serious challenge: the Internet.*

**First cybercafé** *Opened in Beijing, November 1996.*

In 2002, if the present trend continues, there will be 61 million Internet users in China. This will place the nation second only to the United States in the number of citizens surfing the Net. It is an astonishing rate of progress for a country that had only 1.2 million Internet subscribers in 1998 – and an astonishing situation for a country whose rulers have a record of going to any lengths to control the media and suppress criticism. Behind China's information explosion lie a number of factors: a fascination with modern technology, rising economic prosperity, the need to keep up with the rest of the world… and a deliberate political decision.

## The communications revolution

Communication is a buzzword in modern China. For some time the country has been converted to the mobile phone, and in the year 2000 another 43 million were bought. Now the Chinese are taking up web-TV, which allows the user to connect with the Internet via the television screen. Advertising used to be restricted to government announcements and exhortations, but now a stream of advertisements for anything from shampoo to banking services can be seen on the small screen or heard on the radio. Advertising has changed the urban landscape, too: where once there were huge posters of Mao Ze-dong, there are now billboards extolling the virtues of consumer goods – for which viewers can go teleshopping.

Television reached China in 1958, and received its first major boost in 1981, when a good part of the nation was able to watch a re-transmission of the trial of the Gang of Four. Today, it reaches almost every corner of China – 100 per cent of the urban areas and 85 per cent of the countryside. There are nearly 1000 stations, most of them covering regions rather than the entire country. Foreign stations are available only to the privileged classes, such as party members and high officials, as the authorities keep a wary eye on who is allowed to have a satellite dish.

As in other countries, radio has suffered from the advance of television, but China still has an impressive number of radio stations – there were 1363 in 1997. Most are listened to in cars or in taxis. Cinema audiences, too, have dwindled under the impact of television. In an effort to win them back, the government has decided to allow the screening of ten overseas box office hits a year, so Chinese audiences may soon be thronging to see *Titanic*.

During the Cultural Revolution of the 1960s and the ferments following the death of Mao, the Chinese public got its news from wall newspapers or from much-handled copies of *The People's Daily*. Today, China has more than 1000 national and regional newspapers and some 8000 magazines, covering subjects that range from sport to fashion.

**East meets West** *Western television programmes being adapted in the studio for the Chinese audience (above, left).*

**Lucky lad** A Chinese version of Wheel of Fortune.

**Hot off the press** *First edition of the* Liberation of Shanghai, *the city's leading daily.*

# Kung fu conquers the movies

*A new cinema genre emerged in Hong Kong in the 1970s, and soon stormed movie and television screens all over the world. Bruce Lee and Jacky Chan, the kings of kung fu, were heirs to a tradition of unarmed combat that was first practised in a Buddhist monastery some 15 centuries ago.*

Incredible gymnastic leaps through the air, ballet-like pirouettes, lethal blows given with bare hands or from flying feet, human beings fighting against demons and spirits . . . this is kung fu. It first saw the flickering light of the cinema screen in Hong Kong, which by the 1970s had become a haven for a number of Chinese actors, directors and producers who no longer felt safe in Shanghai. They had come under attack from Jiang Qing, wife of Mao Ze-dong and herself a former actress, who did not relish being reminded of her past. Something was needed to entertain the refugees, many of them living in depressing conditions, and that something was kung fu movies – action-packed films that illustrated the eternal struggle between good and evil. One man, virtuous, disciplined and properly trained, could prevail against a host of enemies: it was a heady message for any refugee.

### From a monastery in Shaolin

Hong Kong's first kung fu films were plotted with the aid of simple storyboards. As people of Chinese descent were scattered all over the world, they found a ready-made audience. Soon there was a thriving kung fu film industry throughout Asia and beyond. The first superstar, the supple, athletic and ever-triumphant Bruce Lee, spread the appeal of the genre to Western audiences.

More than half of the kung fu films make some reference to the Buddhist monastery of Shaolin in north-central China, where the monks developed a discipline physically based on the movements of animals, and which was also an aid to concentration. Kung fu and other martial arts were suppressed during the Maoist era, but they came back into favour following the success of kung fu films, and Shaolin is now a major tourist attraction.

Following the first explosion of kung fu on the world's screens, guns began to appear in what began as stories of unarmed combat, and a new generation of film directors took up the genre. By the end of the 1990s they had won international recognition. Director Wong Kar-Waï was acclaimed at the Cannes Film Festival. John Woo went to Hollywood and became a cult director with his stories of gangsters wiping one another out in a welter of blood. And the kung fu cult shows no sign of abating in the new millennium: *Crouching Tiger, Hidden Dragon*, made in China, Taiwan and the USA, and directed by Ang Lee, won an Oscar for best foreign-language film in 2001.

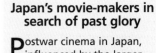

**Hollywood beckons**
*Chinese film director John Woo (right) on a Hollywood film set with John Travolta.*

**The winner** *Wong Kar-Waï, acclaimed at Cannes for his film* Happy Together *(1997).*

**Kung fu superstar** *Bruce Lee kicks out in* Operation Dragon *(1973).*

### Japan's movie-makers in search of past glory

Postwar cinema in Japan, influenced by the larger-than-life dramas of *Kabuki* theatre, made an enormous impression in the West. Akira Kurasawa's *Rashomon* was voted best film at the 1950 Venice Film Festival, and the director went on to make *The Seven Samurai* and other period dramas that were immensely popular with critics and audiences. The output of present-day directors has not had the same impact.

# Sumo: the clash of the demi-gods

*Sumo wrestling, with its origins in a peasant culture, its Shinto rituals and its elaborate etiquette, is the most Japanese of all sports. But in a rapidly changing society, even this deeply rooted discipline is having to fight to maintain its popularity.*

**Before the battle** *Meticulous hair arrangements are part of the elaborate ritual.*

Two behemoths, their hair tied back in topknots, prepare to do battle. First, they raise their legs sideways and crash them down with terrifying force, to 'stamp out devils'. Then they sprinkle the ground with purifying salt. Wearing only loincloth-like *mawashi* aprons, they squat and stare each other out, in a clay ring 15 ft (4.55 m) in diameter. Then they charge, using their overweight bodies like battering rams. For all the time that sumo wrestlers devote to ritual at the start of a match, the bout itself can be over in seconds. The winner is the one who heaves his opponent out of the ring, or who throws or grapples him to the ground so that he touches it with any part other than his feet.

## Rooted in a peasant past

According to an old legend, the first *rikishi*, sumo wrestlers, were gods who did battle to decide who should own the country – and certainly today's *rikishi* are treated like demi-gods by their fans. Sumo has its roots in Shintoism, the earliest religion of the Japanese islands, and is a sport that has emerged from a peasant past. The ceremony performed at the start of every bout contains elements of a Shinto rite meant to placate the gods of the harvest, and the *gyoji*, referee, wears garments based on those of a Shinto priest. In Japan's Middle Ages, combats were arranged between local champions to entertain the villagers as well as to bring a blessing to the crops.

Walk into the *Kokugikan*, the covered stadium in Tokyo, and you will be projected into a noisy, cheering crush of sumo fans. When the crowd likes a fighter, they cry out and applaud; when they adore him, they go wild and throw cushions into the *dohyo*, the ring. After the combat, old women wait to stroke the massive bodies returning to the dressing rooms. Sumo is Japan's national sport, but today two of its most popular *yokozuna*, grand champions, are Hawaiian. One, Akebono, was the first grand champion from outside Japan. A 6 ft 8 in (2.04 m) tall giant weighing 37 stone (235 kg), his body is an abundance of flab overlying a mountain of muscle.

There are some 70 recognised throws, trips, heaves and pushes in traditional sumo, and in December 2000 the sport's governing body approved 12 new techniques. This was their way of giving the sport greater spectator appeal, for although sumo was still immensely popular, empty seats were beginning to appear in stadiums that once had been crammed. Many reasons were put forward for this decline in popularity: competition from baseball and football, match-fixing by gangsters, the predictability of matches in which the winner was usually going to be the heavier man. If the national sport is truly in danger of losing its appeal, the underlying reason could be a simple but ominous one: modern times.

### The making of a sumo champion

Sumo wrestlers are made, not born. Teenagers who decide to make the ring their career are tall and of fairly normal build when they start – but five times a day they tuck into enormous meals. Their staple diet is *chanko-nabe*, a stew of meat, fish and vegetables, eaten with vast mounds of rice. A trainee *rikishi* acts as servant to an established fighter, carrying his towels, preparing his meals and rubbing his back in the bath with a horsehair glove. Like Roman gladiators, the wrestlers live and train together at their *heya*, or stables. The trainees, sleeping in dormitories, have to be up at 5 am to attend to their duties. As they advance in the ranks, they may hope one day to become famous and ride to matches in their own chauffeur-driven cars – filling the back seat with their bulk.

**Changing times** *New grips, pushes, trips and throws have been added to sumo, to extend its appeal.*

# Many paths to the same destination

*According to a long-accepted tradition, all of the martial arts have a common origin. They are based on observations made centuries ago by a Chinese Buddhist abbot, who studied the movements of animals, birds, and even insects, and built them into a system of self-defence that improved the spiritual powers of his monks.*

**All together** *Taiji quan practice in a Shanghai street. The exercises, which can be done at any age, are aimed at achieving inner harmony and increasing energy.*

From Hong Kong to San Francisco, from Paris to Beijing, millions of Chinese rise at dawn, winter or summer, and go into the streets and parks to practise the slow, ballet-like movements of Taiji quan. This gymnastic form of meditation may look unthreatening, but it is the gentle cousin of kung fu, kick-boxing, judo, karate and the other martial arts. All, according to tradition, derive from the same source.

### Moving like a snake or tiger

In the 5th or 6th century AD, the abbot of the Buddhist monastery at Shaolin in north-central China developed a set of self-defence exercises for his monks, based on close observation of the movements of animals. They learned to strike with the swiftness of the snake, leap with the ferocity of the tiger, and move with the agility of the monkey. There was a strong spiritual element to the exercises,

for they helped to improve the concentration needed for meditation. The exercises spread throughout the region and, according to tradition, became the basis of all the martial arts: taekwendo in Korea; kick-boxing in Thailand; jujitsu, judo, kendo and karate in Japan. One legend says that kung fu was developed in the 14th century, when a Chinese Taoist monk rediscovered the importance of animals as models while he watched a snake fight off the attentions of a crane.

Before becoming popular recreations – and in the case of judo, an Olympic sport – the martial arts were blooded on the battlefield and in political

### Legend of the soldier monks of Shaolin

According to legend, the first Shaolin monastery was founded in the coastal province of Fujian, looking out towards the island of Taiwan, in the 4th century BC. At that period it is likely to have been a Taoist monastery. Nearly 1000 years later, another Shaolin monastery was founded by the Buddhists in Shandong. The monks mastered the art of breath control, as an aid to meditation, and modelled their exercises on animal movements. They also developed skills in the martial arts, and several emperors relied on the monks to protect them from the Mongols and other tribes. In the 17th century, when the empire fell to the Manchus, secret societies, the Triads were formed to restore the native Ming Dynasty. Triad members declared themselves to be the true heirs of Shaolin, but their political idealism petered out over the years, and they turned to crime.

**Fists of power** *Kung fu training at Shaolin. The original monks would punch a brick wall to which 1000 sheets of paper had been glued. As the paper wore away, so their fists became harder.*

*Korean karate   Korean children practise a basic move in taekwendo, the way of the foot and fist – the national version of karate.*

struggles. Soldier monks fought off bandits who raided their monasteries, and their fame was so great that they were used as shock troops by great warlords and enlisted by emperors to fight their enemies. Kung fu lost some of its spiritual force when it was taken up by the Chinese Triads.

In today's materialistic China, kung fu has become a profitable business for a number of monasteries, especially Shaolin. Parents take their children there as early as the age of six, hoping that they will be selected for training. The objective is not to turn them into

monks, but to have them trained as potential stars in kung fu movies, or as bodyguards in special units of the army or the police. One day's training costs as much as a month's tuition at an ordinary fee-paying school.

### The ways of Japan and Korea

In Japan, the samurai of the Middle Ages borrowed heavily from the Chinese martial arts, and their fighting styles have become the basis of a number of modern sports. Judo, 'the way of yielding', is a 19th-century development of jujitsu. It is based on the principle of using an opponent's strength to unbalance and defeat him. Kendo, 'the way of the sword', has clear links with samurai training. Karate, a form of bare-handed fighting that can be lethal if not treated as a sport, started in China and came to Japan in 1922, via Okinawa. Aikido has elements of judo, karate and kendo.

The national sport of Korea is taekwendo, 'the way of the foot and fist'. It was banned by the Japanese during their occupation of the country, and so became a symbol of national rebellion. Children are taught the sport from the age of four, and it is used as part of business training.

### The rebirth of traditional sects

New sects, that between them claim millions of adherents, have arisen in China since the early 1990s. They are strongly inspired by Buddhist and Taoist teachings, and many of them practise the martial arts. Mao's successors re-introduced the profit motive into Chinese society, and for many this left a spiritual gap. Shaken by what to other Chinese were long overdue economic reforms, members of the new sects were seeking values other than those of making money and acquiring possessions. The appeal of the martial arts was their combination of spiritual and physical disciplines, with the aim of achieving harmony between body and soul. The regime has seen some of these sects as a threat to its supremacy.

*All in the mind   Lining up the target at kyudo, Japanese archery. A high score is less important than achieving total concentration.*

*Way of the warrior   Two well-protected kendo experts enjoy a sport that goes back to the samurai.*

# Silk, the wonder fabric of the East

*For thousands of years the art of silk-making was a secret known only to the Chinese – a secret guarded so jealously that death was the penalty for revealing it to outsiders. The West was fascinated by this shimmering, lustrous fabric, and legends grew up about its source and manufacture. When, finally, the mystery was solved, new legends arose of how the secret had been stolen from its guardians.*

An ancient Chinese legend tells how Empress Xi Ling, wife of the Yellow Emperor Huang Di, one day let the cocoon of a silkworm fall into a bowl of tea – and pulled out a seemingly endless thread that was gossamer light, shimmering in the air, and surprisingly strong. So began an industry that was to be a Chinese monopoly for many centuries.

### The Land of Silk

Evidence suggests that silk has been produced in China from at least 3000 BC. It was the basis of trade links with the rest of the world, the most famous of which came to be known as the Silk Road. Emperors, nobles and rich people in the Roman Empire had a near-insatiable appetite for the opulent fabric – so much so, that China was known as Serica, the Land of Silk, and the moralist Seneca, who lived during the reigns of the Emperors Claudius and Nero, chastised his fellow Romans for indulging unashamedly in such a luxurious material.

People in the West believed that silk was woven from a fine fuzz, scraped from the

underside of certain leaves. The secret known to the Chinese was that it comes from a caterpillar that feeds on mulberry leaves – the silkworm, B*ombyx mori*. The metamorphosis from moth's egg to worm, from worm to pupa, from pupa to cocoon and from cocoon to silk must have been observed in nature by the Chinese, who commandeered the process, making the silkworm one of the few insects ever to be domesticated. It gave them a docile labour force that reproduced itself, and never demanded anything other than the right temperature and a constant supply of mulberry leaves.

Silk was worth its weight in gold. High-ranking civil servants were paid in bolts of the fabric, and favoured envoys were presented with it as a gift. For anybody who tried to sell the

***Hung out to dry***
*Newly dyed silk is dried in the open air.*

***Willing worker***
*The silk moth and its cocoon.*

***Cocoons by the boatload*** *Silkworm cocoons are taken by water to workshops, where they will be unravelled, then spun into silk fibre, ready for dyeing and weaving.*

### From caterpillar to silk

The eggs of the silk moth hatch into tiny caterpillars whose sole aim in life is to feed voraciously on mulberry leaves. In six weeks they grow to nearly 2 in (5 cm) long and are ready to became pupae. A chemical reaction between the chewed leaves and enzymes produces silk, which is secreted and spun into a protective cocoon. A few pupae are allowed to develop into the next generation of moths, but the rest of the cocoons are unwound by plunging them into warm water. Each cocoon yields a filament 990-3000 ft (300-900 m) long. Twisted with other filaments, it is spun into silk thread, ready for weaving into the world's most luxurious natural material.

precious secret of its manufacture to other lands, there was only one penalty – death. But it was only a matter of time before China's long and profitable monopoly was broken. One story is that around 140 BC a beautiful princess, betrothed to a foreign prince, hid silkworms in the flowers that bedecked her hair when she left China for her new home. Another is that at some time in the 6th century AD, Christian monks smuggled them to the West, hidden in their staves. But although the Chinese lost their monopoly, they never lost their skill in sericulture, the craft of silk farming. Today, China's silk production is based in the south, around Hangzhou, Suzhou and Wuxi.

## The rise and decline of silk in Japan

If there is a single garment that evokes the essence of Japan, it is the kimono. This long, multicoloured robe, shimmering and sensuous, is wound so tightly around the body that its wearer has to walk with short, jerky steps. Kimonos are available in cotton, but the traditional material is silk, which was introduced to Japan in the 7th century, from China by way of Korea. Soon the Japanese had a thriving silk industry of their own and their products won an international reputation. In the 1950s the industry began to decline, with competition from other Asian nations and from the advent of new, man-made fibres. Above all, the times were changing, with more and more Japanese consumers turning away from tradition and wearing Western-style clothes. Today, most Japanese women wear the kimono only on special occasions, such as their 20th birthday, their wedding day, or the New Year festival. Kimonos may be handed down from mother to daughter, or bought secondhand, but buying a new one is an expense that many avoid, for the simplest silk kimono can cost £600, and a new ceremonial *tome-sode* sells at up to £2500.

It takes application and training to tie and wear the kimono in the right way. There are special schools where young women can learn the skills of wrapping the many layers of silk around the body, and securing them with the *obi*, a wide, belt-like sash that folds into a kind of cushion on the wearer's back. The constricting

**Hands of the artist**  *The master, Moriguchi, has been declared a 'living treasure' of Japan for his paintings on silk.*

effect of the tightly wrapped silk kimono makes it unsuitable for the demands of modern life, but one traditional garment that is still fashionable is the *yakuta*, a looser-fitting kimono, made of cotton. Both sexes wear it during the hot summer months, and it makes an elegant dressing gown. When putting on a *yakuta*, the left-hand panel goes over the right – only corpses are dressed wearing it the other way. The garment was rejuvenated during the 1960s when somebody had the idea of decorating it with colourful motifs inspired by Hawaiian beachwear. Then design superstars such as Issey Miyake and Kenzo Takada turned their talents to new motifs and made the *yakuta* a fashion garment, not just in Japan but around the world.

**Colourful lunch-break**  *Surrounded by bolts of dyed and patterned silk, a trader in Tongdaemun market, Korea, waits for customers.*

**Traditional kimono**  *Age-old skills go into making a kimono a timeless work of art. The pine trees symbolise tenacity and longevity.*

CHAPTER 4

# CITIES OF EAST ASIA

As the nations of East Asia move into the modern world, it is their cities that are forcing the pace. It is not just a soaring skyline that has turned Hong Kong into an Asian New York: it is the buzz on the streets, where night and day a swarming, aggressive, success-driven population goes about the serious business of making money. The same frantic imperative operates in Shanghai, a city that stagnated in the Maoist era but is today a showcase for the Chinese version of capitalism. Tokyo has been rebuilt after being flattened by fire, earthquake and the bombs of the Second World War, but still manages to combine the charm of yesterday with the excitement of a modern city. By contrast, Pyongyang, the austere capital of North Korea, is congealed in the past. The future seems to hold more promise for the Mongolian capital, Ulan Bator, where cars are replacing horses in the streets as the city moves into modern times.

*The glare of street lights and neon signs turns dusk into dawn in the Japanese capital.*

# Tokyo: megalopolis of an island nation

**Nightlife** *Clubs and bars compete for trade in Shinjuku.*

*Tokyo is a phoenix of a city, constantly rising anew from its ashes. It was rebuilt after a fire in 1657, built again after the great earthquake of 1923, then rebuilt once more after being flattened by American bombers in the Second World War. In this ever-changing city, rebuilding is still a fact of everyday life, with old buildings constantly being pulled down to make way for new ones.*

Tokyo has 12 million inhabitants, and when the population of greater Tokyo is taken into account, that figure more than doubles, making it the biggest conurbation in the world.

### Land won from the sea

In its headlong rush into modern times the city has engulfed villages and now covers some 32 miles (50 km) from east to west. All that has stopped it from sprawling even further are the Japanese Alps on one side and the sea on the other. And even the sea has not completely blocked the city's expansion, for man-made islands have been built in Tokyo Bay. Land recovered from the sea was used for heavy industry in the 1960s but is now the site of high-tech enterprises and trade centres. The airport is 38 miles (60 km) from the city centre, and visitors have a choice of travelling by underground, by elevated trains or by taxi on a succession of bridges, autoroutes and flyovers that lead straight into the heart of the city.

The citizens of Tokyo have no sentimentality about getting rid of old stones if they stand in the way of progress, but the salarymen who commute each day from the suburbs are making a journey through history. Beginning as a small fishing village called Edo, the core of the city became important when the Tokugawa shogun Ieyasu established his base there in the 17th century. It became the national capital in 1869, when Emperor Meiji moved his court from Kyoto and renamed it Tokyo – the Eastern capital.

**The incense-seekers** *A crowd presses around incense burners outside the Senso-ji temple to the goddess Kanon.*

**Arteries of the city** *Busy overpasses sweep into the heart of a city of tower blocks and skyscrapers.*

**Artificial island** *Desperate for space, Tokyo is building 'stepping stones' into its bay.*

## The 'villages' of Tokyo

For all its ordered chaos of arterial roads, its cacophony of traffic noises and its soaring towers of glass and steel, there is another Tokyo to be discovered. The villages that were swamped during the city's rapid expansion have left their imprint on different districts. There are still temples, shrines and traditional wooden houses not far from more modern developments. Asakusa, for instance, in the north-east of the city, is a prime target of property developers, for it retains some of the character of old Japan. The Buddhist temple of Senso-ji, famous for its red lacquer gate, was founded in the 7th century to house a golden statuette of Kannon, the goddess of mercy, caught by chance in the nets of two fishermen. Monks, on the way to their devotions at the temple, have to pass cheap theatres and striptease bars.

The Imperial Palace, protected by moats and high walls, is set in gardens at the very heart of the city. Some of the gardens are open to the public, but the palace itself is the home of the emperor. The Yasukuni shrine to the north was set up in 1869 in memory of those who died fighting for the emperor during the Meiji restoration. It became a shrine to the spirits of those who fought for later emperors, too – including the kamikaze pilots and others who gave their lives in the Second World War. Ryogiko, the 'low town', has from the 17th century attracted traders and entertainers. It is Tokyo's sumo district, where tourists can see wrestlers in the streets, or sample their diet, the hearty *chanko-nabe* stew.

Farther south, around the Imperial Palace, is the 'high town', where the style was set by the court nobility and by rich merchants. It is still one of the densest concentrations of financial and political power in the world. Ginza is Tokyo's most elegant shopping area by day, and offers expensive restaurants and entertainment for the élite by night. Its old wooden buildings were burned down in 1872 and a British architect and early town-planner, Thomas Waters, built new Ginza of brick, even using it for the pavements.

As in most cities, particular trades have settled in particular areas. Tokyo's fish market, one of the biggest in the world, is at Tsukiji. Jimbocho, the student district, is the place for secondhand bookshops, Nihombashi for kimonos, Harajuku and the red light district of Shinjuku for teenage fashions. The shops of Akihabara are the last word for electronic gadgetry at low prices.

Ueno is the museum district, with the National, Metropolitan and Fine Art museums all set in a park, which becomes one of Tokyo's most popular attractions in April, when the cherry trees

blossom. In 1868 a group of rebel samurai, loyal to the Tokugawa shogun, mounted a last stand against the emperor's army at a temple in Ueno. Japanese gangsters, the Yakusa, congregate in Higashi, and if some of them have missing fingers it is because they have chopped them off to appease their bosses after failing in a mission.

***Away from it all*** *Children discover the fascination of a pond in one of the city's parks – a haven of peace in the Shinjuku district.*

***Buddhist shrine*** *Senso-ji Temple, in the Asakusa district.*

**Hill of Perspective** *The hill, which overlooks the Forbidden City, was built up from the soil dug out when moats were excavated around the imperial grounds. It is sometimes called the 'Hill of Coal' because of what appears to be an unfounded legend that coal was dug up with the soil.*

**Huangji Gate** *The gate opens into the Palace of Tranquil Longevity, which was redeveloped at the end of the 18th century so that Emperor Qianlong could retire there following his abdication. It was his wish not to exceed the length of the reign of his illustrious grandfather, Kangxi.*

1. **Moats**
2. **Gate of the South (Wu-men)**
3. **Bridge of the River of Golden Waters (Jinshuiqiao)**
4. **Hall of Supreme Harmony (Taihedian)**
5. **Hall of Middle Harmony (Zhonghedian)**
6. **Hall of Preserved Harmony (Baohedian)**
7. **Gate of Celestial Purity (Qianqingmen)**
8. **Wall of the Nine Dragons (Jiulongqiang)**
9. **Palace of Tranquil Longevity (Ningshougong)**
10. **Garden of the Palace of Sympathetic Tranquillity (Ciningonghuayuan)**
11. **Palace of Sympathetic Tranquillity (Ciningong)**
12. **Hall of the Nourishment of the Spirit (Yangxidian)**
13. **Palace of Celestial Purity (Qiangqinggong)**
14. **Hall of Shining Benevolence (Zhaorendian)**
15. **Hall of Great Virtue (Hongdedian)**
16. **Hall of Vigorous Fertility (Jiaotaidian)**
17. **Palace of Earthly Tranquillity (Kunninggong)**
18. **Imperial Garden (Yuyuan, or Yuhuayuan)**
19. **Gate of Military Genius (Shen Wu-men)**

**The Emperor's Staircase** *An immense marble ramp, with carvings of dragons and clouds, on a staircase reserved for the emperor.*

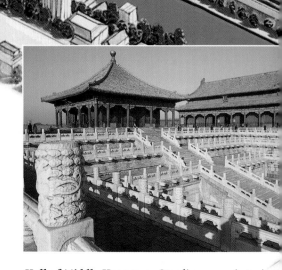

**Hall of Middle Harmony** *Standing on an imposing terrace is one of the Forbidden City's three halls of harmony. The others are dedicated to Preserved Harmony and Supreme Harmony.*

# Imperial splendours of the Forbidden City

The Mongol emperor Kublai Khan moved his court to the site of present-day Beijing in 1266, choosing a place that was not particularly favourable, as it was arid in summer and freezing cold in winter. But it was the Ming emperor Yung Lo ('Eternal Happiness') who established Beijing as China's permanent capital and began, in 1406, to create the Forbidden City – forbidden, that is, to ordinary mortals. Its 9999 rooms, the perfect number, according to the geomantic theory of yin and yang, were for the emperor and a household of wives, concubines, officials and servants – among them some 3000 eunuchs. However, the Forbidden City did not become a favourite imperial residence, both because it lacked comfort, and because of the crushing weight of court etiquette.

**Tiananmen Square**   The square was created in modern times by the levelling of Ministry buildings on either side of the Imperial Way. It was here that Mao Ze-dong proclaimed the founding of the People's Republic in October 1949. The name means 'Gate of Heavenly Peace', but in June 1989 the square saw the bloody suppression of student demonstrators.

**Mao's tomb**   It took some 700 000 volunteers, working for nearly a year, to build the tomb of the 'Great Helmsman' in Tiananmen Square. Crowds still pay homage both before the tomb and before the monument to the Heroes of the People, who gave their lives for the communist revolution.

**Bei Hai park**   Kublai Khan built a palace on the site of the park, but it was already a ruin by 1652, when a bell-shaped tower called the White Dagoba was built on Qiong Hua, a circular island in one of the park's lakes. Where emperors and their retinues once took their courtly pleasure, the ordinary citizens of Beijing now take an evening stroll.

**Summer palace**   The palace, at Yiheyuan on the outskirts of Beijing, was built in the 18th century by the Manchu emperor Qianlong, to escape from the stifling heat of summer in the Forbidden City. It became the favourite residence of the Dowager Empress Cixi, who lavished money on it during the dying years of the Manchu Dynasty.

# Beijing and its surrounding area

**1. The Palace of Eternal Harmony** Now called the Temple of the Lamas, the palace was built in the 18th century for the future Emperor Yongzheng, whose son was an adherent of the Tibetan form of Buddhism.

**2. The Temple of Heaven** Built in 1420, but restored many times since then, this is one of the finest examples of Ming architecture.

**3. The Temple of Confucius** Founded during the Yuan Dynasty (1279-1368), the temple is now a museum.

**4. Wang Fu Jing Street** Here many foreign legations and embassies are sited, alongside smart shops. In imperial times, the street ran through the centre of a district where princes built their palaces.

**5. Tomb of the Thirteen Emperors** The emperors all belonged to the Ming Dynasty (1368-1644), a golden period in China's history. The monuments are a favourite spot for picnickers. The Avenue of Souls, leading to the tombs, is bordered by statues of animals.

**6. The Communications Tower** In recent years, the skyline of China's ancient capital has been taking on an increasingly modern, even futuristic, look.

**7. The home of Lu Xun** One of China's most renowned writers of the 20th century lived in Beijing between 1924 and 1926, and the house is named after him.

**8. Marco Polo Bridge** A little way outside Beijing, the original bridge, built in 1192 before the explorer was born, has since been reconstructed many times.

5

6

7

8

**Imperial throne** *The Golden Dragon throne, in the Hall of Supreme Harmony. Here the emperor sat on great state occasions, such as a coronation, his wedding, the New Year festival, or the appointment of a general.*

**Imperial symbol**
*The dragon with five claws, a symbol of power that appears constantly in the Forbidden City.*

**Palace of the Nourishment of the Spirit** *A room in the palace was altered in the 19th century so that two dowager empresses could listen from behind screens to the emperor giving audience. One of them was Cixi, who lived to see the empire crumble.*

**Palace of Supreme Harmony** *The palace, the largest building in the city, contains the throne room, where the emperor sat amid priceless vases and sculptures.*

**Symbol of longevity** *A bronze tortoise, universal symbol of a long life, watches over the Palace of Supreme Harmony.*

**Imperial Garden**
A Taoist temple in the Imperial Garden, which, like the other gardens of the Forbidden City, is extremely formal in layout and devotes itself to exotic plants.

**Boundary** The Forbidden City is surrounded by a wide moat, both defensive and appealing to the eye.

**Gate of the South** Wu-men, the main gateway of the Forbidden City. Here, after a victorious campaign, prisoners were herded under the stern gaze of the emperor.

**River of Golden Waters** The river was dug out following the precepts of geomancy, to augment the flow of energy through a flat landscape. Its five bridges are in the south of the Forbidden City, where yang energy is believed to be at its highest. Water is a yin element, so it restores the balance.

# Hiroshima and Nagasaki: a reminder and a hope for the future

**Ready for tomorrow** *The Nagasaki of today is a major industrial centre.*

*The two Japanese cities destroyed by atomic bombs have been reborn – one as a symbol of peace and reconciliation, the other as a city of innovation and opportunity.*

Hiroshima was a military base in the Second World War, which made it a target for the weapon that was to break Japan's resistance. On August 6, 1945, the American B29 Superfortress *Enola Gay* dropped the world's first atomic bomb on Hiroshima. It exploded 1900 ft (580 m) above ground, releasing 12 700 tons of TNT and causing a blast that sent tramcars hurtling through the air, and creating a fireball that consumed the centre of the city. As many as 80 000 people died outright, and the deaths that followed, from wounds or from radiation sickness, brought the total above 240 000. Apart from the gutted dome of the Office of Industrial Promotion, at the epicentre of the explosion, the city centre was laid flat. Hiroshima now devotes itself to the promotion of peace. The skeleton of the dome keeps vigil over Peace Park, where children fold paper cranes in memory of a little girl, Sadako, who promised herself that if she could fold 1000 of them she would recover from her radiation sickness. She died after folding 664 paper birds. In front of the Cenotaph, near the Museum of Memory and Peace, burns a flame that will not be extinguished until all nuclear weapons have been abolished.

## Building for tomorrow

A second atomic bomb fell on Nagasaki on August 9, 1945, killing 87 000 outright. More than any other Japanese city, Nagasaki had links with the West. It was an early centre of Christianity in Japan, and was the site of a lone Dutch trading post during the centuries when the country went into isolation from the outside world. The city was not the primary target of the bomb – that was Kokura, at the northern tip of Kyushu Island, where there was a huge arsenal. Heavy cloud over Kokura diverted the attack to Nagasaki. The bomb was three times as powerful as the Hiroshima bomb, but it fell on the outskirts of the city. Even so, 150 000 died from its effects. Nagasaki has memorials to that terrible day – the A-bomb centre and a museum. It has also thrown its energies into building the future. The Kawasaki and Mitsubishi factories are located there, and a ready acceptance of technical innovation has made the city prominent in shipbuilding and engineering. The population is 446 000, larger than it was when the bomb fell.

**Silent city** *Hiroshima soon after the bomb. The Dome is on the left.*

**City of pilgrimage** *The dome watches over the crowds in Peace Park.*

# The re-awakening of Ulan Bator

*Once a crossroads for nomads and a staging post for caravans crossing the Gobi Desert, the capital of Mongolia is today poised on the brink of modernisation.*

Behind the austere face of the administrative capital of a former Soviet satellite, Ulan Bator is a city that looks to the future, for it is one of the youngest cities in the world. Three-quarters of its 600 000 population are under 35, and it is largely under their pressure that the capital, and the country, have shaken off the yoke of communist dictatorship.

## Cybercafés for former nomads

The city, which lies 4265 ft (1300 m) above sea level on the Mongolian plateau, was established in the 17th century as a nomad encampment, centred around a Buddhist temple. Urga, as it came to be called, grew into a religious and trading centre on the trade route between Beijing and St Petersburg. By 1911 it had 50 000 inhabitants, but was still essentially a large encampment of yurts. In the early 1920s Mongolia, with Soviet help, staged a communist revolution and won independence from China. To mark the event the capital's name was changed to Ulan Bator – 'Red Hero'.

The country was a Soviet satellite until 1990, when, with the Soviet empire breaking up, it opted for a democratic regime. The old nomadic pattern of life was changing, and the pace of change was set by the capital. It drew in a quarter of the country's population and began to breathe the air of freedom. Where once they

lived in yurts, the Mongolians have turned traditional skills into a modern industry and now make prefabricated houses. In the Cold War era, nobody had dared to talk to strangers, but now Ulan Bator has been opened up to Western influences, among them satellite television and the Internet. Young Mongolians have been allowed to go abroad to learn how the stock market works on Wall Street. Buddhist monasteries have been re-integrated into the life of the country.

Ulan Bator is now a much livelier city, with a Hard Rock café, four cybercafés, a casino and bars. Mutton is no longer the only item on the menu: it now has to compete with Turkish, Indian, Italian, African and French dishes. The city streets are no longer deserted at night and people no longer need to drink vodka at home. Nightclubs have sprung up in the middle of the city, close to the statue of Lenin.

### Taxis, Mongolian-style

Horses are rarer on the streets of Ulan Bator today than they were in the past, but the cars that are replacing them still fill a role that was an essential part of nomad life. The city is probably the only capital in the world where you can get a lift simply by raising an arm in the street. The driver of the first car that comes along, whether it be a limousine or an old banger, will stop and offer a lift. Young people on a night out use this method to get from bar to bar or club to club. In a country where public transport is rare, every car is a potential taxi. The drivers charge the equivalent of 50p per mile (30p per km), carrying on a nomad tradition of charging fellow travellers.

**Let's dance** *Teenagers in Ulan Bator meet at the movies – one of the few places where they can dance.*

**Yurts and towers** *Circular yurts and wooden shacks surround a city of concrete and cranes.*

# Kyoto keeps its elegance

*Nestling among gently rounded hills, Japan's ancient capital retains the elegance of former days, though it has not been untouched by modern times. It offers a curious contrast between little wooden houses and the glass-sided towers of modern banks and multinational companies.*

In the period when Nara, Japan's first capital, had been forsaken by the emperor, an imperial hunting party stumbled on the site of what was to become Kyoto. Japan at that time was influenced by Chinese culture, and the landscape had features that struck all the right chords with believers in geomancy, the art of feng shui – so much so, that the first name for the new capital was Heian-kyo, 'Capital of Peace and Tranquillity'. In AD 794, Emperor Kammu was installed in the new city, which was laid out in a north-south grid so as to call down the blessings of the spirits.

### An unrivalled cultural legacy

Kyoto was the imperial capital for more than 1000 years, during which an unrivalled legacy of temples, shrines, palaces, pagodas, gardens, craft workshops and little wooden houses were built. After a brilliant start, the fortunes of Kyoto as a power centre were mixed. Real power fell into the hands of warlords, one of whom, Minamoto Yoritomo, made himself Japan's first shogun, and in 1192 moved the seat of government to Kamakura. It returned to Kyoto, but when Emperor Meiji seized control from the shoguns, in 1868, he settled the capital in Edo, soon renamed Tokyo.

Kyoto has never lost its reputation as a centre of culture, and even today, when it has developed into a bustling industrial city with a population of 1.5 million, it preserves the atmosphere of feudal Japan. The pagoda of Daigo-ji, a temple founded in 874, is the oldest surviving wooden building in the city. By contrast, the present-day Golden Pavilion, with its walls of gold leaf, is a faithful 1955 reconstruction of a Zen Buddhist temple founded at the end of the 14th century and burned down by a monk in 1950.

The city has 1600 Buddhist temples, 270 Shinto shrines and numerous quiet gardens for meditation. The Buddhist temple of Ryoan-ji has one of the oldest stone gardens in the world, laid out in 1499, with 15 large stones set in a sea of white gravel that is raked every day.

***Houses of pleasure*** *Traditional wooden houses in Kyoto, which from the 14th century have served tea and cakes, and once offered less innocent delights, too.*

***Restored splendour*** *The Golden Pavilion, built in 1394 as the home of a shogun, and later a Buddhist temple, was burned down by a monk in 1950 – an event that inspired a famous novel by Yukio Mishima.*

***Geishas on parade*** *In Kyoto's Gion district, Geisha girls clitter-clatter along the street on wooden shoes, on their way to entertain rich clients with music, singing and conversation.*

### Snapshots of the ancient capital

Kiyomizu-dera, a spectacular temple raised on a platform over a sea of trees whose colours are ever-changing. White sands in the garden of Ginkaku-ji, the Silver Temple. The Imperial villa of Katsura with its stroll garden. Geishas dancing in the Pontocho district. The house of 20th-century potter Kawai Kanjiro. These are a few of Kyoto's delights.

# Nara: splendours of an ancient capital

*Nara has all the charm of a provincial city where nothing dramatic happens or is likely to happen. But 13 centuries ago it was bursting with creative energy, for this was where Japanese civilisation began. For 74 eventful years, Nara was the nation's capital, its temples alive with gossip, its palaces seething with intrigue.*

**Landmark** *Horyu-ji, founded in 607, is Japan's oldest Buddhist temple.*

Nara entered the pages of history in 710, under the name of Heijo-kyo, 'Citadel of Peace'. It was Japan's first fixed capital, for previously the imperial court had been relocated every time a new emperor came to the throne. By the dawn of the 8th century, such constant moving had become impractical. A Buddhist temple, Horyu-ji, was founded on the site of the future Nara in 610 by Prince Shotoku, a great admirer of Chinese culture. When the new city was built, it borrowed heavily for its layout and architectural styles from Chang'an, capital of China's Tang Dynasty and then the largest city in the world.

## The great bronze Buddha

The Emperor Shomu, the man chiefly responsible for the splendours of Nara, was also a devout Buddhist. In 749 he decreed for the temple of Todai-ji what is still the largest bronze Buddha ever cast. It is housed in the world's largest wooden building, stands 53 ft (16.2 m ) high, and the casting took three years. The statue, though damaged by the ravages of time, is still very impressive.

**Defiant Buddha** *The great bronze Buddha of Todai-ji has been repaired after damage by earthquake and fire.*

Nara and Japanese civilisation went through their golden periods together. Gardens were created, temples sprang up, artistic treasures were wrought to fill them. One of the most spectacular buildings was the Kofukuji Temple, founded by the powerful Fujiwara clan, and famous for its five-storeyed pagoda. But Nara was a troubled capital. It took thousands of skilled workmen five years to build the temple of Todai-ji, and the burden of taxes it imposed led to a peasant revolt. As the monks grew richer, they started intriguing for power. One of them, Dokyo, was the lover of an empress. Civil war broke out, and fires ravaged both temples and houses. In 794, the imperial court moved to Heian-kyo (Kyoto) to get away from the influence of the monasteries. Even after the move, Nara's troubles continued. In 1180, Todai-ji was virtually destroyed by the Taira clan, to punish monks who had supported their rivals. Like many other buildings in Nara it was rebuilt, a symbol of the unique place occupied by the ancient capital in the hearts of the Japanese.

### Treasures of the Horyu-ji

The much-restored Horyu-ji is the oldest Buddhist temple in Japan. Among its many treasures are the Kudara Kannon, a wooden statue of the goddess of mercy, thought to date from the 7th century. The temple also contains the Yumechigae Kannon, reputed to have the power to change bad dreams into good.

**Garden of lanterns** *Tame deer among the 3000 stone lanterns in the garden of Kasuga-Taisha, a Shinto shrine in Nara. The lanterns are lit twice a year.*

**Temple of superlatives** *Todai-ji, home of the largest bronze Buddha in the world, can also lay claim, through its main hall, to the title of the world's largest wooden building.*

# Shanghai: showcase for capitalism Chinese-style

*In the early decades of the 20th century, Shanghai was a byword for crime and corruption. It lost that reputation under communism, but some of its dynamism vanished along with the notoriety. Today, the city's star is rising, as a showcase for China's brand of capitalism.*

**With a little help from abroad** *Japanese and Western shops and styles have made their mark in the new Shanghai.*

Shanghai between the wars, a city of corruption with a whiff of seedy glamour, has almost passed into myth, although today's great metropolis and the city of pre-communist days have one thing in common – an overpowering concern for making money.

### The years of frenzy

In 1842, the Chinese empire lost the first Opium War and signed the humiliating Treaty of Nanjing, by which Hong Kong was ceded to Britain. The legend of Shanghai was waiting to be created: as the city grew rich, so did its gangsters, its secret societies, the proprietors of its opium dens, and the madams who ran its brothels. The contrast between the lives of the privileged few and the misery of the poor majority made Shanghai a breeding ground for unrest, and it was here that the Chinese Communist Party was born in 1921. Shanghai paid heavily for that frenzied era, and was punished by

**The way ahead** *In the 1920s, Shanghai was content to be the 'Paris of the East', but today it has never been more self-confident.*

### Pudong, city of the new millennium

Originally a handful of fishing villages, Pudong is now a Special Economic Zone, an area set aside for fast-track development so as to attract investment from overseas. More than 1184 million sq ft (110 million m²) of office space was completed in less than five years. Such rapid growth came from a combination of low rents, low taxes, ready access to foreign exchange, and freedom from regulation by the bureaucrats in Beijing. Pudong, dominated by the 1535 ft (468 m) 'Pearl of the Orient' television tower, is developing a port that will be as busy as Rotterdam by 2015.

**The powerhouse** *Shanghai is the most populous city in China, with 13.6 million inhabitants, and has become an economic powerhouse for the entire nation.*

the communists after they came to power in 1949, for what they termed its 'excess of Westernisation'. The city suffered particularly in the Cultural Revolution (1966-76), when Mao Ze-dong's wife Jiang Qing, once an actress there, paid off old scores.

Economic reforms were introduced in China in 1978, but the people of Shanghai had to wait ten more years before they began their climb back to prosperity. The official slogan today is 'Capitalism with Chinese characteristics', and the young businessmen of Shanghai have lost none of the entrepreneurial skill of the bankers and industrialists who were their grandparents. In the early 1990s, the city's economy grew at 15 per cent a year as investment capital poured in, both from the government and from abroad. One powerful source of new money was the Chinese who had fled to Hong Kong and Singapore.

**West meets East**  *An ultra-modern, Western-style shopping mall, called 'The 800 Partners', in the heart of Shanghai.*

During the Cultural Revolution there were no funds for new housing, even though the city's population was growing. Now there was an inflow of capital to invest in modernising the silk and other textile industries, and some left over for property development. Old buildings were torn down and new skyscrapers of glass and steel were erected. The city pushed out its boundaries and now extends beyond Huang-Pu, in the Special Economic Zone of Pudong. Within a decade, a neglected city has become a modern megalopolis to rival Hong Kong.

### An economic lighthouse

The gross domestic product of Shanghai is greater than that of all Thailand. Unemployment, close on 15 per cent, may be something of an illusion, for hundreds of thousands work in the unofficial black economy. The physical rebirth of Shanghai is far from being completed, but it has been accompanied by remarkable self-discipline on the part of the population. Inspired by the success of Singapore, the once wild Shanghai has become almost a puritan city, with order, social harmony, cleanliness and discipline as its watchwords. They are respected to the letter: dropping litter in the streets is punishable by a heavy fine. Shanghai has set out to become a model not just to China but to all of Asia – a difficult, self-imposed challenge in a city of 13.6 million that faces all the problems that come with rapid growth. Space for expansion is relatively limited in Shanghai, yet the city still acts as a magnet for peasants seeking to escape from the poverty of rural life. Although casinos, brothels and other reminders of the old Shanghai – even horse-racing – are officially banned, building booms always bring the threat of bribes and corruption. Shanghai, however, knows what the word decadence can mean, and there is no wish to return to the days when its name was synonymous with the word.

### The haven of Yu Yuan

In old Shanghai, away from the bustle of the modern city, with its 6 million mobile phones and its streets a solid mass of bicycles and taxis, residents and visitors alike can find a gentle reminder of yesterday's China. The pools and pavilions, the rockeries, bridges and winding walkways of Yu Yuan, the Jade Garden, offer a haven of quiet. Yu Yuan was created between 1559 and 1577 by Pan Yunduan, a rich mandarin who served the Ming Dynasty. The garden is famed for its 'dragon walls', with overlapping tiles creating the effect of a dragon's scales.

**Link with the past**  *A traditional pavilion overlooks a garden in the very heart of the city of steel and glass that is modern-day Shanghai.*

# Paragons and pacesetters

*When Deng Xiao-ping announced a new economic policy for China, in 1986, with the slogan 'to get rich is glorious', he released energies that had been pent up for a generation. It was the start of yet another revolution in the eventful history of the Middle Kingdom – a revolution that is spearheaded today by such dynamic cities as Guangzhou (Canton) and Hong Kong.*

One of the world's great concentrations of industrial and financial power is situated around the delta of the Pearl River (Zhu Jiang) in southern China. Among its resources are two Special Economic Zones: a thrusting, fast-growing city in Guangzhou, and a pearl almost beyond price in Hong Kong. It is served by ultramodern harbours and by five international airports – at Guangzhou, Hong Kong, Shenzhen, Zhuhai and Macao.

### Hong Kong, the rock that grew rich

When the former British colony of Hong Kong was returned to China, at midnight on June 30, 1997, it was one of the richest territories in the world. Its prosperity came from a blending of the Chinese capacity for industry and entrepreneurship with the British tradition of a corruption-free civil service and respect for the rule of law. Hong Kong had grown in a little over 150 years of British rule from little more than a barren rock into the eighth biggest commercial power in the world.

Hong Kong Island and Kowloon were ceded to Britain after the Opium Wars of the 19th century, and its New Territories were leased for 99 years in 1898. When the colony was returned to China, President Jiang Zemin promised that China would 'unswervingly follow' its pledge to make no change to Hong Kong's social, legal and free-market capitalist systems for 50 years. He also promised to maintain freedom of the press, but with the qualification that 'freedom is relative and limited'. China inherited a city that literally never sleeps, with construction gangs working through the floodlit night to give it a skyline rivalling that of New York. Down below, the streets teem with traffic and the noise of a big city in a hurry to grow even bigger. Foreign banks and multinational businesses queue to join the spree.

*The moneymakers* *One of the richest prizes in the world fell into Beijing's lap when Britain returned the colony of Hong Kong (below) to China in 1997. More than 300 overseas banks compete for business from their skyscraper offices. In the streets, life goes on under a neon blaze of advertising signs – and tradition lingers, with caged birds for sale.*

*A touch of Portugal in China*  With its colonial houses, its squares and fountains, its winding streets and its Roman Catholic churches, Macao has an atmosphere that sets it apart from any other city in Asia.

## Guangzhou: living by trade

For centuries, Guangzhou (formerly Canton) has been China's greatest seaport. Porcelain, silk, tea, weapons, paper, chemicals, textiles, immigrants both legal and illegal – all have passed through its docks. It was a major centre for sea trade as far back as the Han Dynasty (206 BC–AD 220). The Portuguese arrived in 1514, and the British East India Company in the 17th century – and it was the British who extended the range of trade goods to include opium. The city grew rapidly in the 1980s, when thousands of factories and workshops sprang up to turn out products for Hong Kong – for Guangzhou could draw on a vast reservoir of cheap peasant labour from the surrounding countryside.

Today Guangzhou is a city of more than 13 million inhabitants, and what was once a fertile agricultural plain between Guangzhou and Hong Kong's New Territories is vanishing under a network of ten-lane motorways, with a steady traffic of exhaust-belching container lorries. Farmland is being concreted over, too, in the New Economic Zones of Shenzhen and Zhuhai. Taxes are low in these zones, and the tight regulation of economic activity by officialdom that has become standard in the rest of China is relaxed, so as to attract investment from overseas. Among their products are toys, shoes, clothing and electronic components.

### Macao

The Portuguese were the first Westerners to set up trading outposts in China, and the last to leave. They established a colony in Macao as early as 1557, and handed it back to China on December 19, 1999. It became a base for missionary work, as well as for trade, and the 442 years of Portuguese rule left a legacy of churches and classical pink or yellow colonial buildings. Fairly late in the day, the Portuguese tried to turn Macao into a second Hong Kong, but it was far too small to offer serious competition, especially as its harbour was silting up. In the 1970s, refugees from communist China provided a pool of cheap labour that produced clothes, toys and artificial flowers for export, but the trades that flourished best were tourism, smuggling and gambling. On the day after the colony was handed back to China, the Red Army moved in 500 soldiers as the advance guard of a garrison expected to rescue gambling, which accounts for more than half of Macao's revenue, from the grip of the Triad gangs. But the Triads, who enforce their dominion with the gun, have not proved easy to control.

### Hong Kong's glittering prizes

With a population of 6.3 million when it was handed back to China in 1997, Hong Kong had an impressive number of commercial and industrial achievements. They included: the world's biggest container port and second biggest turnover of air freight; the second most important stock exchange in Asia, after Tokyo; the world's fourth largest stock of foreign reserves; a gross domestic product worth US$24 000 per head – higher than that in the former colonial power, and 40 times higher than in the rest of China.

*Every day is market day*  A well-stocked market stall in Guangzhou.

*Baroque glory*  The imposing shell of St Paul's Church, Macao.

111

# Seoul: the supercharged city

*During the Korean War of 1950-3, Seoul was snarled over like a bone by the communist and UN-backed forces. At one stage its population fell to 50 000. Today, after half a century of phenomenal expansion, that figure has risen above 11 million – more than a quarter of the South Korean population.*

The siting of Seoul is far more impressive than the city itself. An autoroute that sweeps into the South Korean capital offers little more enticing than a prospect of undistinguished high-rise buildings and concrete office blocks. But the city was built among craggy hills, some rising above 2600 ft (800 m), and their summits confer a certain natural majesty. So does the mighty Han River, more than 1/2 mile (1 km) wide as it flows through the city.

*Yesterday's city  A jumble of wooden houses with higgledy-piggledy tiled roofs, in one of the few sections of old Seoul still remaining.*

## The roots of civil war

Seoul became the capital of a united Korea in 1394, under the Yi Dynasty, and became a centre of cultural splendour. Japan annexed Korea in 1910, and the country and capital were not freed until 1945, when Japanese troops surrendered, according to whether they were stationed north or south of the 38th parallel, either to Soviet or to US forces. So began the ideological, political and military division between North and South Korea. Seoul stands only 38 miles (60 km) from the 38th parallel, so it was in the front line when, on June 25, 1950, North Korean troops and tanks invaded the South. The war lasted until 1953, with China supporting the North and American-led United Nations forces coming to the aid of the South. Seoul changed hands several times, and most of its wooden houses were reduced to ashes.

What the war spared was for the most part lost in a frenzy of postwar reconstruction. Peasants deserted their villages and moved to the capital to work in its new industries, and tower blocks sprang up to accommodate them. Today, to live in a modern apartment block has become a mark of success. So many people have crowded into the city that it has no room for another influx, but people move to where they can find work, so suburbs and dormitory towns have mushroomed around the capital. Typical is the ultramodern Kangnam, which, with its futuristic skyline, is almost a new city in the making.

Seoul has not been totally destroyed by the war and the reconstruction that followed. It is still possible to stumble across a few old-fashioned wooden houses, carefully preserved and protected from development. The university campuses add a touch of park-like beauty to the city; the Toksu Palace offers a reminder of the glories of Yi architecture; and there is the occasional glimpse of a Buddhist monastery or an ancient Confucian school. And above all, running through the city, there are the mountains.

*Confucian wedding*
*A Korean bride in traditional dress.*

*Where concrete is king*
*The tower blocks of Seoul may not be lovely to look at, but they are a reflection of the city's dynamism.*

112

# Pyongyang: sterile memorial to a dictator

*The North Korean capital is an Orwellian nightmare come true – a city built to glorify the communist dictator Kim Il Sung, the 'Great Leader' who loomed over every aspect of national life, like a malevolent Big Brother.*

***Kim's years remembered*** *The Column of Independence, soaring above the tower blocks, is said to have been built using as many large stones as there were days in the first 70 years of Kim Il Sung's life.*

Pyongyang is more like a vast mausoleum than a living city – a monument to a political theory and to the communist leader Kim Il Sung, who died in 1994. Schools, squares, avenues, even the city's sports stadium and university are named after him. A gleaming 98 ft (30 m) high bronze statue of the man who liked to be called the 'Great Leader' gazes over a vast square near the Museum of the Korean Revolution. The city has broad avenues, and traffic police, but very little traffic. Even bicycles, the ubiquitous form of transport in other cities in the region, are rare on the streets of Pyongyang. After Kim's death, the capital became an even more depressing place under the regime of his son, the 'Dear Leader' Kim Jong-Il, for there hung over it the memory of those who died during the years of famine that followed floods and failed harvests in 1995 and 1996. During those years, the 'Dear Leader' diverted humanitarian aid to the army that kept him in power.

## Inside the silent capital

Kim the elder developed a theory known as *Juche*, self-reliance, and at least he gave the mass of the people work, schools and better housing. For many North Koreans today it is regarded as a privilege to live in the capital. But getting around, both in the capital and in the country, can be fraught with difficulty. Permits are needed to travel, to go on holiday, even to buy food. Pyongyang is an island, surrounded by a wall of prohibitions that can be breached only by corruption or by smuggling. There are no throngs of pedestrians on the streets, as in other Asian cities, and the corridors of the underground railway seem to have more patriotic paintings, in the optimistic socialist-realism style, than they have passengers. The citizens of Pyongyang do a lot of walking, and they do it with little fuss, shouting or laughter. It is

***Personality cult*** *A smiling Kim Il Sung appears against the background of a cornfield. The image is formed by thousands of placards held aloft in a stadium by a well-trained crowd.*

***Traffic cop … but where is the traffic?*** *A uniformed policewoman directs the non-flow of traffic in a surreal scene at a crossroads in Pyongyang.*

impossible for the visitor from abroad to fall into step and strike up a conversation. The only opportunity for meeting people is at the home of an official host – typically a tiny apartment in a dilapidated block, whose interior walls may well have been repainted in honour of the visit. What follows is a session of rice liquor and ginseng, songs, toasts and expressions of eternal friendship between nations. It is hard to get below the surface in a society that has been drained of its vitality and spontaneity.

# CHAPTER 5

# CULTURE AND TRADITIONS

Calligraphy and painting are regarded in China and Japan as being supreme among the arts. Both demand the technical ability and insight to convey beauty and the essence of a subject with just a few strokes of the brush. The compulsion to pay homage to nature that is evident in paintings also applies to gardens. The purpose of a garden is to achieve harmony between the wild and the artificial, to create a miniature world that sets the mood for contemplation. The garden is, in effect, a three-dimensional painting – an idea that reaches its highest expression in the Zen gardens of Japan. Gardens, painting and calligraphy can be admired and attempted by all, but creating a work of high art is only for the enlightened few. With festivals, on the other hand, everybody can join in. Many are based on the ancient lunar calendar and are dedicated to the spirits of nature – either celebrating them or appeasing their anger.

*Schoolgirls in Kyoto, the ancient capital of Japan, wearing traditional costume.*

# Festivals that follow the wandering moon

*East Asia is becoming more urbanised and Westernised, yet in its festivals it holds fast to the old ways. Many of these, such as the Chinese New Year and the Japanese Festival of Souls, are linked to the lunar calendar, following a rhythm set by the moon's phases.*

It may still be bitterly cold in many parts of the country, but on the night of the Chinese New Year, hearts are warmed by the explosion of millions of firecrackers. On the first day of the first lunar month of the year – a date that can vary between mid-January and mid-February – Chinese people everywhere celebrate the chance to make a new start in the new year. Even the smallest villages put on a display of fireworks, and make a boisterous clatter to chase away evil spirits. This is the time to pay off debts, to clean the house from top to bottom, to make resolutions, to sit up late around a table groaning beneath the weight of a gargantuan feast.

### The Year of the Snake

The first day of the new year is set aside for visiting family and friends, wishing them happiness and good fortune, and handing to the children little red envelopes containing their gifts. Fifteen days later, children carry candle-lit lanterns through the streets, and the Festival of the Lanterns brings the new year celebrations to a well-illuminated end.

Each lunar year begins under an animal sign – the rat, the ox, the tiger, the rabbit, the dragon, the snake, the horse, the goat, the monkey, the cockerel, the dog or the pig – and people are believed to take on the characteristics of the animal under whose sign they were born. The year 2001, for instance, is the Year of the Snake, a creature said to combine charm with ruthlessness.

In June or July, on the fifth day of the fifth lunar month, the Chinese celebrate the Feast of the Dragons. Teams of oarsmen on dragon boats race each other in honour of the memory of Chu Yuan, a poet who threw himself into a river and drowned in 280 BC. In Korea, the same date on the lunar calendar sees the Festival of Tano, when families honour their ancestors. In a ritual that dates back to the days of shamanism, Korea's first religion, young

**Religious procession** *In June and October, the Japanese summon the gods in charge of fertility of the land and success of the harvest by beating drums and carrying elaborate shrines through the streets.*

**Buddha's birthday** *On the eighth day of the fourth moon, Korean Buddhists celebrate the birth of the founder of their faith. The day is also known as the Festival of the Lanterns, for lantern parades are held at dusk.*

women put on their elegant traditional dress, the *hanbok*, and dance in the public parks.

The dead are honoured, too, in Obon, the Japanese Festival of Souls, held in July or August, when families gather at the graves of their ancestors. There are also many local festivals. In Nagasaki, for instance, the days when the city was Japan's only bridge to the outside world are recalled at the Kunchi Matsuri Festival, on October 7-9, when floats carrying replicas of Dutch and Chinese ships are pulled through the streets. In Mongolia, tens of thousands of nomads converge on Ulan Bator for the great Naadam Fair of July 11-13. The celebrations, recalling the days when Mongol horsemen conquered the known world, are organised around horse-racing, archery and wrestling, and contestants kiss a horsetail representation of Genghis Khan before their matches.

The Korean Festival of the Harvest Moon – Chusok, on the 15th day of the eighth moon (September or October) – marks the end of the monsoon season. Families gather to feast, to exchange presents, to honour their ancestors and to admire the moon. The same date is marked in much the same way in China, at the Festival of the Moon. Families walk through the moonlight in city parks, and lovers stroll together while eating moon cakes, made with walnuts and sugar.

**Target practice** An archery competition at Ulan Bator's great Naadam Fair.

**New hopes for the new year** Elaborate costume helps to start the Chinese new year celebrations in traditional style.

**Drums of joy** Children run through the streets banging drums during Korea's Festival of Puyeo.

117

# The joy of gardens in China and Japan

*The earliest gardens in China were Buddhist in origin – sacred groves, where life and nature could be contemplated in a silence broken only by the rustle of leaves. The idea of the garden as an aid to meditation has continued down the centuries. It is evident in the lushness of the classical Chinese garden, and in the rocks and gravel of a Japanese Zen garden.*

**A purified sanctuary** At the entrance to a Shinto garden, a stone basin filled with water and a bamboo ladle symbolise purification.

A garden, so they say in China, is a painting in three dimensions. Just as in a landscape, it cannot be conceived without the two essential elements of *shan* (mountains), which can be represented by rocks, and *shui* (water).

## A garden for the privileged

The art is to conceal art – to make a carefully planned arrangement of trees, shrubs, ferns, rocks and water look as if it were a perfectly natural grouping, with no signs of human intervention

beyond an occasional bridge, path or pavilion. The classical Chinese garden was not meant for the mass of the people. It was a hidden world, protected behind high walls; a haven where the cultivated élite, who alone could appreciate it to the full, might study or meditate. It was designed in compartments, so that even in a small garden, every step brought a new delight into view.

The ravages of time, war and revolution have not permitted the most ancient Chinese gardens, those of the Han Dynasty (206 BC-AD 220) to survive, but they are described in poems of that period. Superb gardens from the Ming (1368-1644) and Qing (1644-1911) periods can be found in Suzhou, China's 'town of gardens' in Jiangsu Province. The Garden of the Foolish Politician is renowned for its willow trees and lotus flowers.

## The garden comes to Japan

As with so many other aspects of their culture, the Japanese learned how and why to create gardens from the Chinese. And, as they did with such borrowings as writing and the Buddhist faith, they developed the new art into a totally new form. In an 8th-century compilation of literature and mythology called the *Nihon-shoki*, the word *niwa* was used to designate a garden. It means 'a place purified and set aside for the veneration of the gods', so it is not surprising that the earliest Japanese gardens were built around Shinto shrines.

**Cherry-blossom time**
*The Japanese love of gardens comes to the fore when the cherry trees blossom. Some take out their paintbrushes; others just stand and admire.*

**The mandarin's garden**
*The 16th-century Yu Yuan garden, in Shanghai, was created by Pan Yunduan, a high-ranking official in the Ming empire, to honour his father. It has all the elements that make up a classical Chinese garden.*

## The first 'stroll garden'

The 'paradise garden', dating from the 9th century, was Buddhist in origin: it was an attempt to create a paradise on Earth from rocks and water. The elements that make up a garden came in time to symbolise features of a well-loved landscape – sometimes an actual landscape, sometimes one described in a work of literature. Such was the garden of Katsura Imperial Villa, the country residence of a 17th-century prince. It was created by Kobori Enshu, most renowned of Japan's landscape gardeners. He based his design on an irregularly shaped lake, placing tea houses and pleasure pavilions around its shores, and making paths that invite the visitor to walk from view to view. Katsura was Japan's first 'stroll garden'. A favourite device of gardeners in the Kyoto area was to build into their design a 'borrowed view', so that a person strolling might suddenly have the pleasure of seeing the mountains in the distance, framed by a circular window in a wall or by a studied arrangement of trees.

## Tea gardens and dry gardens

Symbolism plays a key role in Japanese gardens, but sometimes the symbolism has motives other than aesthetic ones. At Nijo Castle, in Kyoto, the shogun Tokugawa Ieyasu allowed no trees to be planted. He wanted to impress the emperor with his power, and falling leaves suggested that all life must come to an end.

Another form of Japanese garden is the tea garden, in which everything is as carefully contrived as the tea

ritual itself. The garden leads to the tea house and is meant to put guests in the right contemplative frame of mind for the ceremony. Every tree, every fern, every lantern, every stepping stone or winding path has been sited to create feelings of harmony and calm.

To Western eyes, the most typical of Japanese gardens is the Zen Buddhist garden. Restrained in its use of colour and of plants, it has clear affinities with painting and calligraphy. As in China, the garden has once more become a painting in three dimensions. Many of the Zen gardens make no use of water, preferring to suggest an entire ocean with the ripples raked over sand or gravel. Kyoto's 15th-century garden of Daisen-in, the smallest dry garden in the world, was designed with the help of a famous ink-line painter, Soami, as a space where Buddhist monks could meditate. It seeks to create the effect of a Chinese landscape painting of the Song period (960-1279). A dry 'stream' flows from a rock that represents Mount Horai, home of the enlightened.

As in a painting, what is left out of a Zen garden matters as much as what goes into it. The dry garden of Ryoan-ji, also in Kyoto, is a sparing arrangement of 15 rocks set in raked white gravel, to represent islands in an eternal sea, mountains rising above clouds – or whatever the observer wishes to make of it.

***World in a bamboo box*** *No matter how tiny the area, the Japanese can turn it into a garden.*

***Islands in the ocean*** *A Buddhist monk creates the effect of an ocean encircling islands.*

# The painter's art

*Chinese painting has evoked a long-lasting confrontation between tradition and innovation, with tradition as the winner. In Japan, the art form began deeply in debt to cultural input from China, but finally found a way to become truly Japanese.*

***Song calligraphy*** *Painting on silk from the Song Dynasty entitled* The spirits meet above the sea.

From its early days, Chinese painting has displayed an aston-ishing mastery of technique. The principles were laid down in the 5th century by Xie He: rhythm and vitality; significant brush-work; realistic form; right colours; good composition; the proper study of good models. Calligraphy was put on the same high level as painting: under the Tang emperors, officials wanting to become mandarins had to prove that they were accomplished calligraphers.

## Tradition versus innovation

All six of Xie He's principles were applied during the golden age of Chinese landscape painting under the Tang Dynasty (618-907). If the human figure appeared in these paintings, it was usually dwarfed against the majesty of nature. Under the Mongol Yuan Dynasty (1279-1368), painting became for some artists an act of defiance against an alien regime. They turned to the past for inspi-ration, especially to the Song period (960-1279). Ni Can's ink paintings on bamboo recalled the work of the Song painter Wen Tong, of whom it was said that he 'melted into the bamboo'. Far from denoting a dead end in art, this led to a cultivated dialogue with the past that was in perfect harmony with a society that val-ued tradition higher than innovation. The technical virtuosity of professional artists in depicting anything from a landscape to plum

***Ladies at a funeral*** *Wall painting of courtesans in a funeral procession, at the tomb of the Tang crown prince Li Xian and his sister, Princess Yongtai, near Xi'an in north-west China.*

***The opulence of Edo*** *A 17th-century folding screen decorated in silver and gold leaf, from Japan's Edo period, when the country was almost completely isolated from the rest of the world.*

blossom had gone so far by the 16th century that a reaction set in. The ideal painter of the day was a gifted amateur, well read and well born, who gave himself to art purely for the pleasure it brought.

In the 19th century, the Shanghai Group broke with tradition and painted flowers, birds and the human figure. Western painting had an impact in the 1920s and Soviet-style socialist-realism took root in the Mao Ze-dong era, with huge canvasses portraying heroic deeds and state occasions. During the Cultural Revolution painting was forbidden and artists were sent to work on farms.

---

### Paper, silk, ink and brush: tools of the trade

Paper and silk, the materials of the painter and calligrapher, are unforgiving mediums. They immediately absorb the paint or ink, allowing no mistakes or second thoughts, so the artist has to set about his work with confidence. The ink, a solid stick of pine soot, is rubbed down on an ink stone, and water is added to get the right shade and consistency. The earliest known brush, a Chinese specimen dating from around 400 BC, was made of animal hair, glued to bamboo.

## The art of emptiness

The notion that emptiness has a value of its own is an essential concept in Taoist thought. It became a major theme in Chinese art during the Song period (960-1279), when painters thought deeply about how to strip a subject to its essentials. Carried over into Japanese art, the notion of emptiness gave masters like Hokusai an enviable economy of line. It can be seen, too, in the design of Zen gardens.

## Japanese painting

Tradition fixes AD 610 as the date when a Korean monk brought the tools and techniques of Chinese painting to Japan. The Chinese influence lasted for more than 1000 years, but alongside it, from the 10th century, a Japanese style developed. Japan's declaration of artistic independence came in 898, when the Heian Court stopped sending ambassadors to Tang emperors. The new national style, *Yamato-e*, used flat blocks of colour and strong lines to depict nature, court life and religious themes. The picture scroll, read from right to left, developed in the 12th century, to illustrate stories. Calligraphy and painting were combined in the *shigajiku* scrolls produced by scholar monks in the 14th and 15th centuries.

The master of a new style – the quickly executed 'flung ink' style, with ink splashes suggesting an entire landscape – was Sesshu Toyo (1420-1506), who had studied in China.

Patronage played a major role in Japanese art. General Oda Nobunaga (1534-82) employed Kano Eitoku to make screens and wall paintings for his castle, and the Kano school that developed made much use of gold leaf against the bright colours of the *Yamato-e* painters.

The Tokugawa shogun Ieyasu moved his capital to Edo (modern Tokyo) early in the 17th century, and began the policy of national isolation that was to last for the next 250 years. But one port, Nagasaki, was allowed to remain open and it was through this loophole that so-called 'literati' painting reached Japan. This style of calligraphic brushwork, with washes of ink and colour, took its inspiration from Chinese ink paintings dating back to the 13th century and the Yuan Dynasty.

After America's Commodore Perry forced Japan to abandon isolationism in the mid 19th century, painters became open to Western influences. Impressionism, Modernism and other movements in Western art all made their impact. A modern style, *Nihon-ga*, seeks to combine Western with Chinese and Japanese traditions.

## The Japanese print

Print-making in Japan had its origins in the use of woodblocks to illustrate novels and in a fashion for illustrating scenes from what was known as *ukiyo-e*, the 'floating world'. This was the realm of pleasure and female company, which the rising merchant classes sought in tea houses and theatres, and sometimes in brothels. The early prints were in monochrome, and the first great master was Mononobu. (1626-94). Full colour prints made their appearance in the work of Haranobu (1730-70). Print-making called for close cooperation between designer, engraver and printer. Among popular subjects were famous beauties and kabuki actors in dramatic poses. Paradoxically, the popularity of the print began to fade when Hokusai (1760-1849) and Hiroshige (1797-1858), the two artists best known in the West, were producing their most admired work. Hokusai, whose *The Great Wave* was one of 36 remarkable views of Mount Fuiji, died in poverty.

**Twelfth-century realism** *Detail of a cockerel, on a Japanese scroll painted nine centuries ago.*

**The waterfall** Mount Jingting with Waterfall, *executed in ink on paper by the Chinese monk Shi Tao (1641-1720).*

**The print-maker's skill** *A young girl peers through silk in this print by the master Utamaro Kitagawa (1753-1806).*

# A night at the Beijing opera

*All theatre has conventions that need to be understood, but those of the Beijing opera are, to Western eyes, baffling when first encountered. Brilliant colours and costumes, loud music, daring acrobatics, garish make-up and fantastic plots intermingle in a form of entertainment that has its roots in China's past.*

**Back-stage check** *A final once-over for one of the gowns that will be worn by an actor on stage.*

The general struts onto the stage to a resounding clash of gongs and cymbals. He is wearing a robe based on the court dress of the Ming Dynasty, and it is red, to show that he is brave and loyal. Another character wears a robe with a complex pattern, which tells the audience at once that he is an enemy. Yet another wears white, a sign that he is treacherous. Then the acrobats take centre-stage, leaping and whirling and brandishing swords in an unforgettable performance of a battle scene. Add music, mime, clowns, garish make-up, clowns with white paint around their noses and eyes, and male actors singing in falsetto voices, and this is Beijing opera. It is the traditional theatre of China, and totally unlike any theatre or opera produced in the West.

## Sumptuous costumes and simple props

Chinese opera is governed by rules and conventions in which the tiniest gesture, from the raising of an eyebrow to the twitching of a finger, conveys a meaning that the audience recognises. The props are minimal but the costumes are sumptuous, and they play a part in the plot. The conventions arose in the days when troupes of players, tumblers and clowns toured villages, marketplaces and town squares, entertaining audiences who had little else to brighten their lives. Because the spectators were often boisterous, the actors pitched their voices in a high register that could be heard above the hubbub. Mime and make-up were developed for similar reasons. The movements made by an actor were a code that told the audience he was getting down from a horse, climbing a staircase or stepping into a house. Make-up revealed the nature of the character.

**Opera lovers** *An opera audience in the provinces watches the local version of a Beijing opera.*

## A change in repertoire

During the Cultural Revolution, the traditional subject matter of the opera fell out of favour and revolutionary operas were staged instead. But the opera is now returning to its traditional repertoire: love stories, palace intrigues, rebellions and fairy stories. Such operas appeal to the popular imagination because they recall the China of the past. Among the most celebrated are *The Legend of the White Serpent* and *The Monkey Creates Havoc in Heaven*, in which the monkey is dressed in yellow to indicate his mischievous nature. The spectators know these classics by heart and appreciate the slightest nuance in the acting, so long as it stays within the boundaries laid down by convention. One convention that until a few decades ago was shared by Chinese opera and the theatre of Shakespeare was that all the parts were played by men.

**Costume . . . make-up . . . action . . .** *Every gesture and every colour has its own meaning in Chinese opera.*

# The enigma and allure of Japanese theatre

*Elaborate masks and make-up . . . unearthly music and guttural cries . . . slow, silent dancing that can be eerily fascinating . . . puppets with human vulnerability . . . This is traditional Japanese theatre, and it comes in three forms – Noh, Kabuki and Bunraku.*

**Female roles** *Women were banned from the Kabuki stage in 1629, and their place was taken by* **onnagata**, *male actors who specialise in female roles.*

In the 19th century, when a Japanese audience saw a Western play for the first time, they were so incensed by the way the villain treated the heroine that they rushed onto the stage, intent on lynching him. Westerners sometimes have similar difficulties in understanding Japanese drama, but the effort is worth while, for it leads to the heart of Japan.

## The skill behind the mask

Noh plays, which began in the 14th century, were meant for an aristocratic audience. Noh is a complex form of drama, mingling poetry, plot, songs, music, dancing, sumptuous costumes and elaborate masks. The plots, drawing on history and mythology, deal with such themes as suffering and loyalty, madness and the world of the supernatural. Interludes of broad comedy, known as *kyogen*, are added to relieve the tension. The performers are born to their trade, for Noh acting passes down in family lines. Their skill lies in the ability to convey the essence of a character even from behind a wooden mask. The principal character, the *shite*, may be a ghost, a madman, an animal, or a more conventional hero. He is masked, as are those playing women and old people. The characters share the stage with the chorus and the musicians – three drummers and a flautist.

## A new theatre for the new classes

Kabuki theatre was aimed at the rising merchant classes. Its early inspiration, at the dawn of the 17th century, came from the licentious movements of a female dancer, O-Kuni, but women were soon prohibited from performing. Kabuki takes its plots from history and from any event that offers the possibility of dynamic action – battles, suicides, tensions between merchants and aristocrats. Movement swirls across a stage that is equipped with gangways, staircases, trapdoors and revolving platforms. The performers tend to come, as in Noh plays, from acting families, and some have achieved the status of 'Living National Treasure'.

In Bunraku, which is performed by puppets about two-thirds the size of humans, stories of blighted love and suicide are popular. The master puppeteer works in full view of the audience, and an astonishingly full range of emotions is conveyed by the marionettes, with the help of a narrator, a lute and a *shamisen*, the Japanese three-stringed guitar.

**On with the motley** *A Kabuki actor starts by putting on make-up, before donning his elaborate costume.*

**The spectacle of Kabuki** *An eye-catching scene from a play presented by the Ennosuke family, who revived the traditional style of Kabuki.*

# Japanese literature, a gift to the world

*Around AD 1000, a high-born Japanese lady wrote the world's first novel,* The Tale of the Genji. *It was the start of Japan's long and fruitful contribution to world literature. Despite more than two centuries of isolation under the Tokugawa shoguns, and rigid censorship during the Second World War, Japanese authors are once again creating work whose appeal is universal.*

**God of writers**
*Tenjin, god of literature.*

Japanese literature began with the spoken word, with storytellers relating how the country was created and how the emperor was descended from the gods. Around 712, these stories were written down in *Records of Ancient Matters*, using a Japanese version of Chinese script in the compilation. But Japan remained in thrall to classical Chinese culture. As late as AD 936, the poet Kino Tsurayuki thought it necessary to apologise to his readers for writing in Japanese. This cultural diffidence had vanished by the dawn of the following century, when Murasaki Shikibu, a lady-in-waiting at the Imperial court, wrote *The Tale of the Genji*. Her book, widely accepted today as the world's first romantic novel, inspired other Japanese authors down the centuries.

### Two thousand haikus in a day

One of Japan's unique contributions to poetry is the 17-syllable *haiku*, in which the poet draws attention to an aspect of life or nature that has caught his imagination. Saikaku, a 17th-century master of the format, was named 'Lord of the 2000' for the astonishing number of *haikus* he wrote in a day.

During the Tokugawa shogunate, which began in 1603, Japan was almost completely isolated from the rest of the world. Internal trade prospered and the focus of literature shifted from the court and the aristocracy to the rising merchant class. The 'floating world' of geishas and pleasure-seeking became a favourite theme. Japan's years of isolation ended in 1853 with the arrival of a US naval expedition, and it was not long before Western books were being translated. One consequence was that Japanese writers turned away from expressing themselves in a 'literary' style to use the language of ordinary people. By the early 1930s, some were turning to the working class for themes and characters.

Police suppression of literature began in the mid 1930s, as the military took over the running of the country, but there were still writers such as Kawabata Yasunari who managed to combine Western and Japanese traditions in their work. During the Second World War censorship became even more oppressive and writers had either to compromise or to remain silent. Kawabata continued writing after the war, and in 1968 won the Nobel prize for literature. He made his reputation with such works as *Snow Country*, which deals with the relationship between a businessman and an ageing geisha. Junichiro Tanizaki sounded a new note after the war in *The Makioka Sisters*, the story of a traditionally brought-up Osaka family. He was critical of those Japanese who were too easily influenced by the West.

**Japan first** *Mishima, founder of the nationalistic Shield Society, was a samurai at heart.*

One of the towering literary figures to emerge in postwar Japan, Yukio Mishima, came from a samurai family and had a vision of a return to samurai values. His *Sea of Fertility* trilogy lamented the passing of the old Japan. In 1970, after a failed attempt to overthrow the government, Mishima committed suicide by hara-kiri. Two years later his friend Kawabata killed himself. Other writers were less despairing. Shusaku Endo, who turned Roman Catholic and was known as the Japanese Graham Greene, examined society

through a moral microscope in *Wonderful Fool* and *Volcano*. Among the younger writers, Banana Yoshimoto took an ironical view that had an appeal beyond the shores of Japan.

**Prize-winner** *Kawabata (far left) won the Nobel prize with his stories of solitude, death and tragic love.*

**The new generation** *Banana Yoshimoto, born in 1964, is a cult figure to younger Japanese readers because of the disturbing, ironical tone of her work.*

# The struggle between literature and the state

*The Chinese have never doubted the power of words to change the world. Their first emperor, Qin Shi Huangdi, had Confucian scholars buried alive and made a bonfire of their books. In modern times, Mao Ze-dong was still insisting that literature should be at the service of the state, and writers suffered in the Cultural Revolution that he set in motion against those marked down as his enemies.*

*The nation's champion*
*Lu Xun wanted his books to help in the revival of a troubled land.*

Mao Ze-dong was following a long-standing tradition when, in 1942, he told his fellow communists that art and literature should follow the party line. The tradition had been established in the 3rd century BC by another strong leader, Qin Shi Huangdi, the first emperor of a united China. The only difference between them was that Mao wanted literature to serve the masses, while Shi Huangdi wanted it to serve his dynasty. He gave orders for all books to be burned, save for those praising the dynasty, or for strictly practical books on such topics as gardening. Anyone publishing a banned book faced the death penalty, and Shi Huangdi is said to have had 460 Confucian scholars buried alive. Some books survived, however, among them the *Five Classics*. This collection of poems, folktales and other writings includes the *I Ching*, a book of divination taken up in the 1960s by New Age believers in the West.

## Poetry for the élite

Poetry was venerated at the Chinese court, reaching its peak under the Tang Dynasty (AD 618-907). The scholarly Li Bai, who gently celebrated nature and friendship, was a typical poet of the time. By the Ming period (1368-1644) fiction had become popular. *The Water Margin*, a cloak-and-dagger story of outlaws fighting injustice, is still read in China today.

The lofty style of the classics was challenged in the 20th century by writers like Lu Xun (1881-1936), whose *True History of Ah Q* was a compelling indictment of the backwardness that allowed China to be dominated by warlords and foreign powers. Mao Ze-dong seemed to be flirting with liberalisation when, in 1956, he proclaimed 'Let a hundred flowers bloom' – but those authors who took him at his word soon had cause to regret their naivety. Writers fared even worse during the Cultural Revolution: they were jeered at and beaten by Red Guards and sent off to farms for 're-education'. Their stories of privation were termed 'wound literature'.

Modern Chinese writers have shown a new vigour, and Western publishers have rushed to translate the work of Mo Yan, Yu Hua, Fang Fang and Su Tong. *Wild Swans* (1991), with its portrayal of communism as an idealistic experiment that went tragically wrong, was a bestseller in the West. The author, Jung Chang, was a former Red Guard.

---

### New words from old

Chinese script uses pictograms (stylised representations of an object) and ideograms (symbols that stand for a concept). In the West, a road sign depicting an elderly couple, warning motorists to take extra care, is an example of an ideogram. Abstract notions are harder to symbolise than solid objects, so the Chinese combine characters to form new words or phrases. In the example below, the character *dao*, a pictogram that stands for the blade of a knife, is combined with the pictogram *cè*, meaning 'book' (bamboo stems, bound horizontally). The result is the new word *shan* ('book' plus 'cutting'), which means 'abridged' or 'condensed'.

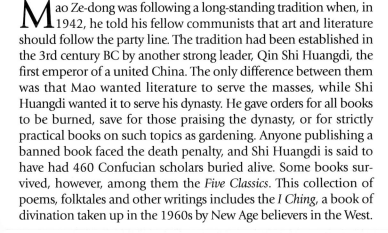

dao (knife)          cè (book)          shan (abridged)

---

*Anguished young man*
*Yu Hua, born in 1960, brings more than a hint of anguish to his work. His novel* Living *was turned into the screenplay for a movie.*

*Man of the people*   Mo Yan, born in 1956 to a family of poor peasants, was a soldier before turning to authorship. His Land of Alcohol was a great success.

# The silent splendour of the Great Wall

*Snaking across the northern mountaintops for 4000 miles (6700 km), the Great Wall is a symbol of imperial China's ability to overcome any obstacle by the sheer weight of manpower. It is also a monument to the folly of overweening ambition, for when the Wall was seriously tested, it failed to keep out barbarian invaders.*

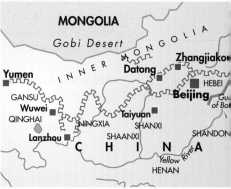

**On guard** *Wall sculpture representing a guardian of paradise.*

**Barrier that failed** *With its watchtowers and battlements, the Wall must have seemed almost impassable to invaders from the north. But its very length meant that its garrison was thinly stretched, and the Wall was crossed by the Mongols of Genghis Khan in the 13th century, and again by Manchu tribes in the 17th century.*

The Great Wall of China ranks alongside the pyramids of Ancient Egypt as one of the greatest feats of building ever attempted by human design and human labour. Built as a barrier against barbarians from the north, it reaches from the Gulf of Bohai on the Yellow Sea to the Gobi Desert. On several stretches there are double, or even triple, lines of defence.

## The 'Wall of 10 000 li'

The imposing, stone-battlemented sections of the Wall that are admired today were built for the most part under the Ming Dynasty (1368-1644), but the story of the Wall goes back to the 5th or 6th century BC. During the Warring States period of China's history, local lords raised walls of tamped earth to protect their territories. Qin Shi Huangdi, China's first emperor, linked, strengthened and extended the original walls in the 3rd century BC, as protection against the terrifying Huns. His 'Wall of 10 000 li' – a distance amounting to about 3300 miles (5300 km) – took ten years to build, using the forced labour of 1 million conscripts and 300 000 soldiers. The work was brutally hard and many died, leaving their bones in the Wall. For well over a thousand years the Wall seemed an effective barrier, but by the 13th century, when

Genghis Khan and his Mongol horsemen were on the advance, it was in a state of disrepair, and the invaders got through without any trouble at all.

## The Manchu invasion

In 1368, a rebellion drove the Mongols out of China and the new dynasty, the Ming, set about rebuilding and extending the Wall. At the peak of its splendour it averaged 25 ft (7.5 m) in height, with ramparts 23 ft (7 m) thick. There were watchtowers every 600 ft (180 m), and five horsemen could ride abreast on the road built along its top. As well as being a barrier, the Wall was a communications link between the east and west of China's vast empire. But in the 17th century it failed once again in its primary purpose. Fierce Manchu tribes took advantage of the decadence and weakness of the last Ming emperor to sweep over the Wall, seize Beijing and set up their own Qing Dynasty. During the years of Manchu rule (1644-1911) the Wall fell into decay. Peasants took away stones to build their houses – a process that was repeated during the Cultural Revolution of 1966-76. The present government recognises the Wall's value as part of China's heritage, and sections have been restored to their original glory.

# Terracotta army of China's first emperor

*In the countryside around the ancient Han capital of Chang'an (modern Xi'an) there had long been stories of ghosts that lay beneath the ground. But when drought struck the area, and a group of local peasants began digging out a well, nothing had prepared them for what they would discover.*

**Still vigilant**  *A terracotta warrior from 22 centuries ago.*

A chance blow with a pickaxe led to one of the most astounding archaeological discoveries in the history of the world: an army of terracotta soldiers, lined up ready for battle on behalf of their dead emperor. The pickaxe was wielded by a peasant digging a well near Xi'an in 1974, and what he had unearthed was a 'giant' – a slightly larger-than-life soldier, modelled in terracotta, who had kept a silent vigil with his 8000 comrades for more than 2000 years.

## The boy king who forged an empire

Qin Shi Huangdi, the first emperor of a united China, died unexpectedly in 209 BC. Ironically, it happened on a journey to the fabled Island of the Immortals, where he hoped to find the elixir of eternal life. In earlier times, a ruler's wives, servants and horses were entombed with him when he died, to continue serving him in the next world. By Shi Huangdi's time, Chinese civilisation had reached the point where humans and horses were no longer sacrificed, and models were buried in their place. The three vaults housing the terracotta army were sited 1¹/₂ miles (2 km) from Shi Huangdi's tomb. The first emperor forged a military machine that was unstoppable, but his successors were less forceful and the Qin Dynasty lasted for only three years after his death.

## Preserved in mud and ash

A rebel general plundered the emperor's tomb and ordered the roofs of the vaults to be set alight. The terracotta soldiers were buried in a slurry of ash and mud that left them in a pitiable condition but also preserved them. It took archaeologists years of work to reconstitute the statues. Their bodies, arms and legs had been mass-produced, but their hands and faces were individually sculpted – some experts believe the faces were portraits from life. Foot soldiers, cavalry, charioteers and bowmen stood in battle formation for a call to arms that

never came. Their metal weapons were still sharp, but the wooden bows of the archers had perished. So, too, had the leather harnesses of the horses, leaving behind their brass fittings. Some 1000 soldiers have been restored, out of an estimated 8000. The wonders of the first emperor's own mausoleum have not been exposed to modern eyes, for full excavations have not yet been started. It is believed, though, that he reverted to the barbaric practice of former centuries and had his gravediggers and those of his wives who had not given birth buried alongside him.

**Bringing the past to life**  *Restoration work on one of the Imperial Guard.*

**In battle array**  *The arrangement of Emperor Qin Shi Huangdi's terracotta soldiers in their tomb has thrown valuable light on the battle formations taken up by a Chinese army in the 3rd century BC.*

# Treasures of the Buddhist caves

*Thousands of Buddhist statues in the caves of Dunhuang, Yungang and Longmen bear witness to ancient China's remarkable capacity for accepting ideas from other cultures and absorbing them in a way that makes them distinctively Chinese.*

When dawn strikes the face of the cliffs of Mogao, near Dunhuang in north-west China, the sun's rays stream into the entrances of hundreds of caves. Inside are Buddhist temples and a treasure trove of statues, dating from the 4th century AD. Dunhuang, a busy staging post on the Silk Road, became a centre from which Buddhism spread throughout northern China.

### A unique find

In 366, a monk named Yuezun applied a building technique that originated in India and began hewing temples out of the cliffs at Mogao and filling them with terracotta statues. Some of the early statues have long noses and curly hair, but over the following five centuries, especially during the Tang period (618-907), their features became Chinese, and the paintings that surround them depict Chinese history and mythology. One statue of the Buddha wears the dragon robe that was otherwise reserved for Tang emperors.

By the 14th century, the Silk Road had declined in importance, and the Mogao caves were abandoned. But in 1900, a wandering monk discovered their greatest treasure, a bricked-up library containing 30 000 manuscripts. Dating back to the 5th century, they were written in Chinese, Tibetan, Sanskrit, Uighur and other languages – an incomparable source of study for historians, theologians and linguists.

### The 10 000 Buddhas

Even more impressive than the cave temples of Mogao were those founded in AD 453 at Yungang, in the northern province of Shanxi, by non-Chinese emperors of the Wei Dynasty. The earlier carvings there show Greek, Persian and Indian influences, with representations of acanthus leaves, lions and the Hindu gods Shiva and Vishnu. But they share the caves with Chinese dragons, and the Indian gods have Chinese features. Monumental Buddhas, sculpted in the late 8th century under the Tang Dynasty, mingle the artistic styles of both India and China.

The caves at Longmen, in central China, were also started under the Wei Dynasty. Well over 1000 caves were hewn in limestone cliffs beside the River Yi and peopled with some 100 000 statues, the biggest 56 ft (17 m) high. The Cave of the 10 000 Buddhas, carved out in AD 680, actually contains more than 15 000 statues. The well-rounded figures of the statues in the Yungang caves give way, at Longmen, to slimmer, more angular shapes – another characteristic of Tang sculpture.

***A prodigality of Buddhas*** *Ornate decoration in a Yungang cave.*

***Miracle in limestone*** *A 56 ft (17 m) high Buddha at Longmen, where 1350 grottoes contain 100 000 statues, carved out of the rock.*

***Where two cultures meet*** *Indian and Chinese traditions are fused in this monumental Buddha at Yungang.*

# Potala, the home of the Dalai Lama

*Perched over the Tibetan capital of Lhasa is the fortress-palace of Potala – once the seat of all power in Tibet, both spiritual and temporal. The Dalai Lama fled the city in 1959, but Potala is more than ever a symbol of his country's unconquerable urge to be free.*

**The great builder** *The fifth Dalai Lama, who began building the Potala palace.*

The setting, against a background of mountains more than 4 miles (6 km) high, is awe-inspiring. This was the capital of the imaginary Shangri-la, where seekers after truth could shed their anxieties and contemplate the meaning of life. Towering over the city was the palace of the Dalai Lama, the sacred leader.

### The 'Yellow Hats'

The palace is still there, a labyrinth of 1000 rooms and corridors, filled with 200000 statues, its walls decorated with murals, its altars covered in gold and studded with diamonds. But its central purpose has vanished, for the 14th Dalai Lama fled to India in 1959, after a failed revolt in Lhasa against Tibet's Chinese occupiers. Until the Chinese invasion, in 1950, the Dalai Lama was Tibet's head of state, as well as its spiritual leader.

The Tibetan form of Buddhism evolved in the 14th century with the foundation of the strict Gelukpa ('Virtuous') sect also known as the 'Yellow Hats'. Devout Tibetans believe all Dalai Lamas to be reincarnations of the bodhisattva Avalokiteshvara, father of the Tibetan people. (A bodhisattva is a saint, who has renounced his own chance of achieving Nirvana in order to save others.) When a Dalai Lama dies, his spirit passes into the body of a newborn child.

In the 7th century, an early Tibetan king, Songtsen Gampo, raised a palace on the site of the present building, but most of it was destroyed during an invasion. The 13-storey Potala was built in two stages: the White Palace in 1645-8 and the Red Palace in 1691-3. It is a fortress as well as a palace, with thick defensive walls. Inside are chapels, meditation rooms, living quarters and vaults for the bodies of former Dalai Lamas, preserved in salt. The tomb of the 'Great Fifth' Dalai Lama is embellished with 4 tons of gold and encrusted with precious stones. During the Cultural Revolution, Chinese Red Guards went on the rampage in Tibet, destroying more than 2000 monasteries, but Mao Ze-dong stopped short of allowing his young fanatics to ransack Potala, and today it is a prime tourist attraction.

**One of a thousand** *A sumptuously decorated stateroom in the Potala palace.*

**Brooding presence** *The Potala palace spreads across the top of Marpr Ri hill, 430 ft (130 m) above Lhasa.*

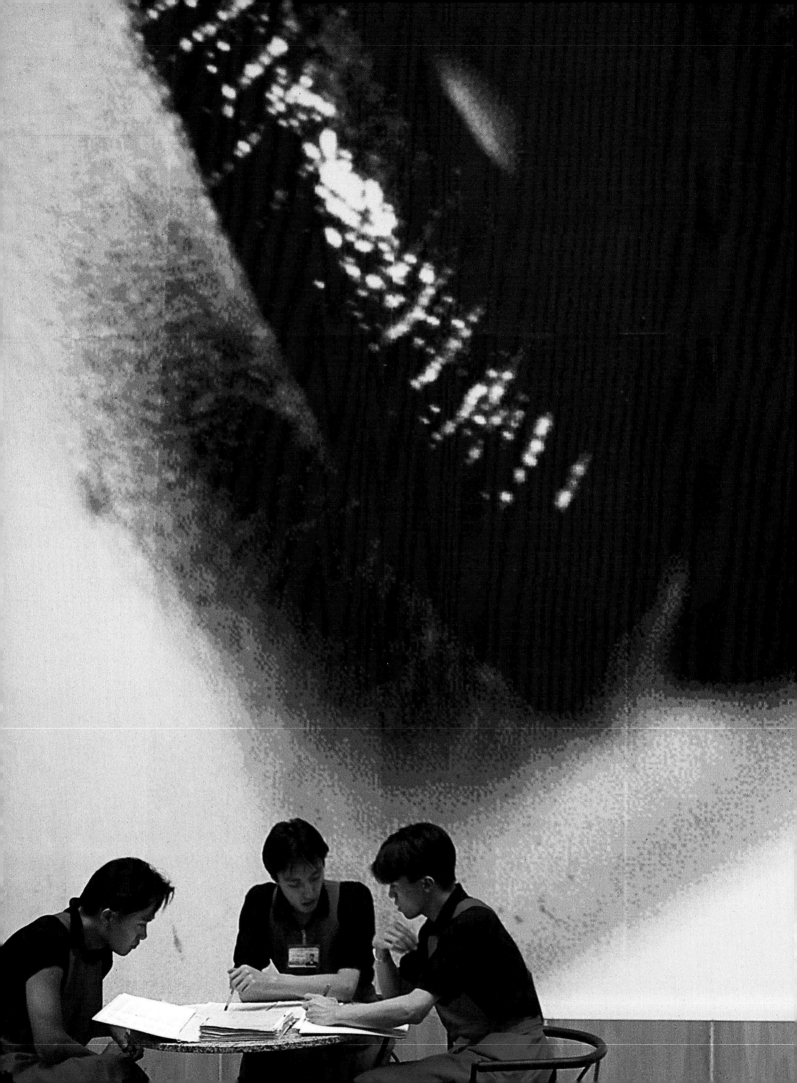

# 6

# THE DRIVE FOR ECONOMIC POWER

Japan, China and South Korea are key players in a high-stakes game whose reward is national prosperity. Japan, woefully short of natural resources, has put its energies into transforming imported raw materials into microchips, video games, televisions and cars for export to the rest of the developed world, building up a huge balance of trade surplus in the process. But since the economic bubble burst in the 1990s questions are being asked about the country that achieved the most spectacular economic miracle of the 20th century. South Korea, too, has faltered in the new century, after throwing up dynamic industries in the previous one. Since the 1980s, China has accepted the profit motive as a force that can drive progress, and made a bid to join the great commercial powers. Her economy, boosted by foreign investment, has finally taken the 'Great Leap Forward' that Mao strived for but never achieved.

*The staff of a Tokyo boutique study the firm's accounts.*

# Investing in the latest technology

*Japan's remarkable recovery after the Second World War was based on an alliance between government and industry, coupled with a readiness to embrace new technology. Today, a nation in recession looks to the latest developments for revival.*

**A helping hand from France** *In the days when 'Japan Inc' was the admiration of the world, firms such as Nissan transplanted their expertise abroad. But after Japan's economy hit choppy waters, the situation was reversed. Here, the heads of Nissan and Renault meet in March 1999 to sign a partnership deal.*

W hen Akio Morita, the charismatic founder of Sony, died in October 1999, the whole nation mourned, for it knew that an era had ended. Morita had started in business in the ruins of postwar Tokyo, repairing radios. He moved into electronics and in 1958 founded Sony (a composite name, from the Latin *sonus*, 'sound' and the English word 'sunny').

## Building a new image

At the time, Japanese products had a reputation for being cheap and unreliable imitations of items produced in the West, but Morita made Sony a byword for innovation and attention to detail. In 1978 he invented a portable cassette player, the Walkman, and where Sony had shown the way in the pursuit of quality, other Japanese firms followed. From the 1970s on, such companies as Panasonic, Toshiba, Sharp, Hitachi, Aïwa, Sanyo, Canon and Epson became household names around the world.

The government went into partnership with industry and the universities to enable 'Japan Inc' to take full advantage of advances in technology, with the result that the country's exports rocketed. Even in the past few years, with Japan in recession, sales of personal computers on the domestic market have held up.

## The explosive success of video games

A walk down any city street in Japan gives an immediate insight into how completely the new technology has taken over everyday life. There are already 40 million mobile telephones in the country, and to the delight of firms like DoMoCo and Matsushita, this number is expected to double by 2010. On trains and buses, young businessmen use mobile phones to check their e-mail. In 1999, DoMoCo introduced the i-mode service – a mobile phone with a screen that allows users to send messages or photographs, play games, or call up instant maps and other information from the Internet. It has two advantages over earlier devices: first, the images are much sharper; second, it gives rapid access to the Internet's information because it is connected 24 hours a day, though

### The end of 'a job for life'

J apan's enterprise culture, founded on loyalty to a firm, a job for life, and promotion according to length of service, is under threat. The economic crisis has forced companies to introduce promotion on merit. Younger employees are now preferred to 'old timers' because their wages are lower. Formerly it took 20 years to reach management level, but now a bright and ambitious employee can climb the ladder in just a few years. In 1999, Japan's unemployment rate was 4.9 per cent – unthinkable in the 1980s. But while older workers can no longer depend on a job for life, there is competition for promising youngsters. Toyota, Toshiba and Nissan all announced in 2000 that they would pay loyalty bonuses to rising stars.

**The workers fight back** *South Korea was hit by the recession, too. Daewoo car workers stage a 'Save Our Jobs' protest in Seoul in December 1998.*

charging only for time actually used. I-mode has made a sensational impact within Japan in the space of a few years – a success that DoMoCo plans to repeat on the export market.

The equally explosive success of video games is not surprising in a country whose traditional written language is based on pictures. Sony brought out PlayStation in 1994, to compete with Nintendo's GameBoy. It catapulted to first place in the market, selling 73 million, against Game-Boy's 29 million. But the launch of the much-hyped PlayStation 2, a few years later, was disappointing. Sony, it seemed, missed the magic touch of its founder.

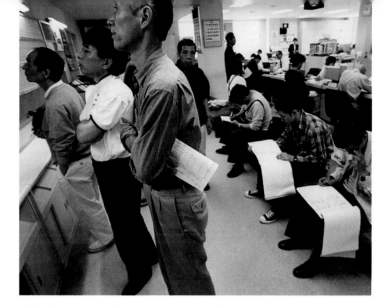

***Job-seekers*** *Out-of-work Japanese search for jobs at an employment agency in Sapporo, capital of Hokkaido.*

***Sleeping rough*** *A homeless man sleeps on the pavement in today's recession-hit Japan, outside a shop selling luxury goods.*

The worldwide web has confounded economic trends and enjoyed a boom of its own in Japan since 1999. The Japanese came late to the Internet, but accepted it with enthusiasm. There are 20 million Internet users in Japan today, a figure expected to treble by 2005. (This estimate was made before the 'dot.com' bubble burst in the West, so it may be optimistic.) The Internet, insatiable for information, and dependent on speedy delivery, has given a boost to manufacturers of semiconductors and fibre optics, which can transport a mass of information – text, images or sound – when it is translated into the form of digital impulses.

The next big step forward for Japan's techno-economy is to transform life both in business and in the home. Banking and shopping from home are already available on line. Home appliances and services, such as the refrigerator, the microwave, television, heating and lighting, will become 'intelligent', switching on and off in anticipation of the family's needs.

## Visions of the future

Japan's Ministry of Trade and Industry (MITI) has a clear vision of where the nation should be in the 21st century: leading the way in the application of new technology to industry. It continues to bring businessmen and the universities together, and to sponsor research into basic science, with robotics and virtual reality high on its list. MITI also sponsors the creation of 'science cities' – clusters of laboratories and research institutes such as the Kansai Science City near Kyoto. Nippon Telephone and Telegraph (NTT), the parent company of DoMoCo, is at the leading edge of research into virtual reality, which could open up new avenues for architecture, surgery and teaching, in addition to its entertainment potential.

It has been estimated that Japan's high-tech economy will be worth around £200 billion by 2003. To make that prediction come true, the country needs more people with the vision of Akio Morita. One man who may fit that description is Masayoshi Son. In much the same way as the founder of Sony, Masayoshi started from practically nothing. But this grandson of Korean immigrants is today the head of Softbank, an investment bank that provides funds for starting up or expanding companies that have good ideas for the Information Age. Within a few years, he has built up the third biggest fortune in Japan. Japan is pinning its hopes on people like Masayoshi and the young entrepreneurs who win his backing to lead the way out of the current recession.

***Building team spirit*** *A break for gymnastics at a Japanese factory.*

# Slowdown for the car makers

*In the 1970s and 1980s, the Japanese motor industry was a dazzling success story. But at the start of the new millennium it has had to call in help from abroad. What went wrong?*

In the 1950s, when Tokyo, Osaka and other big Japanese cities were short of taxis, they had to import small Renaults and Citroëns from France. In 1999, Renault was once again in the news in Japan when it signed a management deal with the troubled Nissan company. The decades in between saw the golden years of an industry that employed 10 per cent of the workforce and made Toyota, Nissan, Datsun and other Japanese makes highly desirable items on garage forecourts in most countries of the developed world.

## A buoyant home market

In the late 1960s, at the start of the 'miracle' years of the Japanese economy, car manufacturers had an armlock on their home market. Only 10 per cent of cars sold in Japan came from abroad – or more specifically, from Germany. Those were the days of euphoria for domestic car buyers, with good wages, high productivity, and (so it seemed) jobs for life. Even those who, for lack of free

**Robots galore**  *The assembly line at Mazda's factory in Hiroshima.*

time, took their car out on the road as little as once a month, looked on it as a status symbol, to be hosed down and spruced up once a week, and traded in to buy a new model every two or three years. Thanks to the seemingly inexhaustible reservoir of the home market, the car manufacturers benefited from economies of scale and were able to break into overseas markets. Japanese cars even stormed that fortress of the automobile industry, the United States. European manufacturers looked on with apprehension when Nissan set up a factory in the United Kingdom. Gloomy forecasts were made about Europe's ability to take on the Asian competition.

Then, in 1997, came what nobody, least of all the Japanese, could have imagined: recession. With unemployment a real threat, families hung on to their savings rather than buying a new car, and the home market plummeted. In the 1980s, the car industry had been restructured, with Nissan buying Datsun and Toyota buying Daihatsu. But this was not enough. In 1999, Nissan announced that five of its plants would close over the next three years, and signed a 'rescue' agreement with Renault. Mitsubishi looked abroad for help, too, and went into partnership with Daimler-Chrysler. It was a crushing blow for Japan's reputation, when, in September 2000, Mitsubishi had to recall 620 000 vehicles and admit that over a period of 20 years it had been covering up defects in its cars. The scandal forced the resignation of the company's president, Katsuhiko Kawasoe. The Japanese continue to make cars, but they are often built with the help of foreign capital.

### Japanese motorbikes are running out of revs

The crisis that hit Japan's car industry has not spared its motorbike manufacturers. Honda, Yamaha, Suzuki and Kawasaki all face lean times, in markets that have shrunk, both at home and overseas. Honda is still ahead of its rivals, with more than half the market, but every motorbike company in Japan was alarmed when mighty Yamaha was taken over by car manufacturer Toyota. An alarm bell sounded for the entire two-wheels sector of the motor industry, which cannot look to high-profile international events such as the Golden Bowl or the Isle of Man TT, for its salvation – for the entrants in races like these are great, snorting monsters, and fashions have changed. Demand is for much smaller machines, and in trying to meet it, Japan faces stiff competition from Europe.

**In the boom years**  *Hundreds of new cars line up at Yokohama docks, ready to swell Japan's balance-of-payments surplus.*

# Economic land of the setting sun?

*One of the world's economic superpowers is in crisis. Growth has stopped, and from the best of times the country quite suddenly found itself facing economic meltdown. Only the information-based 'new economy' offers a gleam of light.*

**Lucky break**  *The recession is good news for fast-food sushi bars, where prices are cheaper than in a restaurant.*

Since 1997 the Japanese economy has been struggling. It has been in trouble before – in 1973, for example, the world price of oil, which provides three-quarters of the nation's energy needs, quadrupled overnight – but the economic juggernaut known as 'Japan Inc' was powerful enough to absorb the shock. This time, it looks as if the machine may have seized up. In 1999, the unemployment rate rose to 4.9 per cent, double the rate of two years earlier. House-building was down, the stock market was down, incomes and prices were down – above all, confidence was down: the Japanese were putting their money into savings, rather than spending it to kickstart the economy. In 1998 suicides rose to a record 32 863, many of them caused by financial worries.

In the 1970s and 1980s, Japan's boom decades, the banks lent money with a singular lack of caution, fuelling steep rises in property prices and share values on the Nikkei Exchange. The first signs that both real estate and shares were overvalued came in the late 1980s. Within ten years, land values in the country as a whole fell by 40 per cent, and in the Tokyo region by a disastrous 50 per cent. It was not only the speculators who suffered: banks were left with crippling bad loans, and some had to close their doors. Finance Minister Kiichi Miyazawa warned that the nation's finances were on the brink of a 'catastrophic collapse'.

**No to Nissan**  *An angry Nissan employee demonstrates in Tokyo against the company's plans to close five of its Japanese plants and sack 21 000 workers.*

Japan's prosperity had been founded on a home market well protected by quotas, high customs tariffs and the innate loyalty of the Japanese to their own products. Pressures against protectionism made themselves felt in the 1990s, and the competition brought havoc to entire sectors of the Japanese economy, from banking and insurance to car manufacturing. In 1997 there came a final blow to the confidence of consumers, when the government introduced 5 per cent VAT on sales.

Faith in the government and the system was further shaken by a series of financial scandals involving bank executives, industrialists, and even government ministers. A typical, but by no means rare, example was the conduct of Labour minister Toshio Yamaguchi, who was given a four-year jail sentence for embezzling money that went into a golf course being developed by his sister. The old notions of loyalty and 'a job for life' were being replaced by a concept new to the Japanese: 'Every man for himself.' The nation's lifebelt in this sea of troubles may be the Internet. Expertise in handling the latest technology has always been one of Japan's great strengths.

## A record public debt

Bad loans have brought the Japanese banking system to its knees. In the three years from 1998 to 2000, the government pumped out 425 billion dollars' worth of stimulus packages, in a bid to bring the economy back to a state of self-sustaining growth, but this had little effect, beyond increasing public debt. In 2001, government debt reached 130 per cent of the nation's GNP. Japan may hold more reserves than any other country. It also occupies first place for issuing bonds to finance its debts.

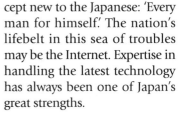

**We are so sorry**  *Directors of the Dai-Ichi Kangyo Bank make a public apology at a press conference called after yet another Japanese bank hits serious trouble.*

# From Great Leap Forward to Open Door

*The Mao Ze-dong-inspired Great Leap Forward of the 1950s was a catastrophe for China. Millions died in the famine it helped to bring about. But the lessons of that failure were not lost on Deng Xiao-ping.*

**Business breakfast** *Executives meet early in a Shenzhen hotel.*

Twenty years ago, the south of China was an underdeveloped land whose inhabitants' only chance of a decent future lay in slipping across the frontier to find work in the British colony of Hong Kong.

### The giant awakens

Today, factories and workshops line the highways of China's golden triangle in the delta of the Pearl River. Containers stencilled 'Made in China' are loaded with textiles, toys and games, shoes and

electronic components for export. Huge lorries take them to the docks at Hong Kong and Guangzhou (Canton), on the first stage of their journey to the big stores and supermarkets of the West. It was from this region that, in 1978, the economic giant that is China began to stir from its slumbers. Deng Xiao-ping, China's new leader, announced an 'Open Door' on trade with the West. He had inherited an economy in a sorry plight, marked by inefficiency and low productivity. Under Mao, the heavy hand of the state had controlled all aspects of economic life, from the number of shoes that could be produced annually down to the price of a box of matches.

**On the catwalk** *Models demonstrate the latest fashions on sale in a big Shenzhen store.*

## The fragility of China's banking system

Chinese banks have lived through anxious days since the 1990s. Under Mao, they had no option but to lend money to state-run enterprises, even if they were inefficient and unprofitable. Such businesses were not permitted to go bankrupt, and the result was bad debts. Nor was the central bank, the People's Bank of China, allowed to control the nation's money supply. The result was inflation. In 1994, an attempt was made to make the banks responsible for their own commercial profits and losses, but it foundered on the bad-debt problem – the state could not pay back the money it had been lent in the years when borrowing was easy because the banks had no choice but to lend. Corrective action has been painful. In 1998, the Bank of China ordered GITIC, the financial arm of Guangdong Province, to cease operations – in effect, declaring it bankrupt. The province's debts amounted to $4.68 billion. The Chinese habit of saving is helpful to the banks, but the Bank of China estimates that 20 per cent of loans are nonperforming – bankers' language for 'paying no interest, and not likely to be recoverable'.

**Lion's roar or Achilles heel?** *Despite the imposing lion, banking is the weak link in China's fast-growing economy.*

In a bid to catch up with the West in a single generation, Mao had tried to bridge the gap in technological know-how by throwing in China's seemingly inexhaustible supplies of manpower. He died in 1976 and the Gang of Four that succeeded him was soon overthrown. Deng saw that China needed both Western technology and Western attitudes – 'Socialism with a Chinese face', as he put it. With the slogan 'To get rich is glorious', he accepted that private profit had a key part to play in improving the living standards of his people. The new approach worked well: in 1978, China ranked 37th in the league table of trading nations; by 1998 it had risen to tenth place. Overseas investment was welcomed, and it came especially from expatriate Chinese in such economic power centres as Hong Kong. Inside China, private businesses set new standards of efficiency and helped to catapult the economy into the 21st century. This was China's true Great Leap Forward. The new class of rich entrepreneurs began to expect a lifestyle like that enjoyed in the West. From Guangzhou in the south to Dalian in the north, people unaccustomed to such comforts were using credit cards to buy cosmetics, washing machines, refrigerators, colour televisions and other electronic products.

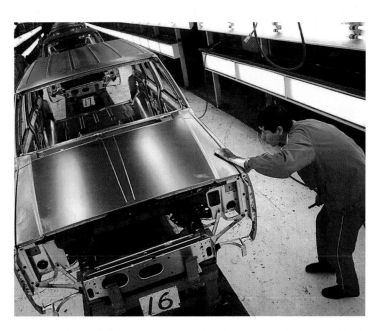

But there were cracks in the façade. Prosperity was concentrated in the cities and along the eastern coast. In a society where communism, with its doctrine of equality, was still the official dogma, poverty was dire in the countryside. Peasants deserted the fields to swell the ranks of the unemployed in the towns. Moreover, the rise of individualism and a 'get rich quick attitude' did not fit well with traditional Chinese notions about the virtues of family life and the duties owed to society.

***Chrysler goes to China*** *Checking a car on the assembly line at the Chrysler car plant in Beijing.*

### Shenzhen, laboratory of economic reform

With their skyscrapers, luxury hotels and factories turning out goods for the world, the Special Economic Zones (SEZs) are prototypes for tomorrow's China. Shenzhen was among the earliest, created in 1979 to show the rest of the country how to grow rich. Enterprise-stifling rules, red tape and high taxes do not apply in the SEZs. Shenzhen appealed to Chinese businessmen in neighbouring Hong Kong, then a British colony, because of its cheap labour force and lack of restrictions. Peasants, huddled into workshops that became sleeping quarters, were happy to earn money to send to their families. The miracle city has prospered so well that wages are much higher than in other parts of China, and the factories turning out textiles and toys are being replaced by new high-tech businesses that attract graduates from all over China.

***Focus on exports*** *Workers in a Shenzhen factory make components for Japan, Hong Kong and Taiwan (centre).*

***Scramble for work*** *Eager young computer graduates in a crush for well-paid jobs in Shenzhen.*

# China sets out to conquer space

*Three decades after launching its first satellite, China is planning to put a robot on the moon, and the ultimate objective is manned space flights.*

China was a latecomer to the space race. In April 1970, almost a year after the USA had put a man on the moon, China launched its first satellite, weighing only 381 lb (173 kg), blasting it into orbit on a rocket named *The East is Red*.

### The benefits and costs of scientific research in space

China has yet to launch a manned spacecraft, but the State Aerospace Bureau is tackling the challenge energetically. The rewards, apart from any military spin-off, are considerable. Some 40 launchings so far have yielded valuable information about various forms of radiation, from cosmic rays to solar X-rays. The opportunity to survey China's landmass from space has improved the country's geological exploration, water conservancy, meteorology and forestry projects. There have also been valuable advances in areas such as metallurgy, electronics and chemical engineering.

The mid 1990s were an unhappy time for China's space scientists. Lives were lost when a number of *Long March* rockets exploded, either on the launch pad or soon after take-off. In August, 1996, a satellite costing $120 million (£85 million) was placed in the wrong orbit and vanished into the emptiness of space. Such incidents did not halt the space programme. The faults were rectified and the space adventure continued. In 1997, China successfully launched a *Long March 3B* rocket.

**Blast off!** *China's* Long March *rocket has launched a spacecraft capable of carrying astronauts.*

***America's open door*** *President Deng Xiao-ping, whose 'Open Door' policy launched China into economic orbit, visits a NASA space centre in Texas.*

### An 'Open Door' in space

In line with its 'Open Door' policy, this once secretive nation has begun to cooperate with other countries in its space programme. In 1999, China and Brazil put an Earth observation satellite into orbit, and Beijing has expressed an interest in cooperating with India to study long-term climate changes from space.

In the 1980s, the United States proposed to Beijing the idea of welcoming a Chinese astronaut aboard an American space mission. Such cooperation depends, of course, on the state of relations between the two countries.

***Yesterday China, tomorrow the moon*** *A popular float at the 1999 parade in Beijing to celebrate the 50th anniversary of the communist victory in China.*

### Robot landing

In October 1999, China's Aerospace Bureau announced its plan to land an explorer robot on the moon to pinpoint sites for a manned mission. Two months later, China launched a spacecraft capable of carrying a human crew. *Shenzhou*, the 'Divine Vessel', was put into orbit by a *Long March 2F* rocket and circled the Earth four times, in a 21 hour flight, before landing in Inner Mongolia. The likely target date for the robot landing is 2005, but unless this date is brought forward, China could be beaten by its small but energetic neighbour. Japan has announced plans to put a robot on the moon in 2003.

# The rise and fall of Korea's mega-companies

*With the region in the grip of an economic crisis, a shadow has fallen across the family-owned businesses that created South Korea's boom years, and their tales of trouble have dominated world financial magazines.*

**Going down** *At the end of the 1990s, the once-mighty Daewoo and other leading* chaebols *were revealed to be deeply in debt.*

Anybody who has been in the market for a car, hi-fi or computer will at least have considered a Samsung, Daewoo, LG (Lucky Goldstar) or Hyundai. These are the heavyweights among South Korea's 50 or so *chaebols* – colossal family-owned business conglomerates, many of which now face a crisis.

### From small beginnings . . .

Chung Ju-yung, the founder of Hyundai, arrived from North Korea in 1947 and started a building firm in the South. In 1960 he branched into car manufacturing, and ten years later he was a force in shipbuilding. Koo Cha-kyung, who founded Lucky Goldstar, began as a manufacturer of soap, toothpaste and face cream. From this unlikely start he launched into electronics in 1970, building LG into a *chaebol* worth $385 billion. Daewoo began as a textile company, created by Kim Woo-choong 30 years ago. It ended owning sectors as varied as automobiles, construction, heavy industry, telecommunications, finance and electronics.

**Power struggle** *Kim Dae-yung, who wants to break the power of* chaebols, *with bosses of Daewoo and Samsung.*

The *chaebol* was above all a family concern, with interlocking directorates to keep control of its many enterprises. Its owners had mutually beneficial relationships with politicians and some had political ambitions of their own. In 1992 Chung Ju-yung stood, unsuccessfully, as a candidate for the presidency of South Korea. The country had made a remarkable recovery, backed by American military and financial aid, after the devastation of the Korean War. It was only when the economy took a downturn, in 1997, that the extent of the *chaebols'* debts was revealed. In 1998, with the crisis deepening, patriotic Koreans queued up to donate their gold and jewellery to the nation's depleted coffers. It was not enough: the *won*, the national currency, lost more than half its value in a year.

South Korea's president, Kim Dae-yung, set out to reduce the crisis to manageable proportions by breaking up the *chaebols*. He ordered that Samsung and LG were to concentrate on electronics, and Daewoo and Hyundai on cars. Daewoo had a mountain of debt, and when 34 of its leading executives were charged with fraud and concealing losses, its chairman and founder, Kim Woo-choong, could not be arrested as he had fled the country, leaving behind the reek of financial scandal. Kim Dae-yung sought to increase the inheritance tax on *chaebols* and to ban cross-shareholdings within families. But taming the *chaebols* was a slow process: the families refused to give up easily, and squabbles broke out over problems of succession.

**Building an image** *In South Korea there is no escaping notices that extol the virtues of the electronic giant Samsung.*

**Indoctrination time** *The workforce of a South Korean* chaebol *line up for their daily lecture on the benefits of working hard for themselves, their employer and the nation.*

# Maps, Facts and Figures

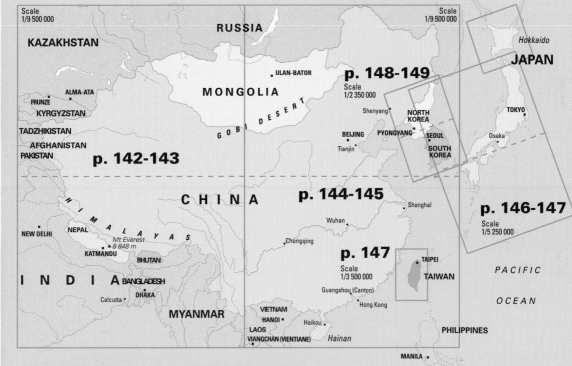

Scale 1/9 500 000

KAZAKHSTAN

RUSSIA

Scale 1/9 500 000

Hokkaido

JAPAN

ALMA-ATA

FRUNZE

KYRGYZSTAN

TADZHIKISTAN

AFGHANISTAN

PAKISTAN

ULAN-BATOR

MONGOLIA

GOBI DESERT

p. 148-149
Scale 1/2 350 000

Shenyang

NORTH KOREA

BEIJING   PYONGYANG

Tianjin

SEOUL

SOUTH KOREA

TOKYO

Osaka

p. 142-143

HIMALAYAS

NEW DELHI   NEPAL

Mt Everest 8 848 m

KATMANDU

BHUTAN

INDIA

BANGLADESH

DHAKA

Calcutta

MYANMAR

VIETNAM

HANOI

LAOS

VIANGCHAN (VIENTIANE)

CHINA

p. 144-145

Wuhan

Chongqing

p. 147
Scale 1/3 500 000

Guangshou (Canton)

Haikou

Hainan

Shanghaï

p. 146-147
Scale 1/5 250 000

TAIPEI

TAIWAN

Hong Kong

PACIFIC

OCEAN

PHILIPPINES

MANILA

## Key to maps

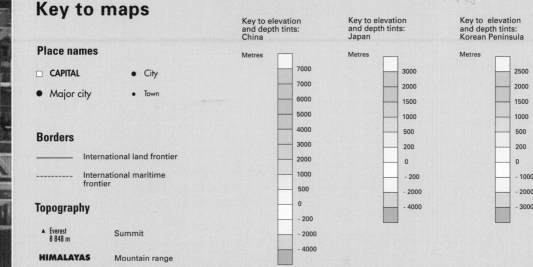

### Place names

☐ CAPITAL

● Major city

● City

• Town

### Borders

International land frontier

International maritime frontier

### Topography

▲ Everest
8 848 m

Summit

**HIMALAYAS**

Mountain range

Key to elevation
and depth tints:
China

Metres

7000
7000
6000
5000
4000
3000
2000
1000
500
0
- 200
- 2000
- 4000

Key to elevation
and depth tints:
Japan

Metres

3000
2000
1500
1000
500
200
0
- 200
- 2000
- 4000

Key to elevation
and depth tints:
Korean Peninsula

Metres

2500
2000
1500
1000
500
200
0
- 1000
- 2000
- 3000

# Western China

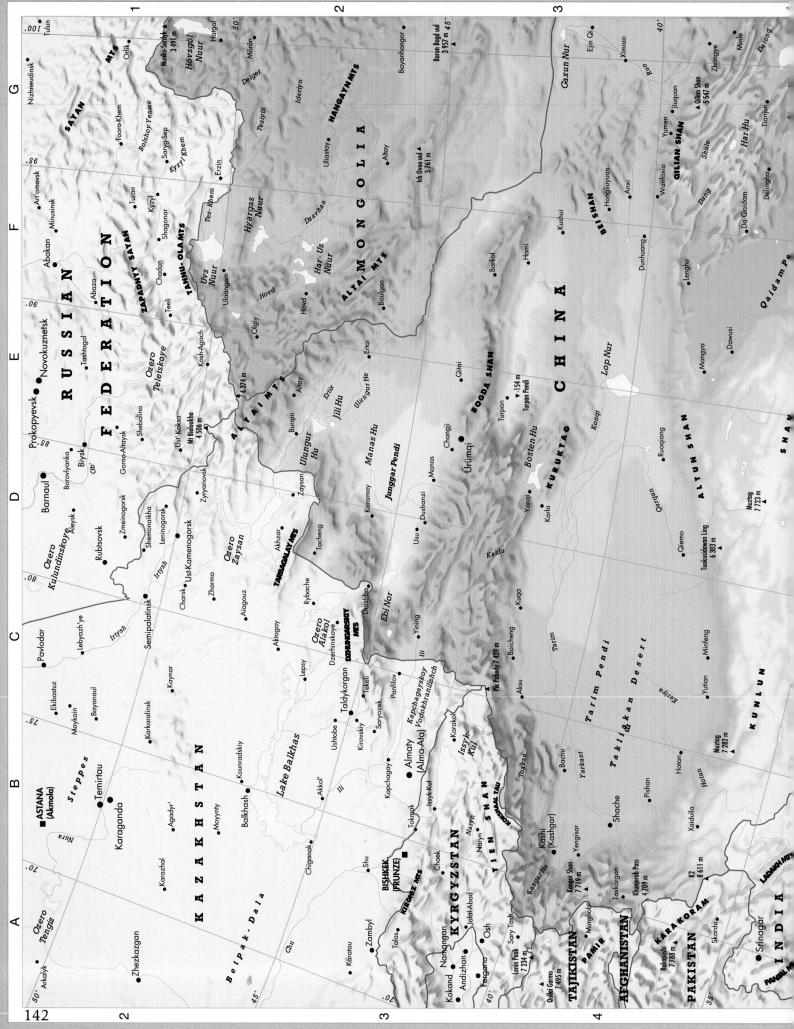

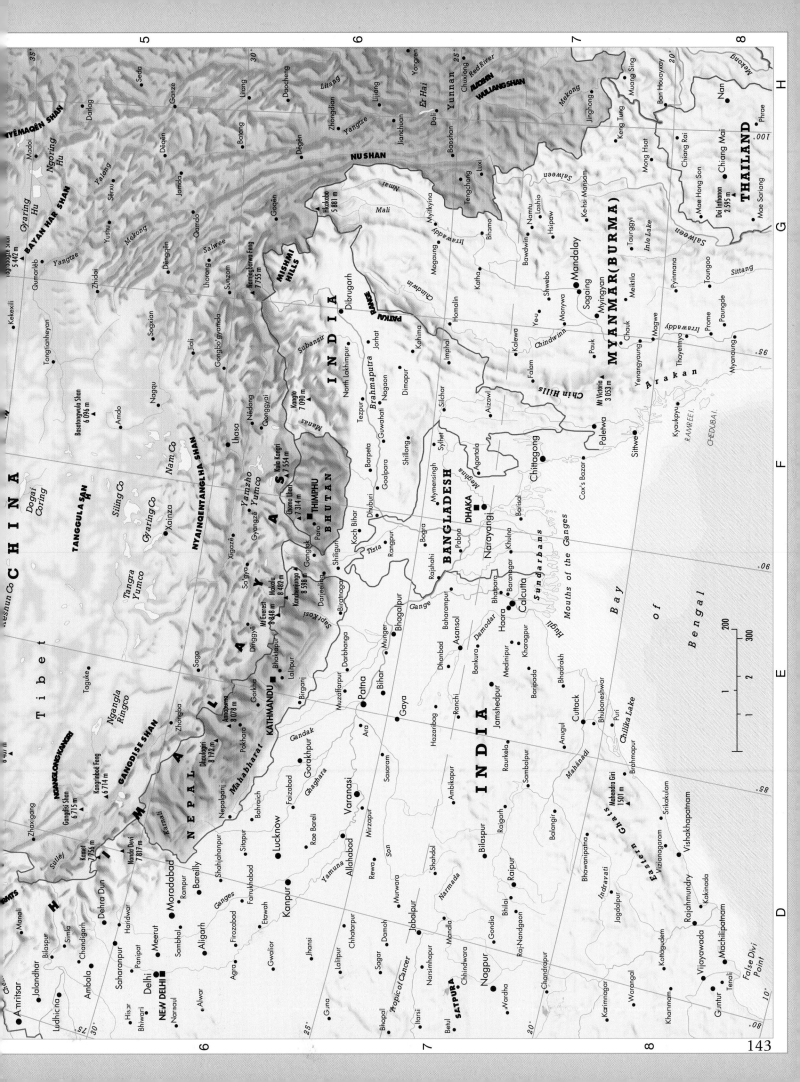

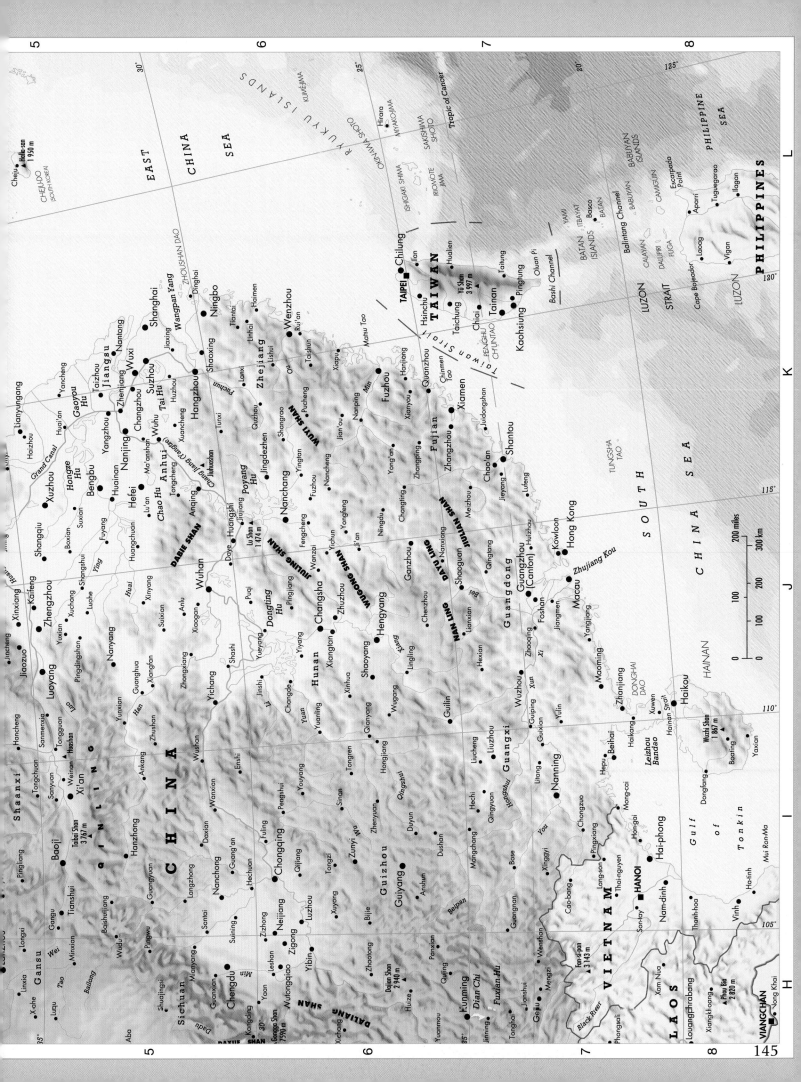

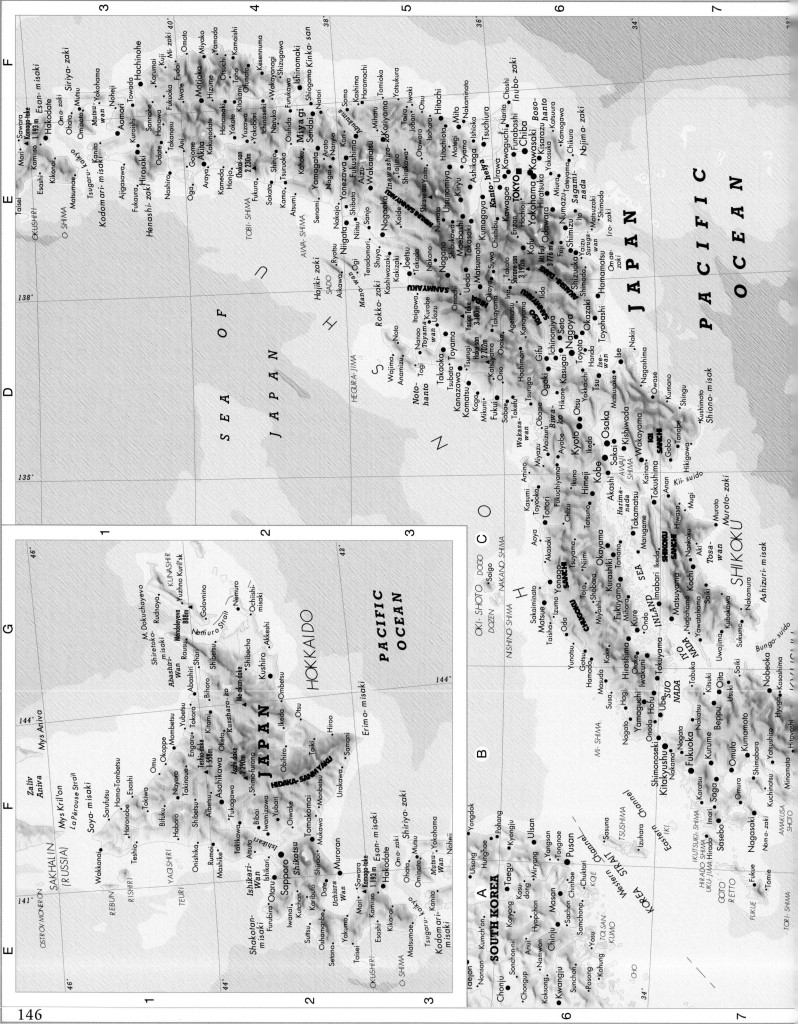

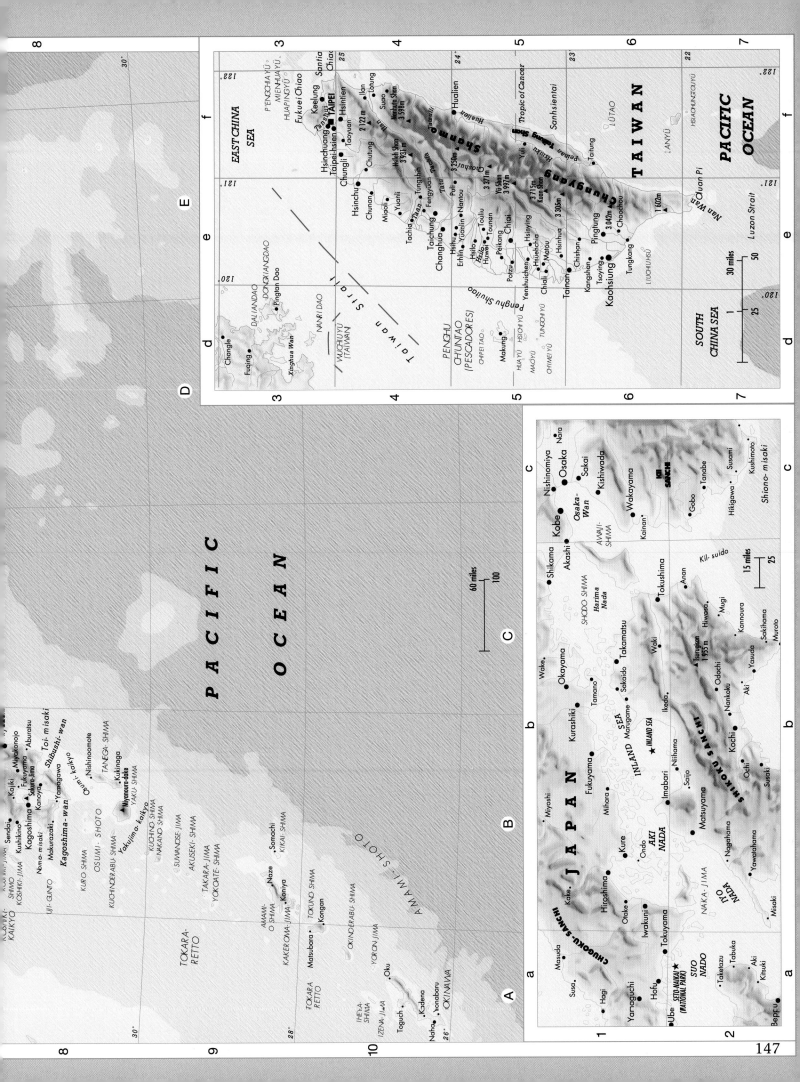

# North and South Korea

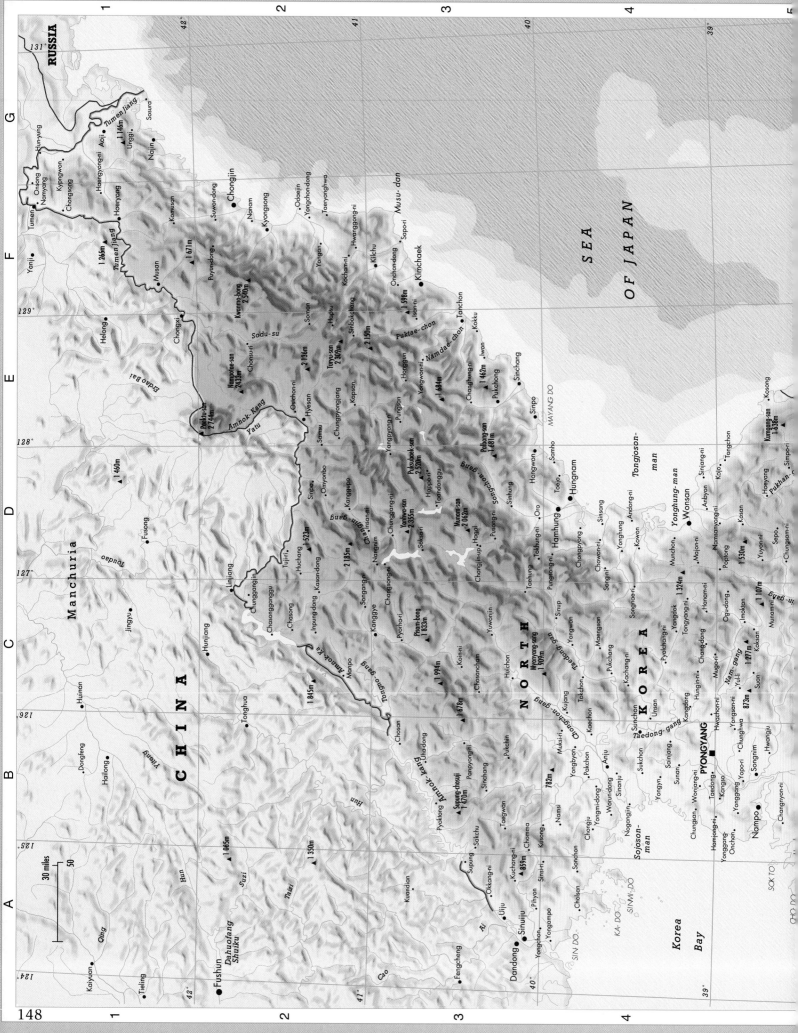

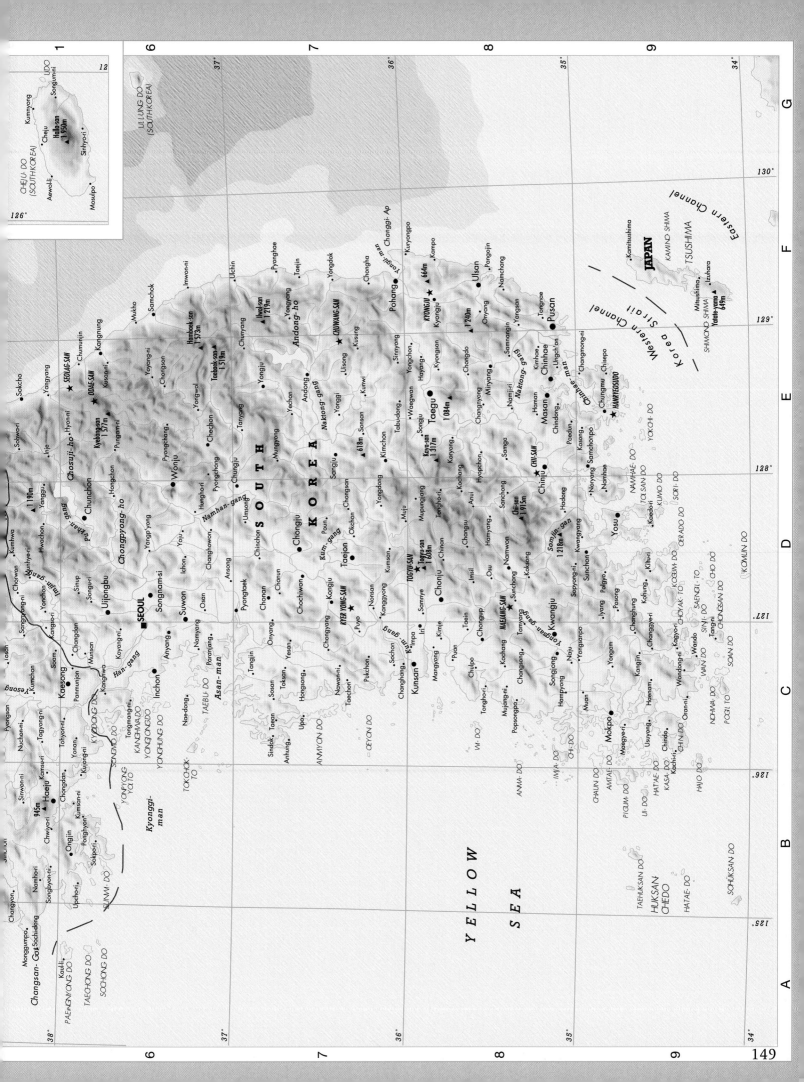

# East Asia: the statistics

*The six countries making up the region provide a rich statistical mix reflecting their varying sizes, ethnicity and political backgrounds.*

## CHINA

**Official name:** People's Republic of China
**Capital:** Beijing
**Area:** 3 704 841 sq miles (9 598 035 km²)
**Population:** 1 254 687 000
**Density:** 337 per sq mile (130 per km²)
**Ethnic composition:** Han 94%; 6% split between 55 minorities (Zhuang, Manchus, Hui, Miao, Uigurs, Kazakhs, Tibetans, Mongols)
**Religions:** Atheist or no professed religion 71.2%, traditional beliefs 20.1%, Buddhist 6%, Muslim 2.4%, Christian 0.2%, other 0.2%
**Currency:** *renmimbi* yuan
**GNP per head:** $820
**Languages:** Chinese (Mandarin and some 50 dialects, including Cantonese), Tibetan, Mongolian, Uigur
**Government:** Single party (Communist) People's Republic, with National People's Congress; the autonomous regions are self-governing in theory
**Flag:** Red with large yellow star (the Party) and four smaller stars (the social classes).

## MONGOLIA

**Official name:** Mongolia
**Capital:** Ulan Bator
**Area:** 603 748 sq miles (1 564 116 km²)
**Population:** 2 458 000
**Density:** 3.9 per sq mile (1.5 per km²)
**Ethnic composition:** Khalka Mongols 77.5%, Kazakhs 5.2%, Dorbed Mongols 2.7%, Bayads 1.9%, Bouriat Mongols 1.7%, Darigang Mongols 1.4%, others 9.6%

**Religion :** Lamaism
**Currency:** Tugrik
**GNP per head:** $390
**Languages:** Khalka Mongol (majority), Kazakh around 6%
**Government :** Multiparty republic with single-chamber legislative assembly, the Great Hural, elected every four years
**Flag:** Vertical tricolour, red-blue-red, traditional symbol in gold on first stripe.

## TAIWAN

**Official name:** Taiwan (Republic of China)
**Capital:** Taipei
**Area:** 13 796 sq miles (35 742 km²)
**Population:** 21 854 000
**Density:** 1582 per sq mile (611 per km²)
**Ethnic composition:** Taiwanese 84%, mainland Chinese 14%, aboriginal 2%
**Religions:** Chinese traditional beliefs 48.5%, Buddhist 43%, Christian 7.4%, Muslim 0.5%, others 0.6%

**Currency:** New Taiwan dollar
**GNP per head:** $12 896
**Languages:** Chinese, Taiwanese
**Government:** Multiparty republic with two chambers (the National Assembly and the Legislative Yuan) sharing legislative power
**Flag:** Red (China) with blue square (the heavens) and white sun.

## NORTH KOREA

**Official name:** Democratic People's Republic of Korea
**Capital:** Pyongyang
**Area:** 47 620 sq miles (123 370 km²)
**Population:** 23 500 000
**Density:** 492 per sq mile (190 per km²)
**Ethnic composition:** Korean 99.8%, Chinese 0.2%
**Religions:** Buddhist 90%, Christian 1%, atheist or no professed religion 9%
**Currency:** Won
**GNP per head:** $800
**Language:** Korean
**Government:** Single party republic, ruled in practice by Korean Workers' Party (Communist), politburo and general secretary
**Flag:** Red, with blue and white bands, and red star within a white circle.

NORTH KOREA

SOUTH KOREA

JAPAN

## SOUTH KOREA

**Official name:** Republic of Korea
**Capital:** Seoul
**Area:** 38 365 sq miles (99 392 km²)
**Population:** 46 400 000
**Density:** 1222 per sq mile (472 per km²)
**Ethnic composition:** Korean 99.9%, other 0.1%
**Religions:** Buddhist 27.6%, Protestant 18.6%, Catholic 5.7%, Confucian 1%, others 1.1%, no professed religion 46%
**Currency:** Won
**GNP per head:** $7970
**Language:** Korean
**Government:** Multiparty republic, with National Assembly elected every four years and president elected every five years
**Flag:** White (peace) with red and blue yin-yang symbol in centre and four black trigrams (heaven, earth, fire, water).

CHINA

MONGOLIA

## JAPAN

**Official name:** Japan (Nippon or Nihon Koku – Land of the Rising Sun)
**Capital:** Tokyo
**Area:** 145 908 sq miles (378 000 km²)
**Population:** 126 000 000
**Density:** 867 per sq mile (335 per km²)
**Ethnic composition:** Japanese 98.9%, Korean 0.56%, Chinese 0.2%, Ainu 0.049%, others 0.3%
**Religions:** Shintoist and derived religions 51.3%, Buddhist 38.3%, Christian 1.2%, other 9.2%
**Currency:** Yen
**GNP per head:** $32 380
**Language:** Japanese (more than 99.8%)
**Government:** Constitutional monarchy with a two-chamber Diet (House of Representatives which chooses the prime minister and passes budgets, and House of Councillors)
**Flag:** Red circle on white background; called Hi-no-Maru (roundness of the Sun).

TAIWAN

# Climate, relief and vegetation

*East Asia (China, Korea, Mongolia, Taiwan and the islands of Japan) covers less than one-tenth of Earth's surface but has roughly a quarter of its people. With its towering mountains, far horizons, vast deserts and ancient civilisations, the region has long fascinated travellers from the West.*

## The extremes of climate

Stretching from the tropics to the frozen north, East Asia contains some of the world's highest mountains, and its central regions lie 1874 miles (3000 km) from the moderating influence of the sea. For these reasons, it has greater extremes of climate than any similar-sized region on Earth – from tropical to near-polar, from continental to oceanic. Its great deserts, the Taklimakan and the Gobi, lie parched behind high mountain ranges that form an effective barrier to moisture-laden winds from the south. By contrast, between the Indian Ocean and the Pacific lie some of the wettest places in the world – the monsoon lands. The monsoon phenomenon is caused by a seasonal reversal of wind direction. In winter, a mass of cold, dry winds blow out from the central plateaus. In summer, warm winds from the oceans, heavy with moisture, bring torrents of rain to the lands in their path. Japan and the two Koreas are on the fringes of the area affected by monsoons, so their rainfall is more evenly distributed between summer and winter. Nevertheless, the south of Japan can have as much as 118 in (3000 mm) of rain a year.

### WHERE THE SUN SHINES
*(in hours per year)*

|  | Total |
| --- | --- |
| Ulan Bator | 2759 |
| Beijing | 2704 |
| Pyongyang | 2673 |
| Seoul | 2373 |
| Lhassa | 2222 |
| Osaka | 2153 |
| Hong Kong | 1982 |
| Shanghai | 1834 |
| Taipei | 1647 |

### ANNUAL RAINFALL *(in inches/mm)*

|  | Total | Wettest month | Driest month |
| --- | --- | --- | --- |
| Hong Kong | 87.3/2217 | 18.9/480 (June) | 0.6/17 (Dec.) |
| Taipei | 82.3/2090 | 12.6/320 (June) | 2.8/70 (Nov.) |
| Tokyo | 61.1/1550 | 8.6/220 (Oct.) | 2.0/50 (Jan.) |
| Osaka | 52.6/1335 | 7.7/195 (June) | 1.8/45 (Jan.) |
| Seoul | 49.5/1257 | 14.2/360 (July) | 0.6/17 (Jan.) |
| Shanghai | 47.2/1200 | 7.7/195 (Sept.) | 1.6/40 (Feb.) |
| Pyongyang | 36.0/916 | 9.3/235 (July) | 0.4/11 (Feb.) |
| Beijing | 24.3/618 | 9.5/240 (July) | 0.1/3 (Dec.) |
| Lhassa | 15.9/405 | 4.7/120 (July) | 0.0/0 (Dec.) |
| Ulan Bator | 8.4/214 | 2.4/60 (July) | 0.03/1 (Jan.) |

**CLIMATIC REGIONS ▼**

**Climate**
- tundra
- subarctic
- continental
- warm and humid
- semi arid
- arid
- tropical

### AVERAGE TEMPERATURES

|  | January | July |
| --- | --- | --- |
| Ulan Bator | -26°C/-14°F | 23°C/73°F |
| Pyongyang | -13°C/9°F | 29°C/84°F |
| Beijing | -11°C/12°F | 21°C/70°F |
| Lhassa | -10°C/14°F | 23°C/73°F |
| Seoul | -9°C/16°F | 29°C/84°F |
| Tokyo | -2°C/28°F | 28°C/82°F |
| Osaka | 0°C/0°F | 31°C/88°F |
| Shanghai | 1°C/34°F | 32°C/90°F |
| Taipei | 12°C/54°F | 32°C/90°F |
| Hong Kong | 13°C/55°F | 31°C/88°F |

## China, the thirsty land

Every year, China needs more than 5 billion tons of water over and above the resources currently available – a shortfall that makes itself most urgently felt in the parched regions of the north. In an effort to remedy the problem, the government has attempted to alter the course of the Yellow River (Huang He), traditionally known as 'China's Sorrow' because of its frequent and disastrous flooding. But this has not been enough. Today, with China embarking on a massive programme of industrialisation, the need for water is more desperate than ever. The state has begun constructing the colossal Three Gorges Dam to harness the turbulent waters of the Chang Jiang (Yangtze-kiang). The dam will also provide much-needed hydroelectric power. But it has aroused controversy because of the impact it will have on the environment and on the million or so people who will be displaced from their homes.

*Growing without soil*
*Hydroponic methods are now used in China to grow vegetables without soil. These tomatoes take up their nutrients in water.*

| THE HIGHEST MOUNTAINS (altitude in ft/m) | |
|---|---|
| Everest (Nepal-China-Tibet) | 29 028/8848 |
| K2 (India-China) | 28 250/8611 |
| Lhotse (Nepal-China) | 27 890/8501 |
| Cho-Oyu (Nepal-China) | 26 906/8201 |
| Xixabangma or Gosainthan (Tibet) | 26 289/8013 |
| Kungur (China) | 25 324/7719 |
| Minga Konba (China) | 24 901/7590 |
| Pik Pobedy (China) | 24 406/7439 |
| Mono Tagh Ata (China) | 24 386/7433 |
| Gauro Shanker (Nepal-China) | 23 405/7134 |
| Fujiyama (Japan) | 12 388/3776 |

▲ PHYSICAL FEATURES OF EAST ASIA

## Mountains, plains and rivers

The Himalayas, the Karakorum and other great mountain ranges that form the western boundary of the Far East were formed some 30 million years ago, when the Indo-Australian Plate ploughed into the Eurasian Plate, setting in motion a colossal buckling and folding of the terrain in between. From the corrugated mountains of the Pamirs in central Asia, four main mountain ranges run eastwards: the Himalayas, Kunlun Shan, Altun Shan and Tien Shan. The Himalayas – the 'Home of Snows' in Nepali – are the southernmost. They sweep across southern Asia for 1500 miles (2400 km) and contain, in Mount Everest (29 028 ft/8848 m), the world's highest mountain. Their northern slopes over-look the Tibetan Plateau which rises to 13 000 ft (4000 m). Completing the isolation of Tibet on the far side of the plateau is the Kunlun Shan, followed by the lower, but still formidable, Altun Shan. The Kunlun Shan stretch from the Karakorum, home of K2, the second highest mountain in the world (28 250 ft/ 8611 m), into China.

Beyond the Altun Shan lies the Tarim Basin, a low-lying area in which the rivers run into the sands and silences of the Taklimakan Desert. The Tien Shan range extends across China's Xinjiang region, and still farther north lie the Altai Mountains, stretching for more than 1000 miles (1600 km) towards the Gobi Desert. East of the mountains lie the great plains of Mongolia and of China. Korea, South China, Taiwan and the islands of Japan are also mountainous. Japan, which lies on a fault zone in the Earth's crust, has more than 50 active volcanoes and is prone to earth-quakes and tsunamis – popularly known as tidal waves, but in fact caused by undersea earthquakes.

## Natural vegetation that vanished

The natural vegetation of the region has long been replaced by crops in the most heavily populated areas. In their natural state, the southern and eastern parts of the region were covered by grasslands and subtropical forests. The rivers that wind across the plains can bring devastating floods in summer, when the waters of the monsoon are added to those brought down by melting snows from the peaks. As compensation, the soil carried by these rivers puts their deltas among the most fertile and most heavily populated regions in Asia.

| FOREST COVERAGE (percentage of land area) | |
|---|---|
| South Korea | 77.2 |
| Japan | 66.8 |
| North Korea | 51.2 |
| China | 14.3 |

| RIVERS (length in miles/km) | |
|---|---|
| Chang Jiang | 3716/5980 |
| Huang He | 3011/4845 |
| Amour | 2900/4667 |
| Ienisseï | 2566/4129 |
| Brahmaputra | 1802/2900 |
| Salouen | 1740/2800 |
| Indus | 1700/2736 |
| Tarim | 1354/2179 |

| LAKES (area in sq miles/km²) | |
|---|---|
| Poyang Hu (China) | 1930/5000 |
| Kokou Nor (China) | 1852/4800 |
| Kossogoe (Mongolia) | 1011/2620 |
| Nam Tso (Tibet) | 755/1956 |
| Tengri Nor (China) | 656/1700 |

*Fantasy landscape* The 'sugar loaf' hills of Guilin, China – fantastic shapes formed by erosion.

# Population, economy and society

More than 1.5 billion people live in East Asia, and the vast majority of them are Chinese. There are enormous disparities between wealthy countries such as Japan, Taiwan and South Korea, and the poorer ones – North Korea and Mongolia. China, a land in transition, has its own contrasts between a prosperous coast and an underdeveloped interior.

## POPULATION DENSITY ▼

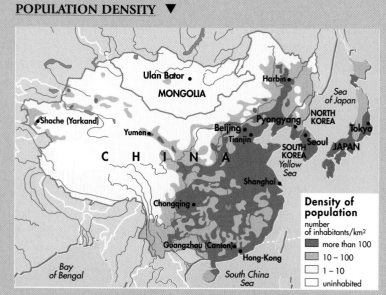

**Density of population**
number of inhabitants/km²

- more than 100
- 10 – 100
- 1 – 10
- uninhabited

### INFANT MORTALITY
*(as percentage)*

| | |
|---|---|
| North Korea | 56 |
| Mongolia | 53 |
| South Korea | 10 |
| Taiwan | 6.3 |
| Japan | 3.8 |
| China | 3.1 |

## THE AGE PYRAMID ▼

**CHINA**

40 %
30 %
20 %
10 %

under 15 · 15 to 29 · 30 to 44 · 45 to 59 · 60 to 74 · over 75

**MONGOLIA**

40 %
30 %
20 %
10 %

under 15 · 15 to 29 · 30 to 44 · 45 to 59 · 60 to 74 · over 75

### LIFE EXPECTANCY

| | Men | Women |
|---|---|---|
| Japan | 77 | 83 |
| Taiwan | 72 | 78 |
| South Korea | 70 | 78 |
| China | 67 | 70 |
| North Korea | 60 | 64 |
| Mongolia | 62 | 65 |

## HEALTH ▼ SERVICES

| DOCTORS | | HOSPITAL BEDS |
|---|---|---|
| *(per 1000 inhabitants)* | | |
| 1.57 | | 2.48 |
| | China | |
| 2.70 | | 11.95 |
| | North Korea | |
| 1.22 | | 3.54 |
| | South Korea | |
| 1.80 | | 13.30 |
| | Japan | |
| 2.70 | | 10.47 |
| | Mongolia | |
| 1.12 | | 4.62 |
| | Taiwan | |

## The sorrows of Tibet

China has regarded Tibet as part of the motherland at least since the early 18th century, when the Manchu Emperor Kang Xi established a protectorate over the country. The Tibetans, though, have resisted the Chinese embrace. In 1950, Mao Ze-dong's Red Army invaded what he regarded as a hopelessly feudal land. The Tibetans, fiercely loyal to Buddhism and to their priest-king, the Dalai Lama, broke out in revolt in 1959. The rebellion was crushed, but the Dalai Lama escaped to exile in India. Tibet, which became an autonomous region of China in 1965, suffered severely during the Cultural Revolution: one estimate is that 1.2 million Tibetans have died as a result of China's invasion. Repression still goes on, though it is less open, and some monasteries have been restored. Tibetan exiles and high-profile sympathisers abroad have turned the spotlight of world opinion onto the sufferings of this ancient land.

### TOTAL POPULATION

| | |
|---|---|
| China | 1 254 687 000 |
| Japan | 126 000 000 |
| South Korea | 46 400 000 |
| North Korea | 23 500 000 |
| Taiwan | 21 854 000 |
| Mongolia | 2 458 000 |

## Transport in China

Considering the vastness of the country, China is a long way from having an adequate communications network. For centuries, its great rivers were the best way of travelling from the coast to the interior. More recently, railways were the predominant form of transport over long distances – a situation that lasted until the 1970s. Even today, the total length of railtrack in China is only 34 000 miles (54 600 km) – a quarter of that in the USA, a country of comparable size. Moreover, only 6300 miles (10 000 km) of China's railtrack is electrified. In 1995, roads took 15 per cent of the country's freight traffic, compared with 40 per cent for the railways. The best roads are those in the coastal regions. Roads in the interior are generally narrow, and only 15 per cent of them are metalled. Air travel in China got under way only with the sixth five-year plan of 1986-90. While the USA has more than 800 airports, China has only 108. For all its slowness, the traditional method of water transport, by river or along the coast, accounted in the mid 1990s for 45 per cent of China's freight traffic. The government has invested heavily in improving the country's transport infrastructure.

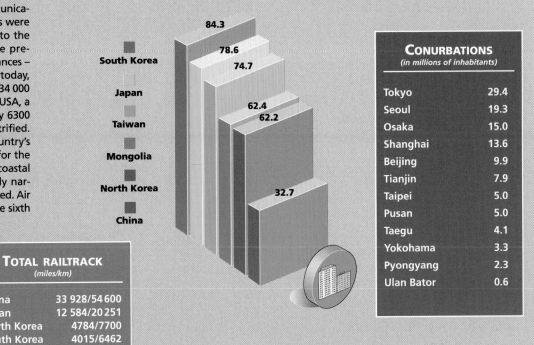

## URBANISATION ▼
*(as a percentage of the total population)*

- South Korea — 84.3
- Japan — 78.6
- Taiwan — 74.7
- Mongolia — 62.4
- North Korea — 62.2
- China — 32.7

### CONURBATIONS
*(in millions of inhabitants)*

| | |
|---|---|
| Tokyo | 29.4 |
| Seoul | 19.3 |
| Osaka | 15.0 |
| Shanghai | 13.6 |
| Beijing | 9.9 |
| Tianjin | 7.9 |
| Taipei | 5.0 |
| Pusan | 5.0 |
| Taegu | 4.1 |
| Yokohama | 3.3 |
| Pyongyang | 2.3 |
| Ulan Bator | 0.6 |

### TOTAL RAILTRACK
*(miles/km)*

| | |
|---|---|
| China | 33 928/54 600 |
| Japan | 12 584/20 251 |
| North Korea | 4784/7700 |
| South Korea | 4015/6462 |
| Taiwan | 1722/2771 |

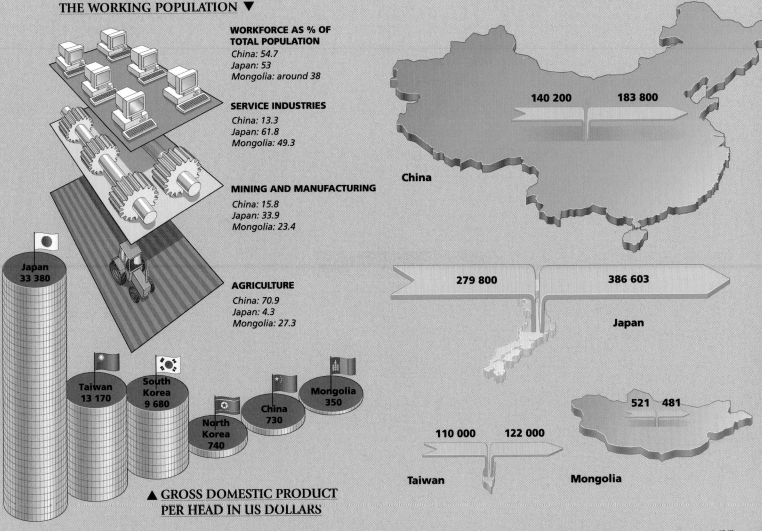

## DISTRIBUTION OF THE WORKING POPULATION ▼

**WORKFORCE AS % OF TOTAL POPULATION**
China: 54.7
Japan: 53
Mongolia: around 38

**SERVICE INDUSTRIES**
China: 13.3
Japan: 61.8
Mongolia: 49.3

**MINING AND MANUFACTURING**
China: 15.8
Japan: 33.9
Mongolia: 23.4

**AGRICULTURE**
China: 70.9
Japan: 4.3
Mongolia: 27.3

Japan 33 380
Taiwan 13 170
South Korea 9 680
North Korea 740
China 730
Mongolia 350

## ▲ GROSS DOMESTIC PRODUCT PER HEAD IN US DOLLARS

## IMPORTS AND EXPORTS ▼
*(in millions of US dollars)*

China — 140 200 / 183 800

Japan — 279 800 / 386 603

Taiwan — 110 000 / 122 000

Mongolia — 521 / 481

# Index

Page numbers in *italics* denote illustrations. The letter and number references in brackets are the co-ordinates for places in the map section, pp. 140-9.

# Acknowledgments

Abbreviations: t = top, m = middle, b = bottom, l = left, r = right.

FRONT COVER: *The mountains of Huangshan in the mist*: IMAGE BANK/Zhi Wu Bian.
BACK COVER: *Geisha girls in Kyoto*: RAPHO/Network/G. Mendel.

Pages: 4/5: BIOS/Oxford Scientific Films/Keren Su; 6/7: COSMOS/SPL/T. Van Sant; 8t: BIOS/Seitre; 8b: DIAF/ Valdin; 9t: COSMOS/P. Lau; 9b: HOA QUI/Donnet; 10: DIAF/M. Vérin; 11t: BIOS/F. Suchel; 11b: COSMOS/F. Perri; 12t: BIOS/S. Kaufman-P. Arnold; 12b: COSMOS/P. Lau; 13: COSMOS/B. & C. Alexander; 14m: G. DAGLI ORTI/Musée Cernuschi, Paris; 14bl: RMN/R. Lambert/Musée Guimet, Paris; 14bm: RMN/Musée Guimet, Paris; 14/15: HOA QUI/M. Troncy; 15t: RMN/P. Pleynet/Musée Guimet, Paris; 15: RMN/Th. Ollivier/Musée Guimet, Paris; 16l: RMN/R. Lambert/Musée Guimet, Paris; 16m: ASK IMAGES/G. Bras; 16/17: HOA QUI/J. Jaffre; 17bl: EXPLORER/Y. Layma; 17mr: DIAF/M. Vérin; 17br: RAPHO/Belzeaux - Horse found at Wou Wei, late Han epoch; 18t: Éditions P.A.F., Paris, 1986 - The Three Kingdoms; 18bl: RMN/R. Lambert/Musée Guimet, Paris; 18br: DIAF/B. Degroise; 19tl: AKG Photo/Musée Guimet, Paris - *The wandering monk*, painting by Dunhuang, 9th century; 19tr: RMN/P. Pleynet/Musée Guimet, Paris; 19bl: RMN/Ravaux/Musée Guimet, Paris; 19br: DIAF/B. Simmons; 20tl: RMN/Musée Guimet, Paris; 20tr: HOA QUI/S. Grandadam; 20bl: DIAF/M. Vérin; 20bm: HOA QUI/J. Hagenmuller; 21tr: AKG Photo/B.N.F., Paris - *Djamil el Tawarik* by Rachid al Din, 14th century; 21bl: G. DAGLI ORTI/Museo Correr, Venice; 21br: G. DAGLI ORTI/Private collection - *Roll of the attack of the Mongols* attributed to Tosa Nagataka, 13th century; 22t: RAPHO/G. Sioen; 22bl: AKG Photo - *Genpei Hokuetsu daigassen* by Utagawa Kuniyoshi, 19th century; 22br: AKG Photo/W. Forman/Coll. Kozu, Kyoto - Costume of samurai, 16th-17th century; 23m: RAPHO/R. and S. Michaud - Father Adam Schall in mandarin costume, engraving from 17th century; 23tr: RMN/Arnaudet/Musée Guimet, Paris - Folding screen, 16th century; 23bl: RMN/P. Pleynet/Musée Guimet, Paris; 23bm, br: RMN/R. Lambert/Musée Guimet, Paris; 24t: RMN/Musée Guimet, Paris; 24ml: G. DAGLI ORTI/Maritime Museum, Rotterdam; 24mm: HOA QUI/P. Wang; 24b: AKG Photo/photo (coloured) by Burton Holmes; 25t: G. DAGLI ORTI/Illustration by A. Beltrame for *la Domenica del Corriere*, 1900; 25bl: CORBIS-SYGMA/*L'Illustration*; 25br: CHARMET, magazine *la Chine*, 1971; 26tl: COLLECTION VIOLLET; 26m: AKG Photo; 26b: KEYSTONE/Ch. Rosecrans; 27t: AKG Photo; 27m: CORBIS-SYGMA/Keystone; 27bl: RAPHO/P. Koch; 27br: CORBIS-SYGMA; 28/29: COSMOS/M. Henley; 30/31: HOA QUI/Bourseiller-Durieux; 32m: EXPLORER/Y. Layma; 32b: BIOS/F. Suchel; 33t: COSMOS/Aspect/Tsune Okuda; 33m: COSMOS/Aurora/P. Essick; 33b: HOA QUI/Bourseiller-Durieux; 34t: HOA QUI/M. Troncy; 34m: GAMMA/ Photographers International; 34b: DIAF/Valdin; 35t: EXPLORER/P. Le Floch; 35m: PHONE/J.-P. Ferrero; 35b: RAPHO/R. and S. Michaud; 36: RAPHO/M. Yamashita; 37t: GAMMA/Chine nouvelle/G. Xinhua; 37tr: CORBIS-SYGMA/J. Van Hasselt; 37bl: COSMOS/Aspect/P. Carmichael; 37br: EXPLORER/Y. Layma; 38t: HOA QUI/*Le Monde*; 38m: AFP/M. Ralston; 38b: EXPLORER/L. Girard; 39t: COSMOS/Aspect/G. Hellier; 39b: EXPLORER/J.-P. Nacivet; 40t: CORBIS-SYGMA/Hashimoto; 40m: CORBIS-SYGMA/*L'Illustration*; 40b: CORBIS-SYGMA/New China Picture Company; 41: CORBIS-SYGMA/Bunyo Ishikawa; 42l: BIOS/Ch. Meyer; 42/43: BIOS/Okapia/H. Reinhard; 43l: EXPLORER/L. Girard; 43r: PHONE/R. Valter; 44/45: DIAF/B. Simmons; 46m: EXPLORER/Y. Layma; 46bl: COSMOS/M. Henley; 46br: HOA QUI/Icône/C. Henriette; 47t: EXPLORER/P. Lissac; 47bl, br, 48l, mr: EXPLORER/Y. Layma; 48br: EXPLORER/L. Girard; 49t: ROGER-VIOLLET; 49b: DIAF/N. Wheeler; 50t: COSMOS/F. Perri; 50m: COSMOS/P. Lau; 50b: EXPLORER/Y. Layma; 51t: AFP/Tsuno; 51m, bl: DIAF/B. Simmons; 51br: DIAF/J.-D. Sudres; 52t: RAPHO/R. and S. Michaud; 52bl: RAPHO/M. Yamashita; 52br: RAPHO/M. Setboun; 53t: RAPHO/G. Sioen; 53m: RAPHO/H. Donnezan; 53b: RAPHO/M. Setboun; 54t: HOA QUI/Donnet; 54m: CORBIS-SYGMA/P. Perrin; 54b: CORBIS-SYGMA/M. Setboun; 55t: CORBIS-SYGMA/Next; 55bl, bm: EXPLORER/Y. Layma; 55br: AFP/Xinhua; 56t: DIAF/J.-D. Sudres; 56bl: DIAF/Eurasia Press; 56/57b: DIAF/B. Simmons; 57t: COSMOS/M. Henley; 57b: DIAF/B. Simmons; 58t: COSMOS/P. Chesley; 58bl: COSMOS/Visum/M. Wolf; 58/59br: CORBIS-SYGMA/P. Landmann; 59tl: COSMOS/Visum/Kaj. Sawabe; 59tr: COSMOS/Aspen/J. Aaronson; 59b: CORBIS-SYGMA/S. Isett; 60/61: DIAF/B. Simmons; 62t: CORBIS-SYGMA/Giansanti; 62m: EXPLORER/Y. Layma; 62b: RAPHO/M. Setboun; 63t, tm: EXPLORER/Y. Layma; 63bl: RAPHO/M.Yamashita; 63br: RAPHO/J.-M. Charles; 64t: COSMOS/Aurora/R. Kendrick; 64mr:

EXPLORER/Globe Press/A. Evrard; 64r: RAPHO/H. Silvester; 64b: EXPLORER/C. Boisvieux; 65t: CORBIS-SYGMA; 65m: CORBIS-SYGMA/N. Hashimoto; 65b: DIAF/Eurasia Press; 66l, r: G. DAGLI ORTI; 67t: HOA QUI/M. Troncy; 67m: HOA QUI/G. Bosio; 67b: RAPHO/F. Le Diascorn; 68tl: CORBIS-SYGMA/ *L'Humanité*/Keystone; 68tr: EXPLORER/Y. Layma; 68m: GAMMA/ Chine nouvelle/G. Xinhua; 68b: COSMOS/C. Wolinsky; 69t: CORBIS-SYGMA/J. Zeng-Huang; 69m: CORBIS-SYGMA/Xin-Hua; 69b: CORBIS-SYGMA/China Features/Zha Chuming; 70t: CORBIS-SYGMA/Keystone; 70bl: CORBIS-SYGMA/L. Stone; 70br: CORBIS-SYGMA/S. Savolainen; 71t: RMN/Th. Ollivier; 71m: HOA QUI/J.-L. Dugast; 71b: RAPHO/R. Scaglia; 72t: DIAF/J. Hervy and N. Tortello; 72m: EXPLORER/Y. Layma; 72b: CORBIS-SYGMA/M. Setboun; 73t: AFP/Wong Sang; 73b: CORBIS-SYGMA/B. Brecelj; 74t: COSMOS/Visum/M. Wolf; 74bl: COSMOS/Visum/M. Wolf; 74bm, br: CORBIS-SYGMA/B. Annebique; 75t: AFP/Jiji Press; 75bl: AFP/Y. Tsuno; 75bm: COSMOS/Impact Visuals/R. Renaldi; 76t: HOA QUI/P. Wang; 76m: HOA QUI/Icône/C. Henriette; 76bl: CORBIS-SYGMA/J. Langevin; 76br: EXPLORER/Y. Layma; 77t: CORBIS-SYGMA/B. Annebique; 77m: RAPHO/R. de Seynes; 77b: DIAF/B. Simmons; 78t: HOA QUI/Donnet; 78m: COSMOS/JB Pictures/P. Charlesworth; 78bl, br: CORBIS-SYGMA/M. Setboun; 79: EXPLORER/Y. Layma; 80t: COSMOS/P. Lau; 80m: DIAF/M. Vérin; 80bm: DIAF/B. Degroise; 80br: COSMOS/Visum/R. Nobel; 81t: RAPHO/M. Yamashita; 81mr: HOA QUI/J. Paoli; 81b: HOA QUI/Icône/C. Henriette; 82t: HOA QUI/E. Valentin; 82m: CORBIS-SYGMA/P. Toutain-Dorbec; 82bl: CORBIS-SYGMA/ Matsumoto; 82br: DIAF/B. Simmons; 83t: HOA QUI/P. Wang; 83m: EXPLORER/Y. Layma; 83b: EXPLORER/C. Boisvieux; 84m: CORBIS-SYGMA/B. Annebique; 84bl: COSMOS/M. Pagnotta; 84br: COSMOS/M. Henley; 85t: ©TEZUKA PRODUCTIONS - *Atomu* by Tetsuka Osamu (volume 15); 85bl: ©SHUEISHA inc. - *Luro Nin* by Nobuhiro Watsuhi; 85br: COSMOS/M. Pagnotta; 86t: COSMOS/F. Perri; 86m: RAPHO/Network/Ch. Pillitz; 86b: CORBIS-SYGMA/B. Annebique; 87t: GAMMA/B. Alistair; 87m: EXPLORER/Y. Layma; 87mr: CORBIS-SYGMA/D. Giry; 87b: CORBIS-SYGMA/J. Van Hasselt; 88bl: CORBIS-SYGMA; 88bm: CORBIS-SYGMA/20th Century Fox - Ch. Slater, J. Travolta and J. Woo during the filming of *Broken Arrow*; 88br: KIPA - *Operation Dragon*, 1973, produced by R. Clouse, with Bruce Lee; 89: CORBIS-SYGMA/B. Bisson; 90t: ASK IMAGES/Trip/T. Bognar; 90b: COSMOS/F. Perri; 91t: DIAF/M. Vérin; 91bl: ASK IMAGES/L. Sechi; 91br: COSMOS/Aspect/M. Yamashita; 92m: DIAF/J. Hervy and N. Tortello; 92b: COSMOS/Leong Ka Tai; 93t: EXPLORER/F. Huguier; 93bl: RAPHO/M. Setboun; 93br: AEDTA, Paris - child's kimono, Japan 19th century; 94/95: DIAF/B. Simmons; 96t: DIAF/Eurasia Press; 96ml: ASK IMAGES/N. Kealey; 96bl: CORBIS-SYGMA/B. Annebique; 96/97b: COSMOS/Visum/Kaj. Sawabe; 97m, b: DIAF/B. Simmons; 98/99: Chinese Embassy, Paris; 98ml: EXPLORER/G. Boutin; 98mr: HOA QUI/M. Troncy; 98bl: HOA QUI/V. Durruty; 98br: DIAF/W. Bibikow; 99t: EXPLORER/Y. Layma; 99m: HOA QUI/M. Troncy; 99bl: DIAF/J.-P. Garcin; 99br: DIAF/Eurasia Press; 100tl: DIAF/J. Sierpinski; 100tr: DIAF/J.-P. Garcin; 100bl: RAPHO/H. Segalen; 100br, 101tl: DIAF/J.-P. Garcin; 101tr: RAPHO/H. Segalen; 101bl: EXPLORER/Y. Layma; 101br: EXPLORER/Y. Layma; 102tl: HOA QUI/N. Thibaut; 102tr: DIAF/J.-P. Garcin; 102m: ANA/Jobin; 102bl: HOA QUI/M. Pell; 102br: DIAF/J.-P. Garcin; 103tm: ANA/J. du Sordet; 103tr: HOA QUI/W. Buss; 103m: DIAF/J. Sierpinski; 103b: RAPHO/R. and S. Michaud; 104t: COSMOS/Dannenberg; 104bl: CORBIS-SYGMA/Nasm; 104br: COSMOS/P. Boulat; 105bl: CORBIS-SYGMA/J. Langevin; 105br: CORBIS-SYGMA/M. Setboun; 106ml: DIAF/A. Even; 106mr: EXPLORER/C. Boisvieux; 106b: RAPHO/Network/G. Mendel; 107t: EXPLORER/Ch. Lénars; 107ml: DIAF/J.-D. Sudres; 107mr: RAPHO/G. Sioen; 107b: EXPLORER/J. Armaya; 108t: RAPHO/E. Barbaras; 108m: EXPLORER/Y. Layma; 108/109b: RAPHO/B. Wassman; 109t, b: EXPLORER/Y. Layma; 110ml: RAPHO/G. Sioen; 110mr: RAPHO/H. Berbar; 110b: ASK IMAGES/S. Fautré; 111t: CORBIS-SYGMA/M. Setboun; 111bl: RAPHO/H. Donnezan; 111br: DIAF/Ch. Bowman; 112t: EXPLORER/A. Evrard; 112bl: HOA QUI/Globe Press; 112br: CORBIS-SYGMA/G. Giansanti; 113t: ASK IMAGES/Trip/J. Sweeney; 113m: CORBIS-SYGMA/M. Abraityte; 113b: RAPHO/R. Scaglia; 114/115t: DIAF/B. Simmons; 116bl: HOA QUI/J.-L. Manaud; 116/117: EXPLORER/K. Straiton; 116ml: EXPLORER/P. Van Riel; 117mr: COSMOS/S. Sibert; 117b: EXPLORER/Y. Layma; 117t: DIAF/M. Vérin; 118t, m: DIAF/B. Simmons; 118b: HOA QUI/W. Buss; 119m, b: DIAF/B. Simmons; 120t: RMN/M. Urtado/Musée Guimet, Paris; 120m: COSMOS/P. Colombel - Frescoes from the funerary city of Chienlang; 120bl: HOA QUI/P. Wang; 120/121: RMN/Th. Ollivier/Musée Guimet,

Paris - Folding screen from the Edo epoch; 121m: G. DAGLI ORTI/Private collection - From the scroll *Hell*, late 12th century; 121bl: RMN/Arnaudet/Musée Guimet, Paris - *Mount Jingting in autumn* by Shitao, 17th century; 121bm: RMN - *Young woman looking through a silk veil* by Utamaro, 17th century; 121br: RMN/Th. Ollivier/Musée Guimet, Paris - *The Big Bridge* (from the series *A hundred famous places of Edo*) by Hiroshige, 19th century; 122t: CORBIS-SYGMA/J. Langevin; 122m: COSMOS/P. Lau; 122b: CORBIS-SYGMA/G. Rancinan; 123: CORBIS-SYGMA/P. Perrin; 124tl: RMN/R. Lambert/Musée Guimet, Paris - Tenjin, kakemono by Hakuin Ekaku, 18th century; 124tr: RAPHO/Pana-Photo; 124bl: RAPHO/S. J. Held; 124br: RAPHO/Grazia Neri/L. Cendamo; 125t: COLLECTION VIOLLET; 125bm, br: RAPHO/Grazia Neri/G. Giovannetti; 126tr: RAPHO/P. Koch; 126m: RAPHO/R. and S. Michaud; 127t: DIAF/B. Régent; 127bm: DIAF/B. Coleman; 127b: ANA/J. Rey; 128t: DIAF/J. Sierpinski; 128m: HOA QUI/Ph. Wang; 128b: HOA QUI/F. Latreille; 129t: RMN/Th. Ollivier/Musée Guimet, Paris - The 5th Dalai Lama, 17th century; 129m: HOA QUI/Ruiz; 129b: ASK IMAGES/ Trip/J. Vikander; 130/131: DIAF/B. Simmons; 132t: CORBIS-SYGMA/F. Pitchal; 132b: CORBIS-SYGMA/Cho Sung-su; 133tl, tr: CORBIS-SYGMA/S. Isett; 133b: CORBIS-SYGMA/D. Goldberg; 134m: CORBIS-SYGMA/J. Van Hasselt; 134b: DIAF/D. Ball; 135t: CORBIS-SYGMA/S. Isett; 135m: AFP/Y. Tsuno; 135b: AFP/Kazuhiro Nogi; 136: EXPLORER/Y. Layma; 137t: RAPHO/Network/F. Hoffmann; 137m: EXPLORER/Y. Layma; 137b: HOA QUI/Icône/C. Henriette; 138tm: CORBIS-SYGMA/A. Grace; 138tr: CORBIS-SYGMA/China Features; 138b: CORBIS-SYGMA/J. Langevin; 139t: AFP/Kim Jae-Hwan; 139ml: AFP/Pool Kyodo; 139mr: AFP/Choo Youn-Kong; 139b: RAPHO/M. Setboun; 140/141: RAPHO/M. Yamashita; 152: COSMOS/A. Dannenberg; 153: HOA QUI/M. Pell.

Printed and bound in the EEC by Arvato Iberia
Colour separations: Station Graphique, Ivry-sur-Seine

160

617-007-02